Nikolaos Papakostas
Nikolaos Pasamitros
(Eds.)

EU: Beyond the Crisis

A Debate on Sustainable Integrationism

Nikolaos Papakostas
Nikolaos Pasamitros
(Eds.)

EU: BEYOND THE CRISIS

A Debate on Sustainable Integrationism

ibidem-Verlag
Stuttgart

Bibliografische Information der Deutschen Nationalbibliothek
Die Deutsche Nationalbibliothek verzeichnet diese Publikation in der Deutschen Nationalbibliografie; detaillierte bibliografische Daten sind im Internet über http://dnb.d-nb.de abrufbar.

Bibliographic information published by the Deutsche Nationalbibliothek
Die Deutsche Nationalbibliothek lists this publication in the Deutsche Nationalbibliografie; detailed bibliographic data are available in the Internet at http://dnb.d-nb.de.

∞

Gedruckt auf alterungsbeständigem, säurefreien Papier
Printed on acid-free paper

ISBN: 978-3-8382-0848-0

© *ibidem*-Verlag
Stuttgart 2016

Alle Rechte vorbehalten

Das Werk einschließlich aller seiner Teile ist urheberrechtlich geschützt. Jede Verwertung außerhalb der engen Grenzen des Urheberrechtsgesetzes ist ohne Zustimmung des Verlages unzulässig und strafbar. Dies gilt insbesondere für Vervielfältigungen, Übersetzungen, Mikroverfilmungen und elektronische Speicherformen sowie die Einspeicherung und Verarbeitung in elektronischen Systemen.

All rights reserved. No part of this publication may be reproduced, stored in or introduced into a retrieval system, or transmitted, in any form, or by any means (electronic, mechanical, photocopying, recording or otherwise) without the prior written permission of the publisher. Any person who does any unauthorized act in relation to this publication may be liable to criminal prosecution and civil claims for damages.

Printed in Germany

Table of Contents

Acknowledgements 7

Abbreviations 9

EU: Beyond the Crisis – Foreword 11

ALBA FERRERI
Armchair Quarterback or Most Valuable Player? – The Italian Parliament:
Debating Economic Planning with a Crisis in the Offing (2006–2014) 11

EMMANUEL SIGALAS
Between the Hammer and the Anvil:
The Impact of the Financial Crisis on the Greek Parliament 35

GEORGE KRITIKOS
Spatial Inequalities and the Rise of the Far-right Wing Euroscepticism
in Southern Europe: the cases of Greece and France 55

MAX LÜGGERT
The Emergence of the ECB as a Political Actor 81

ANNA-LENA HÖGENAUER
The Principle of Subsidiarity after Lisbon:
Towards a Sustainable System of EU Multi-Level Governance? 99

ASIMAKIS TAMOURANTZIS
The Challenges of the European Social Model –
Economic & Political Cohesion in Post-Economic Crisis Eurozone 119

APOSTOLOS AGNANTOPOULOS
(Dis)orienting the Greek Crisis 159

NIKOS PASAMITROS
Conflict of Identity or Conflict of Interest:
The two Facets of the EU North-South Divide 185

VASSILIKI DELLI
EU's Discourse 'Invisibility' on Social Europe and the European Social Model.
Exploring New Legitimacy and Validity from a New Public Discourse Perspective
in the Post-Economic Crisis Period 211

Acknowledgements

The book you are holding in your hands is the result of a collective endeavour of the INTER ALIA Think Tank, *ibidem*-Verlag, the researchers / contributors, the editing team and the proof-readers.

The INTER ALIA team effort was supported by;

Boyka Boneva, a founding member of the organisation that combines energy and hard work and offers them openhandedly to the INTER ALIA cause. Once again, she offered her best to her powers for the best possible outcome.

Max Jakob Horstmann of the *ibidem*-Verlag. He is always available, open-minded and hardworking towards the finest outcome. All the *ibidem* people that worked for this book.

Dr. Apostolos Agnantopoulos, Vassiliki Delli, Dr. Alba Ferreri, Dr. Anna-Lena Högenauer, professor George Kritikos, Max Lüggert, Dr. Emmanuel Sigalas, Asimakis Tamourantzis. They are the quintessence of the volume. Their contribution is the materialization of an idea and at the same time, a meeting point for people that envision, believe and work for a Europe of constant betterment, tireless effort, vivid values, solidarist partners, team players and active citizens.

Our valiant team of proof-readers;
Dr. Babs Williams of Phoenix Social Enterprise, Dr. Jan Sanders from the Arcadia University Center, Athens and Alexia Eastwood

We thank you all for getting involved, working and believing in this volume. We hope the outcome meets your expectations and satisfies you.

We would also like to thank everyone that, directly or indirectly, supported us in the realization of the EU: Beyond the Crisis. Your contribution is greater that you may imagine.

All in all, Europe is our common home and we do the best we can, each one within his own powers, to make it livelier, more beautiful and more open and we are thankful for that.

Nikos Papakostas and Nikos Pasamitros

July 2015

Abbreviations

ALDE: Alliance of Liberals and Democrats for Europe
BL: Basic Law
CALRE: Conference of European Regional Legislative Assemblies
CCD-UDC: Centro Cristiano Democratico - Unione dei Democratici Cristiani e di Centro - Democratic Christian Centre - Union of the Democratic Christians and of the Centre
CDA: Critical Discourse Analysis
CDL: Casa delle Libertà - House of Freedom
CoR: Council of the Regions
DC: Democrazia Cristiana - Christian Democracy
DEA: Directory for European Affairs
DEF Documento di Economia e Finanza - Economic and Financial Document
DFP: Decisione di Finanza Pubblica - Public Finance Decision
DG ECFIN: Directorate General for Economic and Financial Affairs of the European Commission
DIMAR: Dimokratiki Aristera (Democratic Left)
DPEF: Documento di Programmazione Economico-Finanziaria - Economic and Financial Planning Document
EC: European Commission
ECB: European Central Bank
EFSF: European Financial Stability Facility
EFSM: European Financial Stabilisation Mechanism
ELSTAT: Elliniki Statistiki Ypiresia (Hellenic Statistical Agency)
EMU: Economic and Monetary Union
EP: European Parliament
EPP: European People's Party
ESM: European Social Model
ESM: European Stability Mechanism
EU: European Union
EZ: Eurozone
GUE / NGL: European United Left / Nordic Green Left
FdI: Fratelli d'Italia - Brothers of Italy
FI: Forza Italia - Forward Italy
FLI: Futuro e Libertà per l'Italia - Future and Freedom for Italy
GDP: Gross Domestic Product
IDV: Italia dei Valori - Italy of Values
IMF: International Monetary Fund
LC: Law on Cooperation
LN: Lega Nord - Northern League
LTRO(s): Long-Term Refinancing Operations
M5S: Movimento 5 Stelle - Five Star Movement
MEP(s): Members of the European Parliament
MLG: Multi-level Governance

MoU: Memorandum(a) of Understanding
MP(s): Member of the Parliament
NCD: Nuovo Centro Destra - New Centre Right
ND: Nea Dimokratia (New Democracy)
NEET: Not in Education, Employment, Training
NGO(s): Non-Governmental Organization(s)
NPs: National Parliaments
OECD: Organization for Economic Cooperation and Development
OMC: Open Method of Coordination
OMT: Outright Monetary Transactions
PASOK: Panellinio Socialistiko Kinima (Panhellenic Socialist Movement)
PD: Partito Democratico - Democratic Party
PdL: Popolo della Libertà - People of Freedom
PIGS: Portugal, Italy, Greece, Spain
PM: Prime Minister
PNR: *Programma Nazionale di Riforma* - National Reform Program
PPG: Parliamentary Party Group
PS: *Programma di Stabilità* - Stability Programme
QMV: Qualified Majority Voting
RER: *Rapporto sulle Riforme Economiche* - Report on Economic Reforms
SC: Scelta Civica - Civic Choice
SEL: Sinistra Ecologia e Libertà - Left Ecology and Freedom
SGP: Stability and Growth Pact
SMN: Subsidiarity Monitoring Network
SMP: Securities Markets Programme
SYRIZA: Synaspismos Rizospastikis Aristeras (Alliance of the Radical Left)
S & D: Social Democrats
TEC: Treaty of the European Community
TEU: Treaty of the European Union
TFEU: Treaty on the Functioning of the European Union
TSCG: Treaty on Stability, Coordination and Governance in the Economic and Monetary Union
VAT: Value-Added Tax

EU: Beyond the Crisis – Foreword

NIKOS PAPAKOSTAS & NIKOS PASAMITROS

Almost six years after the eruption of the economic crisis, the European Union is still struggling to provide convincing answers that would build trust in the common future of its member states and appease the international market, thus opening the way to normality at all counts. The profound effects of the crisis have necessitated a leap forward, that would irreversibly define the nature of the whole EU project. The policy of extending and pretending that has constituted an oblique economic and political advantage for the Union in the past, now seems unviable and needs to come to an end.

Europe cannot afford introversion. Diminishing competitiveness along with increasing political and economic assertiveness of other players (namely China and, to a lesser extent, Russia) and growing geopolitical unrest, challenge the leading position of the EU in the continent. Perceived as an economic institution, the EU cannot compete with China whose ample liquidity and lack of attached strings in the form of conditionality render it a much preferable partner for European states. Perceived as an envoy of a value system, the EU cannot compensate for its diminishing economic attractiveness as long as it is unwilling or unable to invest in its fundamental principles, such as respect for human dignity, liberty, democracy, equality, proportionality and subsidiarity.

The ongoing crisis has dealt serious blows to the foundations of the European Union and has exposed conceptual, political, economic and institutional weaknesses. While gaining a lot of attention throughout the past years, the financial aspect of the crisis seems to be manageable in the medium term. Regaining the trust of the market means regaining stability. Reversely, the social and political effects are gradually amplified. The enhancement of populism, nationalism and Euro-skepticism in Europe stems, to a large extent, from such political and behavioral inconsistencies. The inability of the European leaders and the current EU leadership to prove that their motives differ significantly and that the EU structure in its current form is viable, has resulted in ostensible reasonability of populist arguments.

Thus, another necessary discourse for the future of Europe relates to political pluralism. Euro-skepticism derives from other political powers and ideologies that have been held accountable for the eruption and escalation of the crisis, the stagnation of European integration process and the lack of a convincing alternative economic policy. It is essential to look into those political spaces, understand the reasons for their demise, and discuss improved alternatives.

What is more, it is worth looking into whether Euro-skepticism is essentially and by default the (only) "other" in the European Union. Alleged political hegemony over the notion of European integration, its characteristics and the rights and obligations that result from it, on the one end, and self-victimization on the other, constitute another ontological threat for the EU. Thus, examining images of the EU and Member States deriving from crisis-related narratives is essential for the future of the Union. The recurrence of stereotypes and in-Europe otherness as a tool for social mobilization, constitute another pressuring challenge for the post-crisis EU. Because, while the goal of the political powers utilizing these tools are usually short-term political benefits, their effects on perceptions of countries and people carry a long-term impact that create intra-EU cleavages.

Shifting the Focus Away from the Crisis

The volume incorporates a variety of issues and approaches that constitute, in total, the sustainable integrationism agenda for the EU. The crisis and post-crisis analyses are set under the prism of specific categorizations, according to their importance and urgency, as perceived by us editors. The "EU: Beyond the Crisis" volume draws attention to three major umbrella categories; a. politics and society, b. institutions and c. notions and perceptions.

Those aspects are considered dually important: on the one hand, because they help contextualizing the notion and impact of the crisis and on the other, because they contribute to the ongoing theoretical discourse, by using the crisis period as a temporal and methodological context for capturing the essence of the EU. The eruption and protraction of the crisis leaves ground for observations, that would arguably not be possible in periods of normality and affluence.

The first batch of articles studies the transformation of European elites and societies. In specific, the contributors research the Italian and the Greek parliament in the EU crisis context and comparatively examine the French and the Greek society vis-à-vis the far-right resurgence.

In "*Armchair Quarterback or Most Valuable Player?*", Dr. Alba Ferreri examines the Italian parliament case and offers an analysis beyond the well-worn "stiff bureaucracy" explanatory approach. Ferreri focuses on the impact of EU policies on the citizens' everyday life, on the enhanced national parliaments that bear the potential to increase the input legitimacy of the EU and on the "Europeanity" of the management of the crisis. On the other hand, Dr. Emmanouel Sigalas in his chapter "*Between the Hammer and the Anvil*", studies the impact of the financial crisis on Greek parliamentarism through fieldwork research and interviews with Greek MPs and decision-makers. Sigalas claims, that the economic crisis has seriously injured parliamentarism in Greece. Detachment of MPs from the citizens, along with high pressure by external actors, led to a greatly weakened representative democracy in Greece. In "*Spatial Inequalities and the Rise of the Far-right Wing Euroscepticism in Southern Europe*", professor George Kritikos attempts to approach the Far-Right phenomenon in two EU cases; France and Greece. Kritikos' contribution accentuates the dormant elements of ethnocentrism and extremist viewpoints inside Europe. Sentiments of injustice along with persistent, tangible problems such as unemployment and criminality in European societies, offered the stage to the Far-right to present itself as the incorrupt, anti-status quo proposal to an EU that is sinking in a multifaceted crisis.

management of the crisis, despite its multi-level implications, constitutes *de facto* as well as *de jure* a European issue.

Introduction

The outbreak of the economic and financial crisis has fuelled a deep need to rethink the whole European governance structure. This brings academic attention to the role that national institutions (should) play in this revised framework. Once more, the capability of the institutions to adapt and fight-back in an attempt to have their voice heard is challenged. The ongoing serious juncture has put into question the democratic legitimacy of the European Union (EU), rendering the contribution of national institutions even more crucial.

The influence of the EU over domestic jurisdiction seems to have reached a point of no return. Particularly, following the introduction of the Lisbon treaty (1 Dec. 2009), new provisions were designed not only to strengthen the role of the European Parliament (EP), but also enhance the power of national parliaments (NPs) and provide for citizens' participation with a view to increase the legitimacy of the EU (Mayoral 2011). Furthermore, with the contextual enactment of the new measures aiming at restructuring the European economic governance, a revival of inter-governmental procedures has emerged (Fabbrini 2013). Such a situation calls upon member states' governments allegedly supported by the legislative bodies to grasp the intermestic[2] character of the crisis. Actually, the predominant role of executive bodies strongly highlights the necessity for better integration of democratically legitimated national legislatures (Riekmann and Wydra 2013). In summation, it is safe to state that the sovereign debt crisis has contributed to putting the issue of European integration on top of the domestic political agenda (Wendler 2013). Consequently, we should expect the national debate on these matters to be livelier, even to the point of boosting the implementation of institutional reforms.

As Fasone and Griglio (2012) rightly state, parliaments are amongst the most adaptable of institutions. They still exist despite long term prognosis of their decline, they are also capable of performing different functions which no other institution has matched. Regarding the NPs' interaction with the European legal and institutional space, a process of institutional adaptation is discernible. This is in reaction to the growing perception of marginalization in the EU decision-making process.

Trying to contribute to the debate on these points, this present paper will trace the recent involvement of NPs in EU governance, focusing on the Italian legislature. This is regarded as a typical case (Gerring 2004), which bears added value for comparative research.

---

[2] An *intermestic* domain is one that concerns itself with both international and domestic affairs simultaneously

Armchair Quarterback or Most Valuable Player? The Italian Parliament: Debating Economic Planning with a Crisis in the Offing (2006–2014)

ALBA FERRERI

Increased academic attention has been devoted to national parliaments within the EU, vis-à-vis the democratic deficit issue. After the outbreak of the economic crisis, scholars recently investigated the ways national legislatures are affected by this event. One basic presupposition is that the pressures arising from the crisis are a disruptive element contributing to the growth of parliamentary controversies. These elements have contributed to starting the debate and raised the profile of EU-related matters. This contribution analyses the so-called 'communicative function', as carried out by parliamentary arenas. In particular, plenary debates on planning documents within the framework of the newly enacted 'European Semester' are analysed. Findings suggest the persistence of domestic stimuli, although the appearance of crisis-specific ones is detectable.

Alba Ferreri is a PhD candidate[1] at the Center for the Study of Political Change of the University of Siena.

Keywords: National parliaments; Italy; EU; Parliamentary debates; European Semester

Editors' Note

Following the eruption of the crisis in 2008, Italy has managed to stay at the outskirts of international media attention and to avoid close EU scrutiny despite suffering from manifold economic and fiscal maladies. Still, the political volatility caused by continual changes of government and leadership, in particular the instatement of the Monti-led technocratic government in 2012, suggests the existence of a crisis-related quandary. This paper discusses the formatory role that the crisis has played within the Italian political system focusing on the intensity of discourse on EU matters and the process of European integration. Beside the usual arguments about Europe's crisis of representation and the "hegemony" of the excecutives, this paper introduces a fresh parameter; the pertinence of the EU's institutional structure for upholding the ongoing discourse. The new competences granted to national parliaments through the Lisbon treaty can increase the input legitimacy of the Union in as much as the parliaments are prepared to take up this responsibility and to handle its political and technical implications. A second conceptual conclusion deriving from the Italian case is that the

---

[1] The views expressed in this publication are the responsibility of the author; any institution the author is part of does not express opinions on its own

gradually falling into self-repetition, banality and quite often self-righteousness. For the editors of this volume, the future of the discourse about the EU lies in the redefinition of the conceptual framework of the EU and its sustainability. The immediate impact of EU policy-making on peoples' lives, as well as the widespread media attention drown by the crisis, has increased scrutiny and has rendered the public a part of the policy-making equation. This process has unleashed manifold pressures, that will unavoidably define the quality and outlook of the EU governance model in the years to come.

"EU: Beyond the Crisis. A Debate on Sustainable Integrationism" attempts to partake in the ongoing academic debate, with a view to provoke action that would counter-balance and challenge the technocratic monopoly over decision-making. It maintains, that the crisis in the European Union is a symptom rather than an underlying condition and an opportunity rather than a menace. The multi-disciplinarity of the volume deprives it from conceptual and methodological certainties. On the contrary, it critically looks at mainstream contemporary perceptions of the EU as well as of the crisis and uses them as a "thread" for setting a new agenda, away from conservative and single-sided narratives. Sustainable integrationism is, in fact, a viable prospect, but it necessitates an in-depth understanding of the specificities of the EU crisis and a synthesis of disciplines and approaches prior to any suggested long-term solutions.

To sum up, the current volume tries to cover big segments of the European reality, without being abstract or excessively theoretical. The contributors attempt to target specific important EU issues and offer fresh, critical viewpoints along with propositions, suggestions and navigation points for a post-crisis Europe. Overall, "EU: Beyond the Crisis" is an effort for a novel roadmap for a Europe which would be political, social and essentially integrationist.

The second set of articles aims to picture the evolution of institutions, regimes and integrationist agreements inside a crisis that causes, and at the same time, demands fermentations.

Max Lüggert in "*The Emergence of the ECB as a Political Actor*", tries to offer a clear overview of the transformation that the crisis and its management brought to the European Central Bank. According to Lüggert, the ECB is rising as a political actor through the ashes of obsolete predecessors and the fire of economic and financial hardships of the crisis. In "*The Principle of Subsidiarity after Lisbon*", Dr. Anna-Lena Högenauer goes over the Lisbon Treaty and its limitations concerning demands of participation and representation of European citizens. Dr. Högenauer examines the role of regional governments and legislative regions in the decision making process and analyzes the capacity of the EU to function as a sustainable system of multi-level governance. Asimakis Tamourantzis in "*The Challenges of the European Social Model*", illustrates the clash between the venture for state economic effectiveness and societal sustainability of the ESM. Tamourantzis stresses the incompatibility of the demands of a globalized economic reality and the need for effective social and welfare provision.

The final category of articles has to do with images and central notions and viewpoints in the EU framework and how they are influenced and reconditioned by the EU crisis.

Dr. Apostolos Agnantopoulos' "*(Dis)orienting the Greek Crisis*", touches the core of stereotypical depictions that torment the EU during the crisis and diachronically prevail, only to re-emerge in harsh times. The case of a non-European Greece inside a company of proper European states is an argument often played across Europe. Dr. Agnantopoulos allocates responsibilities to the causes, in an attempt to struggle against blatant simplifications. According to the author, while structural dysfunctionalities like corruption and tax evasion are part of the problem, Greece does not significantly deviate from the EU average in sectors that it was harshly criticized for backwardness. In "*Conflict of Identity or Conflict of Interest*" Nikos Pasamitros investigates the European North-South divide notion by testing two sets of states (a team of "northern" model states and a team of "southern" problematic ones), in terms of resources data on the one hand, and of perceived well-being on the other. Pasamitros grounds the research on the theoretical models of Realistic Conflict and Social Identity theories. Finally, Vassiliki Delli applies a post-positivist approach to the concepts of the European Social Model and Social Europe. In "*EU's Discourse 'Invisibility' on Social Europe and the European Social Model*", Delli stresses the ambiguity and polysemy of the concepts and suggests that the ESM and SE should be rendered more coherent through political legitimacy, bottom-up approaches and by encouraging and enhancing democratic participation.

A Thorny Path to Sustainable Integrationism

Literature on the European crisis is thriving. The European crisis is the hottest issue in contemporary EU-related bibliography and one of the most debated internationally. However, the discussion about the essence of the crisis and the ways out seems to be

Studying the Impact of the European Economic Governance of National Parliaments

The impact of the European economic governance on NPs has been studied from more than one viewpoint. Most studies being qualitative analyses directed towards evaluating the legal responses of NPs (Neuhold and Strelkov 2012; Griglio 2013. Focusing on the internal changes of parliamentary organisation and functioning. Different parliamentary functions have been referred to, but the great part of the literature has been devoted to scrutiny and oversight (Hefftler and Wessels 2013).

The emphasis here is instead on the so-called 'communicative function' exercised by NPs (Auel and Raunio 2014), appealing to their role as gate-keepers between governmental activities and citizens.

The core question is whether parliamentary discourses are responding to the new forms of governance brought by the mounting European commitment; specifically on the matters of fiscal discipline and budgetary policy.

The concept of 'implementation' is also touched upon, this conceived as a derivative of the thematisation[3] operated by party groups during the parliamentary debates dedicated to various policy issues. Naturally, parliamentarians are the ones actually referring to each policy. In doing so, they are expected to critically refer to the effects of these policies, as well as to the processes and outcomes that the policies bring about. This includes the relationships set up amongst parliament-government.

Within parliament, plenary debates assume a primary importance as they are publicly available and literally transcribed. Therefore, they can be seen as ultimately addressing a wider audience. Accessibility is liable to public resonance, a key-component of politicisation (Auel and Raunio 2014).

Hitherto, studies pertaining to the communicative function (Auel and Tacea 2013) reveal that an active politicisation of the EU issue through NPs has been rather unusual, especially in debates not directly related to the management of the crisis. As Auel (2013: 14) confirms, the crisis led to an increase in the salience of European matters within the plenary, but this is still not the case to 'day-to-day' decisions.

As for the study case, the Italian parliament has recently experienced new patterns of behavior in the conduct of EU affairs. This includes legal updates related to this 'new era'.

Amongst the founding fathers of the European community yet considered a *laggard*, Italy has gone through a period of extreme political polarisation, which has prevented the formation of a real 'bipartisan' consensus. Over the last decade, Italian politics has been '*a permanent warfare between friends and foes of Silvio Berlusconi*' (Fabbrini 2013); more than that, and with particular reference to the Berlusconi IV government (2008–2011), Italy reached a sort of 'marginal position' within the EU decision-making institution.

---

[3] Choice of themes in the parliamentary discourse

Overall, economic decline led to a situation where Monti's[4] technical-coalition government was needed to get away from the political stalemate.

With regard to the salience of 'Europe', Giuliani (2008) famously employed the concept of 'auto-marginalisation' because of the lack of interest and capability of the members of parliament, whereas Borghetto (et al. 2012) concluded, overlooking the impact of European integration on the Italian law making over a 20-year period (1987–2006), that *'it is not possible to talk about the presence of a 'pro-Europe' or 'anti-Europe' split in Italy'* (p. 129).

In the same vein, Pinto and Pedrazzani (2013) analysed of parliamentary debates on the ratification of the ESM and the 'Fiscal compact' in three countries: Italy, France and Germany. This aimed to ascertain the configuration of a common political discourse, in which political parties position themselves. Based on a common supranational dimension, their conclusion highlighted the prevalence of domestic logics.

Based on these premises, this paper will try to map the attitudes of parliamentary parties towards EU-related matters. Particular attention is being paid to the important evolutionary passages concerning the European economic governance. In order to get a complete picture of the most recent patterns of interaction within the parliament, 'EU-driven' incentives will be highlighted, country-specific stimuli and crisis-led inducements.

The time span looked at (2006–2014) analyzes plenary debates on domestic budgetary decisions (the *economic and financial planning documents*).

Planning Documents in Italy: A Rough Journey to Europe?

In Italy, the planning documents serve as an illustration of governmental plans and interventions in the fields of economics and finance. They are designed to match the spontaneous tendencies of public finance with the fixed objectives pre-set by the executive itself (Crescenzi 2007).

The Economic and Financial Planning Document (*Documento di Programmazione Economico-Finanziaria - DPEF*) was introduced at the end of the 1980s[5] and significantly changed later at the end of the 1990s[6]. Contents were streamlined and the deadline for its submission[7] to the NP was postponed.

Alongside the DPEF, two additional documents, prompted by European rules, added to the existing planning 'production'[8]: the Stability Programme (*Programma di Stabilità*,

---

[4] Announced on November 2011, Monti's cabinet was composed of independents and was formed as an *interim* government to replace Silvio Berlusconi to lead a new unified government in Italy in order to implement reforms and austerity measures.

[5] Law 362/1988 modified law 468/1978—the one introducing the 'Financial Law' (*Legge Finanziaria*), which was the normative instrument apt to render budgetary policies somehow more systematic.

[6] With law 208/1999

[7] From May 15 to June 30. More information about this timely evolution available reading Crescenzi (2007)

[8] http://www.dt.mef.gov.it/export/sites/sitodt/modules/documenti_en/analisi_progammazione/documenti_planningi/DPRSPSM.pdf

PS), introduced following Italy's joining of the Economic and Monetary Union (EMU), and the Report on Economic Reforms (*Rapporto sulle Riforme Economiche, RER*), which, since 2005, has been drawn up as part of the 'National Reform Program' (*Programma Nazionale di Riforma, PNR*[9]) relating to the re-launch of the Lisbon Strategy.

In 2009[10], national accountancy was reformed following the new European procedures meant to prevent and correct macroeconomic imbalances as well as to re-organize the budget cycle. The DPEF was substituted by the so-called Public Finance Decision (*Decisione di Finanza Pubblica, DFP)*.

The DFP as such had a life shorter than its own plan (2011–2013) since it was only drafted and approved in 2010. The introduction of the 'European Semester' called for an amendment of the relevant domestic legislation.

With the reform[11], reviewing the structure and deadlines for submitting planning documents, the DEF (*Decisione di Economia e Finanza, DEF*) was designed to supercede the DFP. The deadline for the presentation to the parliamentary chambers was projected to be April 10, twenty days before the deadline for its submission to the European Commission.

Though this little 'jungle' of planning documents might be confusing at first, it is useful to remark how this organization has been flexible enough to react to changes in the international and national economic scenes (Dipartimento del Tesoro 2006). In particular, some observers (Griglio and Lupo 2012) maintain that the new programming cycle featured by the DEF prompted a 'parliamentary activation. The Italian parliament not only is involved in the making of budgetary policies but it also acts more in resonance with the commitment at EU level.

This is not the fact. The government increasingly delayed the submission of the planning documents, and both parliamentary chambers have often found themselves obliged to debate complex policy issues, especially those connected to the crisis, within a few days. This time constraint shackled the parliamentary debate, shortening the dialogue between the NP and its executive, due to the difficulty of examining *complex* documents in such a narrow timespan.

In a recent report, parliamentary staff noted how '*the economic crisis Parliament's decision-making power and representative autonomy have been squeezed between the decisions of the national Government and those of international organisations*', thus confirming the government's predominance. Relevantly, it is stressed how such *'grip on Parliament emphasises the challenge that markets pose to our representative institutions, as they strive to meet social demands and represent voters'* (Piccardi 2012: 6)

---

[9] The National Reform Programme is presented in parallel with its Stability / Convergence Programme, which sets out the country's budgetary plans for the coming three or four years.
[10] Law 196/2009
[11] Law 39/2011

Parties Debating Planning Documents: Working Hypotheses

There is no doubt that the process of European integration and the creation of a new, supranational and increasingly loaded policy can influence political parties. Alongside this, the development of the crisis has recently contributed to increasing the degree of public awareness of domestic factors in EU affairs. This situation has dared the assumption about low salience[12] of EU affairs or the scarcity of information which domestic factors are offered.

Political parties are still important but no longer retain a monopoly of representation in Europe. This is why questions relating to who is representing whom and on what basis are particularly pertinent, especially when dealing with the EU-level and its interplay with the domestic one (de Wilde 2009).

It follows that:

- **(H1)** *if Europe matters, one could expect an increase in the salience of EU-related matters as the EU commitment mounts over time—e.g. following the occurrence of the crisis.* More specifically,
- **(H1a)** *the outbreak of the crisis may have brought 'Europe' back to parliamentary debating, contributing to focus the debate on specific themes amenable to the current critical juncture.*

A change in thematization in the discussion of union activities and policies has been brought about by the crisis. This assumption can be tested through the analysis of specific *frames*—arguments used by MPs to justify statement (H1a).

The analysis would primarily deal with measuring the *salience* of European matters, which is simply understood as the level of attention devoted to European matters. According to saliency theory, parties compete by giving emphasis to certain issues or making a claim to 'issue ownership' and de-emphasizing others (Budge et al. 2001: 78–87). Saliency theory contrasts with the main assumption of spatial theories, which see parties competing and taking distinct positions along issue dimensions (Nanou and Dorussen 2013); moreover, the EU pressure cannot be seen as a uniform force, affecting all the domestic systems and factors in the same way.

Alongside 'European issue salience', the preferred level for understanding the importance of the EU-related (salient) issue mentioned is deemed high, with a view to specify the basic conception of the EU commitment.

Accordingly, it is hypothesized that **(H2)** *the 'European' competence-level will be increasingly preferred, since parliamentarians would progressively approve a (partial) transfer of competences from the national to the European level.*

The hypotheses presented have to be considered as specifically referring to the Italian case. Further recalling Lijphart, this research may be also regarded as a 'hypotheses

---

[12] Salience is conceived as the level of attention devoted to European matters (either in a positive, neutral or negative way).

generating' case study, because it aims to produce first empirical evidences, in order to refine theories and hypotheses to be tested onto a larger sample (*N*) (Collier 1993).

Methods: A Brief Introduction to 'Claims-Making Analysis'

Claims-making analysis (Koopmans and Statham 2002; Della Porta and Caiani 2007) is a specific form of qualitative content analysis[13] that combines quantitative protest event analysis (Franzosi 2008) and qualitative frame analysis (Gamson and Modigliani 1989). It allows an examination of variables relating the factor-level and those dealing with themes and frames using a single dataset.

As de Wilde (2013) affirmed, this methodological alternative is the most promising from the viewpoint of representation studies, since it combines a focus on the factors, policy positions and framing of claims, including attention for the 'addressees' who are called upon to enact the claim into policy and 'object actors' (which are the represented constituencies). Reference is made here to the work of Saward as the main advocate of the claims-making approach. He conceives representation as *a constitutive activity or an event* (Saward 2010: 14), rather than as a mere result of an election. Furthermore, he depicts the relationships between representatives and represented as a 'three-party interchange'—the representatives, their claims offered to an audience of prospective represented, and those who are actually 'subjects' to the decisions made by the representatives.

Taking stock of recent projects based on similar textual material[14], the present research proposes and adopts an original coding scheme. The latter is designed to take into account the specificities of the EU issue salience—identified through the analysis of parliamentary debates on budgetary policy in Italy.

---

[13] Different from discourse analysis, content analysis looks at specific aspects of the text. First, the unit of analysis is one single text or smaller units (e.g. the MP's single intervention, but also a sentence or a claim); secondly, hand-coding is still quite lengthy but less subjective, in that is led by a codebook including 'standardized' variables and values—allowing for inter-coder and intra-text reliability (as well as replications or across space / time comparisons among texts coded using the same codebook). Last, inductive approaches deem content to emerge in the making of the research itself, by means of conducting the analysis relative to a particular context. For this reason, texts simply 'do not speak' to the researcher if not 'treated' before: in doing so, it is fundamental to take into account that meanings can change accordingly to the contexts and purposes of the speakers—but also of the 'coder - interpreter'. Therefore, two specific aspects are crucial on content analysis: the context in which the message is produced and the importance of making inferences from a body of texts to their chosen content.

An act of claim-making can normally be broken down into the following elements: a *claimant*, that is, an actor who makes a demand, proposal, appeal or criticism; an *addressee*, who is the target of the criticism or support; *an object actor*, whose interests are affected by the claim; and finally the *substantive content* of the claim, which states what is to be done (aim) and why (frame). In textual terms, a claim may correspond to a few words, or go on through several paragraphs, as long as it is the same claimant making a single argument on a single topic.

[14] Mainly, the 'Europub' project (http://europub.wz-berlin.de), the RECON project (http://www.recon project.eu/projectweb/portalproject/Index.html) and the ongoing Comparative Agendas Project (CAP; www.policyagendas.org)

As for the data, independent variables (for instance, institutional factors) have been just qualitatively assessed in the previous sections, since the present paper focuses its attention on the measurement of the dependent variable.

Once the text is divided into claims, a code is assigned to each relevant claim under three main categories, namely: 'EU salience' (Y / N, dummy-wise); 'thematic variable' (matching with the policy sector mentioned) and 'frame'.

Tone is also codified: following Hurrelmann (et al. 2009), negative tones are seen as having de-legitimating effects while positive tonalities are considered as entailing legitimizing effects[15].

When the claim is salient and expresses proposals of policy reform, the sector mentioned is identified. Every sector is further specified with the 'competence level', that indicates the preferred level of governance for handling a certain matter (modalities: European; mixed; domestic). As indicated when formulating the hypotheses, the competence levels are useful because they allow the coder to discern which of the pertaining arenas the claimant herself favors; thence, they are central to H1b testing.

Last, when the sentence coded under the 'thematic variable' category also entails reference to either the 'European' or the 'mixed' competence level, 'frames' are activated.

Following previous researches applying frames alongside 'traditional' codes, the present work understands 'framing' as an act performed by the claimant precisely in order to *make sense of the claim itself*. Essentially, framing is *an emphasis in salience of certain aspects of a topic* (de Vreese 2005: 53). It is believed that frames constitute good proxies for evaluating MPs' attitudes towards the EU commitment, at least in terms of support or criticism (Closa and Maatsch 2014).

The codebook attributes great importance to the frames, intended as 'means' to thematize the debate along broad subject areas. Those frames are descriptive and the areas they refer to are exhaustive and do not overlap, yet do not demand completeness.

In the present contribution, the frame area 'implementation'[16] will be usefully recalled, because it is linked to the validation of H1a, advancing the presence of crisis-specific, implementation-related, themes. Thus, the following frames, coming from the 'implementation' area, would be inspected:

- 'implementation / policy outcomes': (a) general reference to the implementation / lack of implementation of the provisions foreseen in the previous planning document / documents connected to the national budgetary maneuver; (b) pressure towards preferring changes prompted by feedbacks received from the EU arena (e.g. modification of policy goals and means in light of the economic governance framework / the EU institutions response to national conducts on

---

[15] Neutral tone entails 'ambiguity'
[16] For analytical reasons, the codebook groups the frames into the following thematic areas: (a) implementation: failures and policy outcomes; (b) governance and budget; (c) principles to action; (d) crisis-specific management issues. Please see the Appendix

macro-economic matters); (c) reaction to changes prompted by feedbacks received from the EU arena (e.g. rigidity towards modifications prompted by the EU-level)
- 'Excessive Imbalance Procedures / Infringements of EU laws / Misfit in the adaptation to the European commitment': this frame deals with the implementation of EU law. Each Member State is responsible for the implementation of EU law (adoption of implementing measures before a specified deadline, conformity and correct application) within its own legal system. It refers to the allocation of responsibility for implementation failures: (a) general reference to EIPs / infringement procedures, without any explicit 'blaming' action; (b) blaming the executive (government / opposition 'classic' cleavage) for the current economic situation; (c) blaming the inaction / length of decision-making processes of the parliament; (d) blaming the European Commission's misuse of its discretionary power when determining the existence of infringements; (e) status quo maintenance (e.g. statements in line with the current executive's choices)

Findings: Insights into European Issue-Salience and Implementation over Time

Prior to the computation of those elements, some basic structural data regarding the documents analyzed.

Table 1: Plenary Sessions' features and votes by Chamber

Legislatures	XV		XVI					XVII	
Cabinets	Prodi II		Berlusconi IV				Monti I	Letta	Renzi
Years	2006	2007	2008	2009	2010	2011	2012	2013	2014
Documents	DPEF 2007–2011	DPEF 2008–2011	DPEF 2009–2013	DPEF 2010–2013	DFP 2011–2013	DEF 2011	DEF 2012	DEF 2013	DEF 2014[17]
SENATE – Sessions (no.)	2 Plenary sessions[18]	2 Plenary sessions[19]	3 Plenary sessions[20]	3 Plenary sessions[21]	3 Plenary sessions[22]	4 Plenary sessions[23]	1 Plenary Session[24]	2 Plenary Sessions[25]	1 Plenary Session[26]
Votes (Resolution)									
Yes	154	159	161	152	174	145	170	209	156
No	147	147	127	121	129	117	24	58	92
Abstention	-	1	5	3	-	3	4	19	2
Mission	-	-	-	1	6	-	-	-	-
Presents over total (%)	95.56%	97.46%	93.02%	87.62%	96.19%	84.13%	62.86%	90.79%	79.36%

---

[17] *At the Senate*: speaking of the vote for the connected resolution (6-00048) on the 're-entry plan' and the delay in the achievement of budgetary balance, in that occasion there were more favourable votes (YES: 170; NO: 87; ABSTENTIONS: 1) as compared to the 'yes' received by the 2014 DEF. The presents were also slightly more numerous (159, as compared to the 251 senators who were present during the 2014 DEF vote) www.senato.it/leg/17/BGT/Schede/ProcANL/ProcANLscheda29826.ht
At the Chamber of Deputies: speaking of the vote for the connected resolution (6-00064) on the 're-entry plan' and the delay in the achievement of budgetary balance, in that occasion there were more favourable votes (YES: 373; NO:114; ABSTENTIONS: 4) as compared to 'yes' received by the 2014 DEF.
[18] Sessions n. 25–26 (26am–26pm July 2006)
[19] Sessions n. 203–204 (25–26 July 2007)
[20] Sessions n.31–32–33 (8/9 July 2008)
[21] Sessions n. 246–247–248 (28/29 July 2009)
[22] Sessions n. 438–439–440 (13–14–19 Oct 2010)
[23] Sessions n. 547–548–549–550 (3/5 May 2011)
[24] Session n. 716 (26 April 2012)
[25] Sessions n. 18–19 (6/7 May 2013)
[26] Session n. 233 (17 April 2014)

Armchair Quarterback or Most Valuable Player?

Legislatures	XV		XVI					XVII	
Cabinets	Prodi II		Berlusconi IV			Monti I		Letta	Renzi
Years	2006	2007	2008	2009	2010	2011	2012	2013	2014
CH. OF DEPUTIES sessions (no.)	3 Plenary sessions[27]	2 Plenary sessions[28]	2 Plenary sessions[29]	2 Plenary sessions[30]	1 Plenary session[31]	1 Plenary session[32]		1 Plenary Session[33]	2 Plenary Sessions[34]
Votes (Resolution)									
Yes	302	291	292	254	297	283	389	419	348
No	248	205	240	233	256	263	56	153	143
Abstention	2	-	4	2	3	1	11	17	-
Mission	33	42	34	48	29	29	38	9	-
Presents over total (%)	87.62%	78.73%	85,08%	77,62%	88,25%	86,83%	72,38%	93.4%	77,94%

Looking at the table above, votes are reported. The parliamentary resolution coming out of the dedicated parliamentary sessions is fundamental for the DEF construction. In fact, the DEF is integrated by the resolution approved by the parliament. Moreover, voting patterns are here considered as an important supplement to the textual analysis: in fact, as Close and Maatsch (2014) recall, the thematization operated by parliamentarians during plenary debates shall be a useful proxy for establishing the justifications beyond those voting patterns.

Table 1 also displays parliamentarians' attendance, which has been quite high—with percentage values above 70% with only one exception, the 2011 DEF session at the upper Chamber. The 2013 is the year when the turnout is higher: the new legislature (XVII[35]) had just started, and a new actor, the lively Five Star Movement (M5S, Movimento 5 Stelle[36]), was impatient for expressing itself within the parliament. Newborn in the arena, the latter might have been impatient for expressing itself within the parliament.

As for votes, it is important to note how contested the voting act has generally been, and how consensual the pattern lately becomes—though, consensuality seems less consistent in 2014 as compared to 2011–13. As noticeable as it is, the number of sessions is overall low (1–2 session), especially at the Chamber of Deputies. Moreover, the 2013 DEF sessions are quite noteworthy not only for the turnout, but also for abstentions. To be sure, the text was quite controversial when it came for discussion at the parliament— since the outgoing technical executive led by Monti[37] had drafted it, but the discussion

---

[27] Sessions n. 30–31–32 (24/26 July 2006)
[28] Sessions n. 197–198 (31–31 July 2007)
[29] Sessions n. 29–30 (7/8 July 2008)
[30] Sessions n. 210–211 (28/29 July 2009)
[31] Session n. 382 (13 Oct 2010)
[32] Session n. 469 (28 April 2011)
[33] Session n. 626 (26 April 2012)
[34] Session n. 13 (7 May 2013)
[35] This legislature has begun on 15 March 2013—thereafter the first sessions of the parliamentary chambers. The composition of the parliament naturally mirrors the electoral results of the round held on 24–25 February 2013.
[36] Indeed, the Italian political elite has experienced a profound renovation following the rise of the movement named 'Movimento 5 Stelle' (the Five Star Movement led by the blogger and comedian Grillo) at the 2013 political elections which preceded the beginning of the XVII legislature.
[37] Announced on 16 Nov 2011, the technical government ran the country for eighteen months until after the elections in the spring of 2013 and then was replaced by the Letta Cabinet that was formed by Enrico Letta on 28 April. The latter cabinet is composed of members of PD, PdL, Civic

took place after the beginning of Letta's mandate. It is likely that this situation has produced much puzzlement on behalf of the parliamentarians—called to evaluate a text prepared by a government that was not accountable anymore.

The graphs below deal with the units of analysis, namely the claims, showing the percentage of the 'salient' ones.

Figure 1: EU-salient claims: majority and opposition (2006–2014)

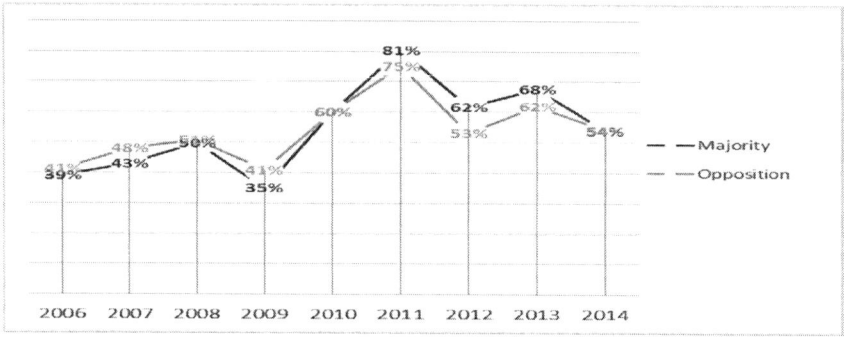

Figure 1 shows the amount of salient claims over time, dividing the trends for majority and opposition lines. The level of European salience seems fairly distributed between the two groups—with a slight drop in 2009 and shared picks in relation to year 2011, when most of the anti-crisis measures were debated and the *'austerity packages'* were at the top of Monti's political agenda. Those years were characterized by marked consensual patterns—especially for what the technical government (Monti) and the *grand coalition* executive (Letta) were concerned. Overall, it seems fair to state that salience increases over time, and the zenith of the crisis might have had a role in this upturn (H1; H1a).

Choice (Scelta Civica, SC), the Union of the Centre (Unione di Centro), one member of the Italian Radicals (Radicali, Rad) and three non-party Independent

Table 2: Salient Claims (% on the totals per PPG)

	2006	2007	2008	2009	2010	2011	2012	2013	2014	Totals
FI / PDL	45.58%	50.13%	50.37%	31.12%	71.04%	77.36%	74.13%	79.55%	46.58%	55.44%
IDV	22.54%	59.38%	40.85%	35.19%	61.02%	65.38%	51.97%	--	--	49.12%
LN	28.00%	44.60%	47.33%	39.57%	43.90%	81.90%	49.65%	60.84%	60.67%	50.77%
M5S	--	--	--	--	--	--	--	53.67%	59.11%	55.29%
NCD	--	--	--	--	--	--	--	--	57.69%	57.69%
PD-ULIVO-MARGHERITA-SD / SE	41.05%	44.62%	52.17%	45.39%	59.22%	73.70%	56.10%	68.42%	63.16%	55.25%
UDC-DC-TERZO POLO	35.74%	45.15%	51.88%	35.90%	66.90%	87.66%	71.54%	58.65%	43.84%	53.07%
Totals	39.63%	46.84%	50.00%	39.66%	60.91%	75.80%	59.12%	63.17%	53.91%	53.98%

When looking at table 2, showing percentages of salient claims per major[38] parties, a series of comments can be made. The center-left-sided Democratic Party (*Partito Democratico, PD*) has been characterized by a fair level of European issue-salience over the years examined (with a minimum percentage value of 40% - EU salient claims at the Chamber of Deputies in 2006, and a maximum percentage value of 76% in 2010 and 2011). Concerning the level of competence preferred, there is a diffused preference—on behalf of PD—of the mixed / domestic competence level. In mere numerical terms[39], PD is the group that counts sensibly more EU salient claims as compared to other parliamentary parties[40], regardless of its position within or outside the government. In other terms: the PD 'speaks more' of EU-related issues over the timespan analyzed.

Observing the liberal-conservative People of Freedom (*Popolo della Libertà, PdL*), it is primarily fair to say that the overall number of claims detected and codified is far smaller than the ones relating to the other 'big party', PD: this may be enough to denote a lower level of attention for EU related issues. That said, the salience shows lower levels in 2009 (28% at the Senate).

In 2011 PdL still led the governmental coalition (government Berlusconi IV[41]): the 'European competence level' was mostly preferred in 2011 (at the lower chamber), with an average of salient claims counting 89% of claims at the lower chamber.

---

[38] 'Major' in terms of longevity within the parliamentary arena.
[39] The detailed table showing percentages and amount of claims per party and per year is available upon request from the author
[40] With the exception of year 2013, where the newborn Five Star Movement distinguishes itself for the highest number of claims stated during plenary sessions in both the chambers. The coming out of M5S is unsurprising, as the party is a newborn, therefore willing to 'show off' and be as active as a participant as possible.
[41] Berlusconi IV Cabinet lasted from 8 May 2008 to 16 November 2011. It was a coalition government composed mainly by two parties, PdL and LN

As of 2013, PdL broke down[42]. Berlusconi rebranded his party (again) as *Forza Italia*[43] (FI), whereas the group led by Angelino Alfano established the New Centre Right (NCD, *Nuovo Centro Destra*[44]). While FI located itself at the opposition in 2013–2014, NCD firstly supported Letta's cabinet, and then entered Renzi's government[45] with three appointed ministers[46]. Both the parties showed a rather high percentage of salient claims, on average 57% (NCD) and 58% (FI) at the lower chamber—the competence levels being mainly mixed-domestic. In the case of FI, it has to be noted a definite decrease in the percentage of salient claims as compared to the instances where the party has been part of the government (30 percentage points fewer on average).

Relating to the right-wing populist Northern League (*Lega Nord, LN*), an interesting consideration could be made: when member of the majority (government Berlusconi IV), the mere number of EU salient claims is medium-high (level of competence preferred: mixed), with a peak in 2011 at the lower chamber (average of 93% EU salient claims)— significantly decreasing when at the opposition during 2012–2014. This indicates a sort of 'pragmatism' (Kopecky and Mudde 2002)—more pronounced as compared to the PdL—when shaping its attitudes towards Europe.

On the contrary, both 'Union of the Centre' (*Unione di Centro, UDC*) and 'Civic Choice' (*Scelta Civica, SC*)[47] are characterized by a good level of European salience, with peaks in terms of EU salient claims in 2011 at the lower chamber (UDC reaching an average of 92 % EU salient claims).

For what other opposition parties are concerned, in 2013 the democratic-socialist party Left Ecology and Freedom (*Sinistra Ecologia e Libertà, SEL*) and the national

---

[42] Berlusconi faced expulsion from parliament over a tax conviction. Speaking at a congress to rebrand People of Freedom (PDL) as *Forza Italia*, the name of his original political movement, Berlusconi said his impending expulsion from parliament, with the support of Letta's Democratic Party (PD), meant the left-right coalition created in the wake of February's deadlocked election could not continue.

[43] The party stems from People of Freedom (PdL), in that it is a successor of the Forza Italia party which has been active from 1994 to 2009, when it was merged with National Alliance (AN) and several minor parties to form the PdL.

[44] Led by Angelino Alfano, former PdL national secretary, the group initially included 30 senators and 27 lower house deputies. NCD ensured enough support in parliament for Letta, who even survived a confidence vote with the help of the PDL rebels. This notwithstanding, Berlusconi declared the break with Alfano and the other rebels was down to personal differences rather than deep policy disagreements and he considered the group as potential allies in future. In February 2014, after the fall of Letta's government, NCD joined the new coalition government led by Matteo Renzi. http://www.reuters.com/article/2013/11/16/us-italy-berlusconi-idUSBRE9AE15M20131116

[45] The cabinet, in office since 22 February 2014, is composed of members of PD, NCF, SC, UDC and three non-party independents. The new government is basically supported by the same majority as the precedent. Letta used to be vice head of PD and was forced to resign from premiership after Renzi called a party meeting to oust him for ineffective pace in dealing with the economic crisis.

[46] Alfano himself at the Interior, Lupi at Infrastructure and Transport, and Lorenzin at Health. Those ministers survived from Letta's cabinet alongside with two PD figures, Dario Franceschini at culture and tourism (during Letta's cabinet, he was minister of relations with parliament and coordinator of governmental activities) and Andrea Orlando at justice (during Letta's cabinet, he was minister of the environment).

[47] SC is included in the group labelled 'UDC-DC-TERZO POLO'.

conservative Brothers of Italy (*Fratelli d'Italia, FdI*), are characterized by a medium level[48] of EU salience (being preferably 'domestic' as competence level)—even though in some cases the number of claims is too low for any, even superficial, conclusion.

In order to allow for a deeper account and discuss the levels of competence preferred, figure 2 displays the levels over the time span considered:

Figure 2: Competence levels over time: area graph (2006–2014)

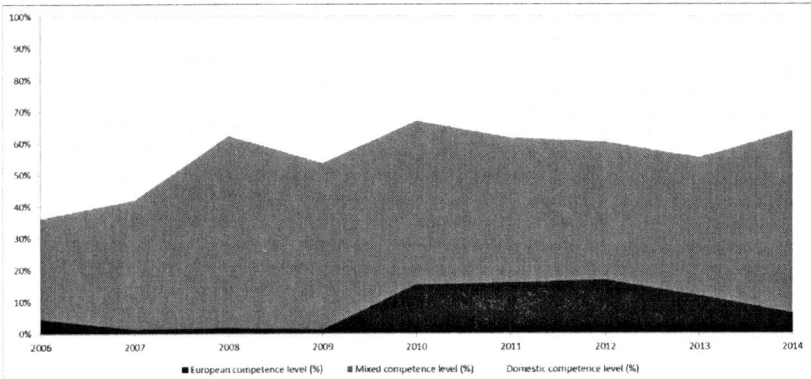

The European competence level is marginally preferred in the most recent years—in concurrence with the onset of the economic crisis. However, the prevalence of the domestic / mixed competence levels is conspicuous, as the areas in figure 2 reveal.

All this appears to disconfirm the expectation put forward by H2. Yet, this is rather unsurprising: although EU-related issues are salient, parliamentarians remain members of a domestic kind of elite. Thence, when the claim is dealing with European issues (*the claim is salient*), the levels at which it is suggested / preferred to handle them are prevalently the 'domestic' or, at best, 'mixed' ones.

For what the area '*implementation: failures and outcomes*' is concerned, the following graphs shed some light on the thematization anticipated in H1a.

Figure 3 looks at claims specifically mentioning failures taken place when implementing EU law, e.g. meeting specified deadlines, infringements, etc.[49].

In order to better define the claimant's attitude towards the EU commitment, it seemed useful to keep count of the statements where the actor indicates *the responsibility* for implementation failures, and, more prominently, whether the national government is seen as liable for the letdowns.

---

[48] The average percentage is 69%. However, the number of salient claims is low.
[49] Overall, those claims are 12% on the total number of salient claims codified.

Figure 3: Blame-shifting? Allocating responsibility for implementation failures (2006–2014)

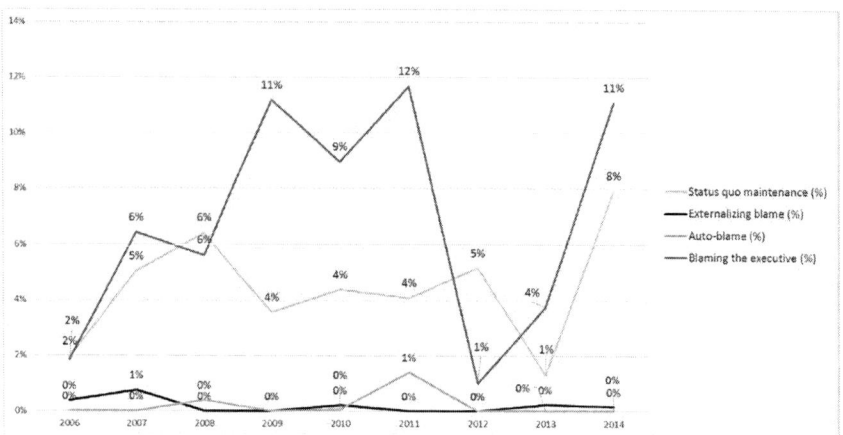

The 'lasting fiber' of the 'majority / opposition' cleavage is confirmed, even though—in 2011 and 2013—it is also noticeable how members of the majority progressively express more criticisms towards governmental actions and decisions. This may be due to the nature of the executives in charge, namely Monti's *technical-coalition* executive and Letta's *grand coalition* one—but also to the disputed character of decision-making 'in times of crisis'. Monti and Letta achieved necessary results in terms of economic equilibria, but implemented rules in a sort of 'political void': acting 'policies without politics', the results accomplished did not correspond to a full politicization.

Looking at the overall occurrences over time[50], one could appreciate how the 'auto-blame' (*blaming the inaction / length of decision-making processes of the parliament*) is rare, if not absent. Same for the 'externalization of blame' (*blaming the European Commission's misuse of its discretionary power when determining the existence of infringements*). What is instead comparatively more common is the mention to the executive's actions, either negatively (*blaming the executive*) or positively (*status quo maintenance*) connoted.

Aiming to expand the analysis, the items of this frame area were factor analyzed and one rotated factor was extracted through varimax rotation[51]: figure 4 explores this factor, which theoretically hints to a sort of 'mainstream consent' attitude. The rotated factor adds the total number of claims supporting the national government's actions to overcome implementation failures to expressions of supportive attitudes towards changes decided at the EU-level[52]

---

[50] These are percentages on the total amount of salient claims
[51] The Varimax rotation has been run with STATA 13. Results and dataset are available upon request.
[52] These are percentages on the total amount of salient claims

Figure 4: Majority / opposition lines: 'mainstream consent' (merged variable, 2006–2014)

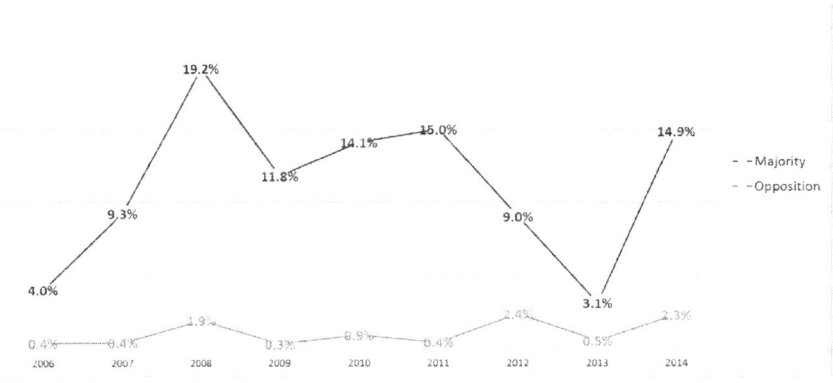

The merged variable (*'mainstream consent'*) is presented per majority and opposition lines: parties belonging to the majority first presented an increasing support, then—along with the peak of the crisis (2011)—became rather negative and critical towards governmental actions and EU-driven change. In 2014, the new cabinet somehow restored the lost enthusiasm, but the overall number of EU-related claims did not exceed 20% in any case.

As a whole, however, the claims ascribable to the area 'implementation', even if not numerically irrelevant (N=1092), do not allow the formulation of appropriate conclusions, but it could be anyway said that a focused thematization on crisis-specific issues linked to the implementation area—as envisaged in H1a—did not occur, or at least not as frequently as expected.

Conclusive Remarks: European Awareness but lack of clear Political Horizon?

The analysis repeatedly confirmed the resilience of country-specific patterns (*government / opposition; mainstream / peripheral logics*), which still tend to play a key-role in the political discourse about planning documents hereby considered.

However, the data about European issue-salience are rather satisfactory, as parliamentarians could be defined 'more than averagely aware' about EU-related issues—the mean percentage of relevant claims being 53%. Based on issue-salience, it appears that the Italian NP has managed to become a venue where European governance issues are discussed—with peaks, in terms of attention, which are clearly amenable to the occurrence of the socioeconomic and financial crisis.

However, while the crisis as such has seemingly acted as a *catalyst* for what the salience of EU-related issues is concerned, the Italian parliament has not managed to fully articulate and thematize those topics. Such a situation could be a valid corollary to the findings about issue-salience, as the increase in the references to European matters happens in response to crisis-driven impulses, but the lack of a profound articulation of crisis-related issues seems to underline the absence of a clear political horizon and in-depth analysis of the current situation on behalf of parliamentarians.

As a whole, this piece has tried to assess the efficacy of the aforementioned 'communicative function', as it emerged within the parliamentary arena. Inter alia, it is shown that the relevance of external commitments, such as those that are EU-driven, have implied a reduction of policy decidability (Lupato 2014). Finally, the codebook proposed by the present contribution could be applied to other, analogous, parliamentary debates, covering a larger time span or including other study cases. In the latter instance, the adoption of a comparative perspective would be informative, in order to have a wider overview of parties' attitudes towards EU-related matters. Hopefully, the present research has managed to provide useful insights for further research project of this kind.

References

Auel, K., (2013). *De-Parliamentarisation Re-Considered: 'Representation Without Corresponding Communication' in EU Affairs*, paper prepared for the 13th Biennial Conference of the European Union Studies Association, Baltimore, 9–11 May

Auel, K. and Raunio, T. (2014). Introduction: Connecting with the Electorate? Parliamentary Communication in EU Affairs, JLS, Volume 20, Issue 1, Special Issue: 'Connecting with the Electorate? Parliamentary Communication in EU Affairs'

Auel, K. and Tacea, A. (2013). *'Fighting Back? And if Yes, How? Measuring Parliamentary Strength and Activity in EU Affairs*, 13th Biennial Conference of the European Union Studies Association, Baltimore, 9–11 May 2013.

Borghetto, E., Giuliani, M. and Zucchini, F. (2012). Leading Governments and Unwilling Legislators: The European Union and the Italian Law-Making (1987–2006). In Brouard, S., Costa, O. and König, T. (eds), *The Europeanization of Domestic Legislatures*, New York, Springer, pp. 109–130.

Budge, I. Klingemann, H., Volkens, A., Bara, J. and Tanenbaum, E., (eds), (2001). *Mapping policy preferences: Estimates for parties, electors and governments, 1945–1998*, Oxford University Press

Cavatorto, S. (2012). Il trattato di Lisbona nel Parlamento italiano, oltre il permissive consensus. In Bellucci, P. and N. Conti, N., *Gli Italiani e l'Europa. Opinione pubblica, élite politica e media*, Roma: Carocci editore, pp. 83–109.

Cavatorto, S. (2015). A new era in the making of EU policies by Italy? In Hefftler, C., Neuhold, C., Rozenberg, O., Smith, J. and Wessels, W. (eds.), *The Palgrave Handbook of National Parliaments and the European Union*, London: Palgrave Macmillan (forthcoming).

Closa, C. and Maatsch, A. (2014*). In a spirit of solidarity? Justifying the European FinancialStability Facility (EFSF) in National Parliamentary Debates*, JCMS, volume 52, number 4, pp. 826–842.

Crescenzi, A. (ed.), (2007). *I documenti programmatici: una lettura della politica economica in Italia dal Piano Marshall al DPEF 2008–2011*, LUISS University Press.

Della Porta, D. and Caiani, M. (2007). *Talking Europe in the Italian Public Sphere*, SES&P, Vol. 12, No. 1: 1–21

de Vreese, C. H., (2005). News framing: Theory and typology, *Information Design Journal + Document Design, 13*(1), 51–62

de Wilde, P. (2009). *Designing Politicization How control mechanisms in national parliaments affect parliamentary debates in EU policy-formulation*, ARENA Working Paper, no. 13, August

de Wilde, P. (2013). *Representative claims analysis: theory meets method*, JEPP, 20:2, 278–294

Fabbrini, S. (2013). *Intergovernmentalism and Its Limits: Assessing the European* Union's *Answer to the Euro Crisis*, Comparative Political Studies, 46, 1003–1029.

Fasone, C. and Griglio, E. (2012). The setting up of the Fiscal Councils and the perspectives for the National Parliaments. Comparing Belgium, Germany and the UK, paper presented at the European University Institute Dissemination Conference "the Euro Crisis and the State of European Democracy", Florence, 22/23 November.

Franzosi, R. (2008). *Content Analysis: Objective, Systematic, and Quantitative Description of Content. Introduction* in *Content Analysis*, SAGE Benchmarks in Social Research Methods series, Sage Publications, four volumes.

Gamson, W. and Modigliani, A. (1989). Media discourse and public opinion on nuclear power: a constructionist approach, *American Journal of Sociology, vol. 95*, pp. 1–38

Gerring, J., (2004). What is a case study and what is it good for?, *APSR, vol. 98*, no.2, May.

Giuliani, M. (2008). Patterns of Consensual Law-making in the Italian Parliament, *SES&P, 13*(1), pp. 61–85.

Griglio, E. and Lupo, N. (2012). Parliamentary democracy and the Eurozone crisis, *Law and Economics Yearly Review, volume 1*, part 2, 2012.

Griglio, E. (2013). *The role of national parliaments in the new European economic governance: the parliamentary scrutiny of budget and public finance*, paper presented at the LUISS workshop "Parliamentary democracy within the new European economic governance: the European parliament and the national parliaments" held on May 21st

Hurrelmann, A. et al., (2009). Why the democratic nation-state is still legitimate: A study of media discourses, *EJPR, 48*(4), 483–515

Koopmans, R. and Statham, P., (2002). Political Claims Analysis: Integrating Protest Event and Public Discourse Approaches, *Mobilization 4*(2): 203–222

Kopecky, P. and Mudde, C. (2002). The Two Sides of Euroscepticism. Party Positions on European Integration in East Central Europe, *European Union Politics* 3(3); 297–326

Lord, C. and Pollak, J. (2013). The Pitfalls of Representation as Claims-Making in the European Union, *Journal of European Integration*, 35(5), 517–530

Lupato, G. F., (2014). Talking Europe, Using Europe—The EU's role in Parliamentary Competition in Italy and Spain (1986–2006), *The Journal of Legislative Studies* 20(1), Special Issue: 'Connecting with the Electorate? Parliamentary Communication in EU Affairs'

Nanou, K. and Dorussen, H., (2013). European integration and electoral democracy: How the European Union constrains party competition in the Member States, *EJPR* 52: 71–93.

Neuhold, C. and Strelkov, A. (2012). *New opportunity structures for the 'unusual suspects'? Implications of the Early Warning System for the role of NPs within the EU system of governance*, OPAL Online Paper No. 4.

Piccardi, C. (2012). *The economic crisis and the national parliaments: the Italian experience*, conference of the European Centre for Parliamentary Research and Documentation (ECPRD) – Working group on Economic and Budgetary Affairs, Rome, June 7–8.

Pinto, L. and Pedrazzani, A. (2013). L'attività del Parlamento nell'anno del governo tecnico. In Di Virgilio, A., Radaelli, C. (eds.), *Politica in Italia*, Bologna, Il Mulino.

Saward, M. (2010). *The Representative Claim*, Oxford: Oxford University Press

Wendler, F. (2013). *When Europe hits Parliament Explaining variation in the communicative responses of four EU Member State legislatures to European integration*, Paper prepared for the EUSA Biennial Conference, Baltimore, 9–11 May.

Between the Hammer and the Anvil: The Impact of the Financial Crisis on the Greek Parliament

EMMANUEL SIGALAS

The present chapter examines the impact of the financial crisis on parliamentarism in Greece. In particular, it addresses the following questions: (1) How much did the post-2009 economic crisis affect the legitimacy of the Hellenic Parliament? (2) To what extent was the legislative performance of the Hellenic Parliament affected by the crisis? The chapter draws on extensive fieldwork research and a combination of quantitative and qualitative data. The latter include personal interviews with former presidents of the Hellenic Parliament who are normally difficult to interview for academic purposes. The empirical analysis reveals that the crisis delivered a major blow to parliamentarism in Greece. Public trust toward the parliament and its members declined rapidly, while its legislative function was eroded. A weak and problematic parliament came under pressure from two sides, the citizens and the government, raising concerns about the future of parliamentary democracy in Greece.

Emmanouel Sigalas is a visiting professor at Carleton University (Canada) and senior research fellow at the Czech Institute of International Relations (Czech Republic).

Keywords: Greece; Parliament; Economic Crisis; Parliamentary Democracy; Legitimacy

Editors' Note

Somewhere between hot debates on huge, unviable deficits and fiscal paraphernalia, the Greek political system was furiously hit by the global economic crisis. Austerity brought the rapid consumption of political personalities and the dissolution of several political parties. What is more, the very essence of the Greek political system was fiercely tried by the outbreak of the domestic crisis; questions of legitimacy of the Greek parliament where posed, issues of democratic deficit were set and old, long-lasting deficiencies of the Greek parliamentary and political system returned as Erinyes, to haunt an already gloomy social and political reality. In *"Between the Hammer and the Anvil"*, Professor Emmanuel Sigalas attempts to analyze the great impact of the economic crisis to the Greek parliamentary system.

Introduction

The 2008 global financial crisis may have started in the USA, but it was the repercussions in one of the smaller European countries that had everyone holding their breath. Greece's economy started unravelling in 2009 and by 2012 it was at the brink of bankruptcy. The decline of the GDP, the rise of unemployment and the explosion of the public debt left no doubts that the economic recession in Greece was severe, threatening not only Greece's membership in the Eurozone, but also the Eurozone itself.

Naturally, much of the international attention evolved around the economics of the Greek crisis. However, the political dimension is equally important. It is not only that political reforms are a precondition for economic reforms and growth (Acemoglu and Robinson 2013), but also that democracy is a valuable yet vulnerable good in itself (Fukuyama 2013).

In this respect, Greece is a particularly interesting case of a parliamentary democracy suffering as an indirect consequence of its membership in the European Union (EU). Given that one of the reasons why several countries joined the EU is the consolidation and flourishing of their democracy, this is a disconcerting development. It is ominous not only for the individual member states, but also for the future of the EU as a whole.

Greece has so far been spared a return to authoritarianism, but the post-2009 developments leave no room for complacency. As soon as the economic crisis erupted, the legitimacy of the Hellenic Parliament and of its members to take decisions in the name of the Greek people was questioned. The effectiveness of representative democracy was put in doubt and the deficiencies of Greek parliament came to the fore.

The current chapter draws on original and secondary data to demonstrate that the economic crisis in the Eurozone injured the cornerstone of parliamentary democracy in Greece, the Hellenic Parliament, by exacerbating pre-existing problems. While the economic crisis triggered a series of parliament-related developments (e.g. the fragmentation of the old party system, the rise of extremist and populist parties, the formation of coalition governments), the chapter concentrates on its impact on the performance, autonomy and legitimacy of the Hellenic Parliament. Without an autonomous and legitimate parliament, representative democracy remains vulnerable regardless of which party wins the elections.

Personal interviews with key figures of the Hellenic Parliament (four former presidents and the secretary general) confirm the quantitative evidence I collected, and point to the fact that since the outbreak of the crisis some of the maladies of parliamentarism in Greece intensified. Working under unprecedented domestic and international pressure, the government abused its legislative prerogatives, in order to expedite its work. In combination with survey findings that public trust toward the Hellenic Parliament has almost vanished, the wounded autonomy of the Hellenic Parliament leave its legitimacy, and consequently its future, exposed to the volatility of the national and international economic indicators.

The chapter commences with an outline of the Hellenic Parliament's pre-existing deficiencies; then, I present my research questions and the data I used to answer them in some detail. Following that, I explain why the Greek parliament is in the precarious position the chapter's title suggest.

The Context: The Deficiencies of the Hellenic Parliament

With a few exceptions (Andeweg 2012, Longley and Davidson 1998), there seems to be a consensus that parliaments as institutions are today in decline or even in crisis (Baran and Fox 2010, Beetham 2011, Costa et al 2012, Ilozinski and Papp 2012, Leston-Bandeira 2012a, Russo and Verzichelli 2012, Saalfeld and Dobmeier 2012). This is not a particularly new observation (Manin 1997). Already in the 1920s Carl Schmitt was making a powerful argument that the parliaments of his day no longer served the original spirit of parliamentarism. In short, Schmitt (1998) maintained that parliamentarism was in crisis, because it was at odds with party loyalty, a feature of democracy that undermined the autonomy of the members of parliament (MPs) and consequently of the whole house. Despite changes over time in the understanding of the role of parliaments, and despite the benefits the advent of mass parties brought to democracy, the strengthening of the executive and the diminishing of parliamentary autonomy are being identified as the key factors behind the continuing decline of parliaments (e.g. Grosser 1964, Wheare 1969, MacGuigan 1978, Norton 2000, Baran and Fox 2010).

In an era where most representative assemblies seem to be struggling to remain relevant, the parliament of Greece is no exception. Like its European counterparts, the Hellenic Parliament suffers in terms of autonomy and power in relation to the national executive and to the EU. However, compared to most other legislatures, the Hellenic Parliament appears to be particularly vulnerable. Independent studies classify it as one of the weakest, not only in Europe (Pennings 2000), but also in the whole world (Elkins et al. 2009). The empowering of the national parliaments resulting from the EU Lisbon Treaty was meant to partially compensate for the negative effects of the European integration, but the Hellenic Parliament thus far proved unable to benefit from the new provisions (Auel and Christiansen 2015).

Greek experts too have argued that, in terms of institutional strength, autonomy and output, the Hellenic Parliament lags behind other European parliaments, and that is without taking into account the influence of the post-2009 crisis in Greece. In particular, Contiades (2009) maintains that before the economic crisis the quality of the legislative control and deliberation functions of the Hellenic Parliament had already declined sharply. The Greek parliament, in his view, has become a mechanism for rubberstamping decisions that are taken at the international or the EU level. Furthermore, Contiades (2009) continues, the Hellenic Parliament acts as an arbitrator of different sectoral interests, instead of promoting the general interest.

Foundethakis (2003) observes that although some improvements in the Hellenic Parliament's legislative and control powers took place following the 2001 revision of the Greek constitution, many of the structural deficiencies remain. Neither the subsequent revision of 2008, nor the changes in the standing orders over the years addressed important and longstanding defects, such as the government's discretion to include irrelevant articles and amendments in a bill (often only minutes before being put to vote in the plenary), or to bypass the ordinary legislative procedure (which allows time for two readings and for debate in the plenary) and use cloture motions instead. Similarly, the fact that the parliamentary committees are weak, that the opposition has no right to set up investigation committees, or that such committees rarely conclude in a single cross-party resolution, impede the transformation of the Hellenic Parliament from a talking to a working representative assembly. Even if the Hellenic Parliament is better understood as a deliberation forum, as Foundethakis (2003) proposes, it is not unusual for government ministers to be absent from the parliament during question time. Likewise, the 2008 constitution introduced the Prime Minister's (PM) question time, but it is up to him to decide if a minister can answer the question instead. In other words, it is in the PM's discretion to attend the plenary, in order to answer any questions.

Chrysogonos (2011) argues that the Greek political system suffers from a crisis of representation as a consequence of atrophic political institutions, including the Hellenic Parliament, that have been dominated by the two bigger (until 2012) parties, PASOK and Nea Dimokratia. Real politics, Chrysogonos (2011) claims, have long ceased to take place in the Hellenic Parliament, since the political parties and subsequently the MPs simply execute the decisions of the party leaders.

Alivizatos (2013) also talks of a representation crisis, and criticizes the previous constitutional revisions for further strengthening the government in relation to the parliament. In particular, he is highly critical of article 86 of the Greek constitution that renders the criminal prosecution of ministers impossible in practice. He is equally critical of the provisions allowing MPs, in practice, unrestricted parliamentary immunity. Until recently the Hellenic Parliament almost always refused to lift the immunity of any of its members, partly as a result of the stringent conditions that are associated with the procedure. As Fotiadiou (2011) informs us, out of 831 requests for immunity waiving that had been filed between 1974 and 2006 only 17 were granted.

Even Greece's Prime Minister between 1996 and 2004, Mr. Kostas Simitis (2007: 17), accuses the MPs of having a 'shameless guild-like attitude' that damages democracy in Greece. The abuse of the parliamentary immunity system, the refusal for any political reforms that might threaten their re-election and the behaviour akin to other professionals who are interested in safeguarding their privileges, are all undermining democracy, he argues. The Hellenic Parliament, Simitis (2007: 19) concludes, is distant from the citizens, who feel that in between the elections they matter little.

Research Question and Data

This short summary of the ills of Greek parliamentarism leaves no doubt that the Hellenic Parliament suffered from many problems long before the outbreak of the economic crisis. Given its very limited autonomy, the popularity of the parliament is closely intertwined with that of the government. Therefore, when the repercussions of the global economic crisis reached Greece in 2009 and the country's economy started to rapidly deteriorate, the Hellenic Parliament found itself in the middle of a storm of popular discontent. The threat to Greece's parliament was at moments so grave, as I demonstrate in the following section, that it can only be compared to the threat of a violent overthrow of a political system. At the same time, the government pressed the parliament even harder than before, in order to ensure that unpopular legislation would go through as quickly as possible. This must have undermined the public support toward the Hellenic Parliament even further.

Although I distinguish here between public and government pressure on the parliament, there should be no misunderstanding that these forces can be traced to a single source. The pressure, which indirectly injured the Hellenic Parliament's functions, is a consequence of the country's dire economic situation. The need for drastic fiscal tightening, in combination with the explicit demands of the troika (European Commission, European Central Bank and International Monetary Fund) resulted in highly unpopular austerity measures. Soon the crisis transformed from economic to political, undermining the legitimacy of not only the government, but of the whole political system, and inevitably of the Hellenic Parliament as well (Mavrogordatos and Mylonas 2011).

The following sections outline the nature and magnitude of the pressure that was exerted on the Hellenic Parliament and its members, and how it affected a crucial aspect of its operation, namely, its legislative function. The goal is to focus not on the electoral or party political consequences, which has been dealt with by others (e.g. Dinas and Rori 2013, Teperoglou and Tsatsanis 2014), but on the institutional framework that is the necessary condition if democratic politics are to take place at all. Thus, the present chapter answers the following research questions: (1) How much did the post-2009 crisis affect the legitimacy level of the Hellenic Parliament? (2) To what extent was the legislative performance of the Hellenic Parliament affected by the crisis? To compare the post-crisis with the pre-crisis legitimacy and performance levels, the analysis stretches over the period 2004–2014. Some tentative predictions about the post-2014 period are presented in the concluding section.

Taking into account Beetham's (1991) definition of legitimate power, I use both secondary and primary data to gauge the "evidence of consent by the subordinate [the Greek citizens] to the power in question [the Hellenic Parliament]"(Beetham 1991: 16). In particular, I rely on electoral turnout and levels of public trust, instruments that have been used by other scholars before (e.g. Leston-Bandeira 2012b), to demonstrate how rapidly the Hellenic Parliament was delegitimized following the implosion of the national economy and the signing of the memoranda agreements with the troika. Personal testimonies from Greek parliamentarians (see below) are used in a complementary way to confirm the quantitative evidence.

Whereas scholars have identified in the past infringements on the Greek parliament's powers (e.g. Foundethakis 2003, Contiades 2009), systematic and, especially, quantitative data are hard to come by. Unless the administration of the Hellenic Parliament responds positively to individual data requests, the minutes of the plenary (but not of the parliamentary committees) are the only available source of parliamentary performance data. I need not explain how labor-intensive the latter option is. This is probably one reason why much work on performance and output of the Hellenic Parliament is of qualitative nature (e.g. Contiades and Spyropoulos 2011, Karavokyris

2014), and another one is that in Greece the study of parliamentarism has been traditionally the remit of constitutional lawyers or historians rather than of political scientists.

Thankfully, the office of the Secretary General of the Hellenic Parliament (Mr. Athanasios Papaioannou) kindly agreed in providing me with numerical data with regard to the parliament's legislative function over the period 2004–2014. These data measure the number of bills that were submitted under the ordinary (Bills) or extraordinary legislative procedures (Urgent Procedure Acts, Legislative Content Acts).

The personal interviews (conducted in Athens in 2014) record the views on the economic crisis and its political repercussions of Greek politicians who were or, at the time of writing, still are formally responsible for the Hellenic Parliament's operations and procedures. These are:

- Mr. Evangelos Meimarakis (President of the Hellenic Parliament, 2012–2015)
- Mr. Filippos Petsalnikos (President of the Hellenic Parliament, 2009–2012)
- Mr. Dimitrios Sioufas (President of the Hellenic Parliament, 2007–2009)
- Mr. Apostolos Kaklamanis (President of the Hellenic Parliament, 1993–2004)
- Mr. Athanasios Papaioannou (Secretary General of the Hellenic Parliament since 2009)

Public Pressure on the Parliament

Anyone who is even slightly familiar with daily life in Athens will know that demonstrations are a part of the city's daily routine. However, what happened between 2010 and 2012 in the streets of Athens and outside the parliamentary building in particular can be hardly called ordinary or usual demonstrations. In my view, the nearly successful attempts to storm the parliament and the attacks against MPs mark the pinnacle of the crisis of the Hellenic Parliament. In combination with the electoral turnout and public trust evidence, there is little doubt that parliamentarism in Greece suffered badly.

The Impact of the Financial Crisis on the Greek Parliament

Figure 1: Electoral turnout in the Greek parliamentary elections

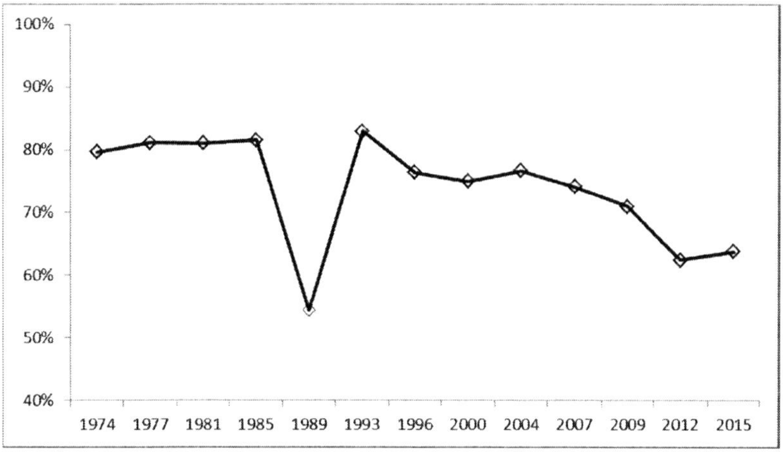

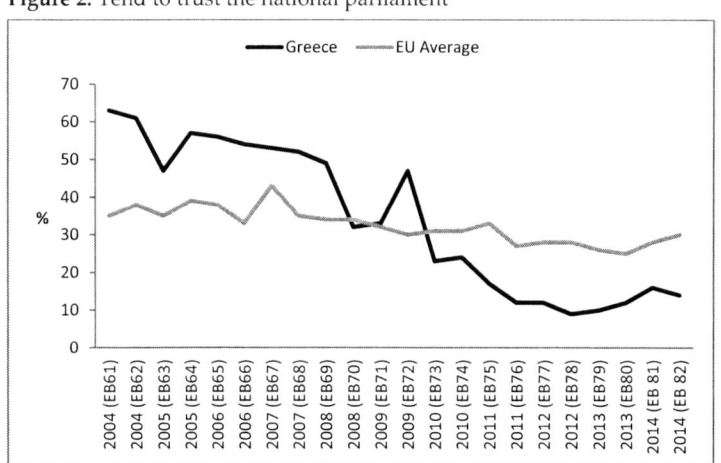

Source: IDEA http://www.idea.int/vt/countryview.cfm?CountryCode=GR

Figure 1 displays the electoral turnout in the Greek parliamentary elections since the restoration of democracy in 1974. Until recently Greece had one of the highest electoral turnouts in Europe partly thanks to the compulsory nature of the vote. For about 10 years the turnout stayed at a high of 80% only to fall dramatically in 1989. This was a turbulent year for Greece marked by high profile political and economic scandals involving even the prime minister. The political instability prompted three parliamentary elections between 1989 and 1990. It was an extraordinary time and the popularity of different political institutions suffered, but the legitimacy of the parliament was not put into question.

Figure 2: Tend to trust the national parliament

Source: Standard Eurobarometers 61–82.

In 1993 voter turnout returned to the previous levels, but the decline has been inexorable ever since. From 82.9% in 1993 the turnout has fallen to 62.5% in 2012. Therefore in just under 20 years there was a 20 percent drop. To some extent this development is attributable to the same reasons of falling turnout in other established democracies. For example, Austria's turnout fell continuously from 92.9% in 1979 to 74.9% in 2013, but it is difficult to argue that Austria is suffering a major parliamentarism crisis. Nevertheless, a closer look at Figure 1 will reveal a slope change between 2009 (70.9%), a year before the Greek prime minister declared publicly that the country was only a short step before bankruptcy, and 2012 (62.5%), when the Greek parliament had approved of the second memorandum of understanding between the troika and Greece and the crisis was at full swing. A drop of turnout by as much as 8.4 percent in just 3 years cannot be called ordinary.

Figure 2 looks at the development of trust in the national parliament in Greece between 2004 and 2013. The year 2004 was not chosen arbitrarily. It was the year the Summer Olympics were hosted in Greece, an event symbolising the apogee of Greece's economic growth and prosperity. Although the decline of public trust had started already before the outbreak of the crisis, as Figure 2 illustrates, Greeks were until recently among the most trustful of their parliament in the EU. In 2004 63% of the Greeks tended to trust their parliament, as opposed to only 45% in the EU. In the next 4 to 5 years, public trust in the parliamentary institutions remained largely stable in the rest of the EU, but in Greece it was deteriorating. Apparently Greece was quickly catching up with the older EU member states in terms of not only purchasing power, but also of political dissatisfaction and estrangement as well. In other words, 'parliamentarism in decline' was in the process of becoming a phenomenon in Greece as common and as casual as in other parliamentary democracies in the EU.

Figure 3: Tend NOT to trust the national parliament

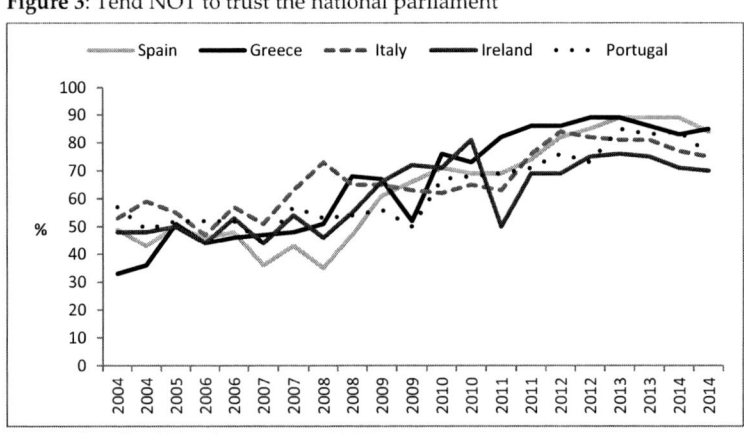

Source: Standard Eurobarometers 61–82.

After 2008, however, the developments in Greece have been dramatic. The parliamentary trust level fell from 50% to nearly 30% in just one year. At the same time

(2008–2009) the EU average started to decline as well, but by no means as sharply as in Greece. After a brief respite in 2009, trust toward the Greek parliament fell by nearly 40 percent. In 2012 less than 10% of the Greeks trusted the parliament compared to 30% on average in the EU.

The fact that the Greek case is unique is exemplified in Figure 3. Where although the number of people who tended not to trust their parliament in Spain, Portugal, Ireland and Italy was growing after the outbreak of the crisis, in Greece the growth was larger and faster. Almost continuously since 2008, proportionately the Greeks have been unhappier with their country's parliament than the Spanish, Portuguese, Irish or Italian nationals.

If the survey and the electoral turnout findings reflect Greeks' attitudes, the large scale demonstrations between 2010 and 2012 revealed their actual animosity towards the parliament. Wikipedia provides a record of what happened in front of the parliamentary building in Athens and around Syntagma Square, but those who did not witness the violent incidents first hand, probably watched them on television thus sparing me the need to go into details.[1] Other than the extent, persistence and intensity of the public demonstrations, which were often marred by violent clashes with the police, what is worth noting here are the repeated, and sometimes nearly successful, attempts of the demonstrators to force their way into the parliament and the physical attacks against MPs and government ministers.

As the Secretary General of the Hellenic Parliament explained in the personal interview, "while once the [public] critique focused on the government at the time, or on the bipolar party system, or on the two big parties, now the critique focuses on the parliament and on the MPs. The relationship with the citizens has been broken".[2] In the recent past, Mr. Papaioannou said, the site of any demonstrations was "the ministries and the American embassy. There were no demonstrations against the parliament. They didn't show the finger [*moutzonan*] to the parliament. They didn't try to enter the parliament".[3]

Although the repeated sieges of the parliament and the physical threats did not frighten Mr. Papaioannou, as he maintained, they saddened and worried him. Being surrounded by tens of thousands of angry demonstrators is intimidating enough, but the possibility of parliament's security breach added to the pressure everyone inside the parliament felt. "There were times I was waking up in the morning and I had to go to the parliament. I knew that there would be a demonstration, that there would be chaos, and I [nevertheless] went. You can't do your job. A distance that normally takes me 20 minutes it took me 1 hour. And secondly, you can't do your job […] when your concern

---

[1] http://en.wikipedia.org/wiki/2010%E2%80%9312_Greek_protests (last accessed on 6 April 2014).
[2] Mr. Papaioannou has been the Secretary General of the Hellenic Parliament since 2009. He is the head of the parliament's administration and responsible for all its operations. It is a semi-political post in the sense that the general secretary is appointed directly by the president of the parliament who is in turn elected by the MPs.
[3] This and the following quotes from the personal interviews have been translated from the Greek original by the author.

is if the parliaments' policemen will do their job properly [pushing the demonstrators back]. Psychologically it was difficult".

Mr. Sioufas, an MP for 31 years until 2012 and the president of the Greek parliament for the period 2007–2009, also maintained in the personal interview that "he knows not what fear is", but he knows that the political situation between 2010 and 2012 was very tense. Similar to the other interviewees, he confessed that he was worried, and that he was cautious when he was walking in the streets in fear for his safety.

Mr. Kaklamanis, the longest serving MP (40 years) and president of the parliament (1993–2004), was even more explicit. "The 2010–2012 years saw the worst institutional crisis thus far. Worse than the 'dirty 1989' "when the parliament was again put to test [...] Now the rates of people who think that getting involved in politics is a (financially) rewarding activity grows. A feature of the current crisis is the dominance of the belief that getting involved in politics conceals always a pursuit for financial gains. This has been imprinted on the citizens [...] The people spit against the parliament. Many inspire the people the sense that the parliament is a public spittoon".[4]

Like his predecessors, Mr. Petsalnikos (president of the parliament during the crucial 2009–2012 years) is also of the opinion that the Syntagma Square events were unprecedented and the attempts to storm the parliament transferred the tension inside. Sharing his views on the causes of the delegitimation of the Hellenic Parliament, he claimed that, "the financial crisis forced the MPs and the parliament to shoulder a weight that was not theirs. The sense that they [the MPs] are to blame is everywhere. Secondly, the image of parliamentarism in the media; in no other country was this depreciation to be found, not in Portugal, Spain or in Cyprus. In no other country was there such a wave of attacks from the media. This does not excuse the political world from their responsibilities, but the attack is unfair and unacceptable".

Whether the attack is unfair and unacceptable is a different discussion, but it is clear that all former presidents and the Secretary General agree that the Hellenic Parliament has been under attack by the media and the public at large. As if such pressure on the Hellenic Parliament was not bad enough, the stance of the Greek governments after 2009 made matters worse.

Government Pressure on the Parliament

On 31 March 2014 the leader of the parliamentary group of SYRIZA Mr. Alexis Tsipras, currently Greece's Prime Minister but head of the opposition at the time, filed a censure motion against the Hellenic Parliament President, Mr. Evangelos Meimarakis. A hopeless as much as symbolic move, it was meant as a protest act against the President's decision to refuse registering SYRIZA's censure motion against the finance minister the day before. The procedure included a debate in the plenary where Mr. Tsipras declared

---

[4] The 'dirty 1989' refers to a Greek 'mega-scandal', as Koutsoukis (2006: 132) calls it, that unfolded mostly during 1989. It involved a Greek banker who allegedly bribed not only ministers of the PASOK government, but even the Prime Minister (Andreas Papandreou) himself. Whilst the Prime Minister was acquitted, some of his close associates were eventually convicted. The scandal shook the whole country and undermined the legitimacy of Greece's political class (ibid.).

to his peers and, thanks to media coverage, to the electorate, that because of the way the government handled the consequences of the economic crisis, parliamentarism and democracy in Greece had been badly damaged.

> "There is no doubt, that in society's conscience the parliamentary process has been discredited, and what we are experiencing during the past years is a dehydration of democracy itself. Of course history teaches, that in periods of crisis the depreciation of the parliament and of the institutions grows enormously. It teaches also, that the policy against the people demands, and imposes, a discredited parliament. What we are going through in this country, however, [...] is without precedent. I will speak in numbers. Four hundred executive laws have come through here [the plenary]. One hundred and eighty of them only during the past two years. Forty acts of legislative content have gone through. Nine bills under the very urgent procedure, that is [examined and voted] just in two days, during the past two years. The Prime Minister shows up only to vote. He never comes to [answer] the questions that are submitted by the [parliamentary group] leaders or the MPs. He abolished the PM Time. The government ministers follow his example. The parliament no longer deliberates, it does not discuss in a political sense, it has acquired a strictly implemental role. Amendments [are submitted] in hiding, in the night, past the deadline. Bills of hundreds of pages in a single article!"

(Hellenic Parliament 2014: 9567).[5]

Taking it at face value, the picture emerging from Mr. Tsipras's speech about the state of parliamentary autonomy and subsequently of democracy in Greece is disconcerting. According to Mr. Tsipras, the coalition government (Nea Dimokratia, PASOK and DIMAR) that was formed after the 2012 elections and led by Mr. Antonis Samaras (ND) chose to ignore and side-line the parliament as much as it could.[6] By favoring extraordinary legislative procedures, the "parliament no longer deliberates", as Mr. Tsipras put it, the PM shows up only to vote and the parliament has been reduced to rubberstamping decisions that have been taken elsewhere. Four years after the signing of the first memorandum of understanding with the troika and two years after Mr. Samaras came to power Greek parliamentary democracy, in the view of the SYRIZA leader, had reached an all-time low.

It is not the first time the Greek executive has abused its prerogatives to expedite its business, and it is not an exclusively Greek phenomenon either (Karavokyris 2014). In all parliamentary democracies there is an inherent tension between the government's desire for efficiency and the parliament's orientation for autonomy and control of the executive (Norton 2000). However, according to Mr. Tsipras, by 2014 the government of Mr. Samaras surpassed in abuses all the governments since the restoration of democracy in 1974. This is a strong claim, but is it true? After all, one would expect to hear no less from the leader of the main opposition party whose interest lies in eroding the popularity, if not the legitimacy, of the incumbent.

---

[5] Author's own translation.
[6] DIMAR withdrew its support from the government in June 2013.

Interestingly enough, all the former presidents of the Hellenic Parliament confirmed in the interviews that the Hellenic Parliament has been heavily affected by the economic crisis. What makes their account so interesting is that it supports the claims of a political opponent rather than the interests of the government that was supported by their own parties. Thus, Mr. Kaklamanis (PASOK) talked of the "worst institutional crisis" the Greek parliament has experienced thus far. His successor, Mr. Sioufas (ND), argued that "the crisis of the parliament grew from 2009 onwards reaching its height in 2012". Mr. Petsalnikos, the parliament's President during George Papandreou's PASOK government, admitted that "parliamentarism is in crisis", albeit not only in Greece. And last but not least, the President during Mr. Samaras' premiership, Mr. Meimarakis (ND), explained, that "the whole political system has been discredited" of which the parliament is naturally a major, if not the main, component.

Likewise, all four interviewees argued that crisis changed important characteristics of the parliament's functions. Some even went as far as arguing that "decisions are no longer taken in the parliament" (Petsalnikos), or that the Hellenic Parliament "was confined to a ratifying role" (Meimarakis). Malpractices of the past, such as adding lengthy and numerous amendments, that sometimes amount to whole bills, to bills that have nothing to do with the topic of the amendments, intensified greatly (Kaklamanis). Where there is clear consensus among all four former presidents is that after the outbreak of the economic crisis, and especially after the 2012 parliamentary elections, the government abused its constitutional prerogative to legislate by presidential decree, by cloture motions or by resorting to the very urgent procedure acts.

According to the Greek constitution (article 43), presidential decrees are executive acts issued by the President of the Republic after proposal from a minister. They are valid only if they bear the signature of the proposing minister(s), and they are supposed to be acts that facilitate the implementation of already existing laws. As such, presidential decrees do not go through the Hellenic Parliament. Cloture motions, known formally in Greek legal parlance as 'legislative content acts', are again issued by the President of the Republic "in extraordinary cases of very urgent and unforeseen need upon proposal of the minister cabinet" (article 44 of the constitution). As soon as they are published in the government's official gazette, such acts acquire legal status. However, they have to be submitted to the parliament for ratification within forty days. If they are not submitted in time, or if the parliament fails to ratify them within three months after submission, then they become void. Until then they are treated as if they have been ratified, i.e. they are legally binding. The main advantages the legislative content offer to the government are: first, that they have immediate effect, second, that they are quicker and easier to produce than ordinary bills and, third, that the plenary is asked to give its assent to the act as a whole. Finally, the 'very urgent procedure acts', as the term implies, are the outcome of an extraordinary legislative procedure that fast-tracks legislation. According to article 109 of the Hellenic Parliament's standing orders, the appropriate parliamentary committee examines such acts in a single session, and they are subsequently debated and voted upon in the plenary during a session that can last no longer than ten hours.

The aforementioned instruments, of which only two relate directly to the parliamentary process (legislative content acts and the very urgent procedure acts) and are therefore examined here, allow the government to speed up law making, but they come at a cost. The very urgent procedure acts are synonymous to hastily drawn legislation. Whereas two readings are the norm for ordinary legislation, which allows for mistakes and omissions to be corrected, the parliamentary committee needs to conclude its work in a single session. Similarly, debate in the plenary has to be concluded in just one and session within ten hours at most. If, as Foundethakis (2003) maintains, one of the more important functions of the Hellenic Parliament is to deliberate publicly so that citizens can hear all sides of the argument before casting their vote in the next elections, then limiting parliamentary debate to a minimum, especially concerning important matters, offers poor service to democracy.

The legislative content acts are even more problematic. Firstly, they overturn the constitutional hierarchy between the different forms of law, because executive acts substitute parliamentary laws (Karavokyris 2014: 159). More importantly, they disturb the balance between the executive and legislative power. Legislative content acts allow the government to legislate quickly and in a sense without the MPs, at least for three months. That is particularly useful if the act's content is contested, putting at risk the government's cohesion in the parliament. And it is exactly for this reason why the opposition would insist on the government following the ordinary procedure, hoping that it could expose the fragility of the governing majority. Instead, parliamentary assent is given with significant delay, and the already limited manoeuvring space of the opposition is limited even more.

Expedient as it may be, this process, which according to the Greek constitution should only be used rarely and only in unforeseen and urgent cases, undermines the legitimacy of the parliament, and consequently that of the government as well (Kaklamanis). The excessive or abusive use of the legislative content acts, although legal in the strict sense, makes a mockery of the parliament and of its members, including those supporting the government. The fact that it is up to the government to decide if and when legislative content acts may or may not be used (Karavokyris 2014), and the fact that the parliament has no other choice than to accept the government's judgement and the consequences deriving from it, suggest a weak, and therefore irrelevant, parliament. If the parliament is irrelevant then parliamentary elections become meaningless. As a result, the whole edifice of parliamentary democracy starts trembling and the government's own legitimacy is questioned. To put it differently, the government needs a strong parliament not only to formally approve its proposals, but also to legitimize its decisions in the eye of the citizens who have given a mandate to all MPs. Legitimation from a stronger parliament is more potent and therefore more useful to the government for pursuing its agenda, especially in times of crisis.

The quantitative data on the development of its legislative output between 2004 and 2014 show that the economic crisis prompted successive Greek governments to make an increased use of the extraordinary legislative procedures. As Figure 4 demonstrates, there were very few legislative content acts and hardly any under the very urgent procedure prior to 2010. After 2010 the picture changes considerably. From an average of 106.5 ordinary bills per year between 2004 and 2009, the number falls to 89.2 between 2010 and 2014. In contrast, the average number of very urgent procedure acts and legislative content acts rises from 0.17 and 1.33 to 3.8 and 5.2, respectively. In other words, after the outbreak of the economic crisis the Greek government, especially that of Mr. Samaras, made a greater use of the extraordinary legislative procedures at the expense of the ordinary procedure.

Thus, one can conclude that the economic crisis affected the legislative performance of the Hellenic Parliament in a negative way. At a time when the Greek government could use all the parliamentary support it can get, in order to legitimize the painful, unpopular yet necessary, at least in its view, decisions, it opted instead to marginalize the parliament.

Figure 4: Legislative Output of the Hellenic Parliament (2004–2014)

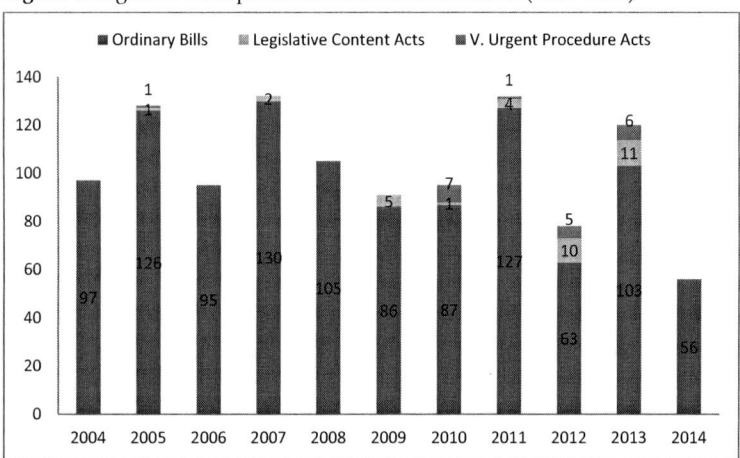

Notes: Data for 2014 are until 2 May.
Source: Author's own data.

This is exactly what happened with three pieces of very important legislation that are associated with the bailout agreements and the two memoranda with the troika (laws 3845/2010, 4046/2012 and 4093/2012). Justifying its decision in terms of time pressure and the need to secure international funding, the governments of PASOK in 2010 and of ND, PASOK and DIMAR in 2012 used the very urgent act procedure to pass legislation that was a precondition for financial assistance from the troika. As a result, Karavokyris (2014: 147) explains, MPs were asked to study, debate and approve lengthy and complex legislation in a very short amount of time, when the importance and consequences of these laws demanded instead greater caution and consequently more time than ordinary legislation.

Providing the government with the possibility to resort to extraordinary legislative procedures when extraordinary circumstances demand it is a sensible precaution.

Democratic processes can be complex and time-consuming, while social developments are sometimes unexpected and urgent demanding immediate action on behalf of the government. Thus, one could perhaps forgive the Greek government for rushing legislation that was a precondition for securing urgently needed funding from the troika. However, the issuing of legislative content acts was not confined to "extraordinary cases of very urgent and unforeseen need", as the Greek constitution prescribes. Karavokyris (2014: 157) names four examples of legislative content acts that were tackling neither urgent nor unpredictable problems. There is no need in repeating them in detail here. A brief outline of the most representative cases is enough to show that the Greek government used extraordinary legislative means for reasons of political expediency rather than genuine need.

For instance, there is nothing unpredictable or urgent in the annual evaluation of military officers for their promotion. Similarly, there is nothing unforeseen in the prolongation of a social policy programme that was set to expire on a known date, or in the need for buildings to house the impoverished immigrants who crossed the borders illegally years ago. Nevertheless, the government of Mr. Samaras chose to deal with these issues as if they were exceptional showing little interest in engaging the opposition or even its own members in the parliament.

The real motives of the government for sidelining the parliament are not known, but the consequences are. Some of them have been already mentioned, and important as these may be, they are not fatal. Hasty legislation is usually poor quality legislation, but this can be corrected. Equally, alternative forms of public deliberation can compensate for the lack of debate within the assembly. And even though the government would probably benefit from having its legislation approved by the parliament beforehand, it can rely on alternative sources for the legitimation of its policies. What cannot be repaired, though, is the damage to the public image of the parliament as a guardian of democracy. Because in a globalized world of multilevel governance it is not so much its actual powers that make the parliament so important for democracy, but its perceived powers. In other words, the parliament remains relevant in the modern world to the extent it can convincingly present itself as the heart of democracy. When the executive exercises self-restraint and respects the autonomy of the parliament, then the latter can serve its symbolic function. In contrast, when the government legislates without the parliament it strips the parliament off its symbolism potential. From a king meriting respect from the people, it becomes a king with no clothes on.

Having established the nature of the wound inflicted upon the Hellenic Parliament, it would be useful to establish also its extent. Unfortunately, this is not possible here. It is unclear if the government's legislative abuse concerns all the legislative content acts after 2010 or only a selection. However, the careful reader will have noticed that the numbers mentioned by Mr. Tsipras in his plenary speech and the numbers reported in Figure 4 do not match! Whereas he referred to as many as 40 acts of legislative content, the data given to me by the Hellenic Parliament reveal that only 21 such acts have been issued since 2012 and 36 in total since 2009. Without revealing his sources, Karavokyris (2014: 156) claims that the government issued 28 legislative content acts in 2012. The disagreement between three different and independent sources on the real extent of the use of legislative contact acts raises serious questions about the accuracy and reliability of any parliamentary data. If it is not possible to establish simple facts right, what hope is there that the Hellenic Parliament can perform its functions properly and regain its lost credibility? Of course, it may be the case that both Mr. Tsipras and Karavokyris (2014) consulted inaccurate sources. It is impossible for me to tell. In any case, there is consensus on one matter: following the outbreak of the economic crisis in Greece the 2010 and 2012 Greek governments overturned the balance between ordinary and extraordinary legislation. As a result, it is possible to conclude that the Hellenic Parliament was not only pressured by the Greek people, but also by the governments that had to administer the consequences of the crisis.

Conclusion

Hardly anything is known about the sources of public support toward the Hellenic Parliament, but it seems to be tied to the government's economic performance. As soon as the latter plummeted following the outbreak of the global economic crisis in 2008, public trust to the Greek parliament vanished. Between 2010 and 2012 thousands of Greeks sieged the Hellenic Parliaments for whole weeks. The violent clashes with the police were combined with repeated attempts of groups of protesters trying to force themselves in the parliamentary building. Whilst Athens is no stranger to demonstrations, this has not happened before. For the first time since the restoration of democracy in 1974 Greek MPs had to fear for their safety not only outside, but also inside the parliamentary building.

On top of the destabilizing developments taking place in the streets, another drama was unfolding inside the parliament. Faced with the spectre of imminent bankruptcy two governments since 2009, both of them the product of snap elections, were compelled to meet the troika demands to secure vital international funding. These demands included highly unpopular austerity measures that required new legislation in a short amount of time. As a result, the use of extraordinary legislative instruments and procedures is not that surprising. However, as I have shown in my analysis there were some legislative proposals that had nothing to do with the economic crisis, yet the government opted to use its prerogative to legislate by presidential decrees. As a consequence of this strategy, the autonomy and credibility of the Hellenic Parliament suffered. Given the parliament's poor record in several dimensions (deficiencies in the control function, excessive MP privileges etc.), the marginalization of the Hellenic Parliament made it look like more powerless than before. It is only natural, therefore, for the citizens to be asking themselves why they should be bothered with a parliament that appears increasingly irrelevant.

I have been referring to parliamentary developments related to the economic crisis in the past tense, even though while writing these lines, there is no end to the Greek crisis in sight. In 2015 a new coalition government was elected headed by a party that has been highly critical of the stance of the previous government toward the Hellenic

Parliament. One would have expected and hoped that the SYRIZA-led government would not follow the footsteps of its predecessor. It is too early to pass a judgement, but the first signs from the new government are discouraging. Unlike other Eurozone governments, the Greek government refused to bring the much-advertised Eurogroup agreement of 24 February 2015 to the Hellenic Parliament for ratification. The government's spokesperson Mr. Sakellaridis maintained, that the agreement refers to the extension of an already agreed upon programme thus making a parliamentary ratification superfluous, but it is in the government's intention to bring the agreement to the plenary for discussion (TA NEA, 2/3/2015). Political predictions during turbulent times can be nothing but precarious. Nonetheless, given the government's reluctance to bring the Eurogroup agreement for vote, one can only be cautious regarding its intention to fully respect, let alone upgrade, the autonomy of the Hellenic Parliament.

Hence, the parliament of Greece is likely to remain between the hammer and the anvil for the foreseeable future. With political legitimation at an alarmingly low level, it is doubtful if the Hellenic Parliament can withstand another major wave of political (and possibly physical) attack. Therefore, I can only end with the pessimistic conclusion that not only did the economic crisis weaken parliamentary democracy in Greece, but that there is an imminent threat that it will deteriorate even more.

The primary focus of this chapter may have been Greece, but it is obvious that there are long-term implications for the EU as well. If Greece's economic woes are associated to its membership in the Eurozone, then a strong case may be made that its parliamentary problems are due to its membership in the EU. A reductionist argument such as this one can become a powerful weapon at the hands of the opponents of European integration, regardless of its validity. With Euroscepticism on the rise nearly everywhere in Europe, this is a possibility worth taking seriously into consideration.

References

Acemoglu, D. and Robinson, J. (2013). *Why Nations Fail*, London: Profile Books.

Alivizatos, N. (2013). *Poia Dimokratia gia tin Ellada Meta tin Krisi?* [What Democracy for Greece after the Crisis?], Athens: Polis.

Andeweg, R. (2012). A Least Likely Case: Parliament and Citizens in the Netherlands, *Journal of Legislative Studies* 18 (3–4), 368–383.

Auel, K. and Christiansen, T. (2015). After Lisbon: National Parliaments in the European Union, *West European Politics* 38 (2): 261–282.

Baran, Y. and Fox, G. (2010). Fixing Parliament, from Committees to QP: A Conversation about Parliamentary Reform, *Policy Options* (September), 43–49.

Beard, Ch. and Lewis, J. (1932). Representative Government in Evolution, *American Political Science Review 26* (?), 223–240.

Beetham, David (1991). *The Legitimation of Power*, Basingstoke: Macmillan.

Beetham, D. (2011). Do Parliaments Have a Future?. In Alonson, S., Keane, J. and Merkel, W. (eds.), *The Future of Representative Democracy*, Cambridge: Cambridge University Press, 124–143.

Contiades, X. (2009). *Elleimmatiki Dimokratia*, Athens: Sideris.

---- and Spyropoulos, F. (2011). *To Mellon tou Ellinikou Koinobouliou*, Athens: Sideris.

---- and Tassopoulos, I. (2013). The Impact of the Financial Crisis on the Greek Constitution, in X. Contiades (ed.) *Constitutions in the Global Financial Crisis*, Farnham: Ashgalte.

Chrysogonos, K. (2011). Koinovoulio kai Krisi Antiprosopeysis. In Contiades, X. and Spyropoulos, F. (eds.) *To Mellon tou Ellinikou Koinovouliou*, Athens: Sideris, pp. 85–95.

Costa, O., Lefébure, P., Rozenberg, Ol., Schnatterer, T., Kerrouche, E. (2012). Far Away, So Close: Parliament and Citizens in France, *Journal of Legislative Studies* 18 (3–4), 294–313.

Elkins, Z., Ginsburg, T. and Melton, J. (2009). *The Endurance of National Constitutions*, Cambridge: Cambridge University Press.

Fotiadou, Al. (2011). Eleytheria tou Koinobouleytikou Logou kai Vouleytiki Asylia. In Contiades, X. and Spyropoulos, F. (eds.) *To Mellon tou Ellinikou Koinovouliou*, Athens: Sideris, 113–123.

Foundethakis, P. (2003) The Hellenic Parliament: The New Rules of the Game, *Journal of Legislative Studies* 9 (2), 85–106.

Fukuyama, F. (2013). Democracy and the Quality of the State, *Journal of Democracy* 24 (4), 5–16.

Grosser, Al. (1964). The Evolution of European Parliaments, *Daedalus* 93 (1), 153–178.

Hellenic Parliament (2014) Minutes of Plenary Session of 31 March 2014 (Nr. 117).

MacGuigan, M. (1978). Parliamentary Reform: Impediments to an Enlarged Role for the Backbencher, *Legislative Studies Quarterly* 3 (4), 671–682.

Mavrogordatos, G. and Mylonas, H. (2011). Greece, *European Journal of Political Research* 50 (7v8), 985–990.

Ilozinski, G. and Papp, Z. (2012). The Paradoxes of Parliament Citizen Connections in Hungary: A Window in the Political System, *Journal of Legislative Studies* 18 (3–4), 334–350.

Karavokyris, G. (2014). *To Syntagma kai i Krisi*, Athens: Kritiki

Koutsoukis, K. (2006). Political Scandals and Crisis Management in Greece, 1821–2001. In Garrard J. and Newell, J. L. (eds.). *Scandals in Past and Contemporary Politics*, Manchester: Manchester University Press, 123–136.

Longley, L. D. and Davidson, R. H. (1998). Parliamentary committees: Changing perspectives on changing institutions, *Journal of Legislative Studies* 4 (1), 1–20.

Leston-Bandeira, C. (2012a). Parliaments' Endless Pursuit of Trust: Re-Focusing on Symbolic Representation, *Journal of Legislative Studies* 18 (3–4), 514–526.

Leston-Bandeira, C. (2012b). Studying the Relationship between Parliament and Citizens, *Journal of Legislative Studies* 18 (3–4), 265–274.

Manin, B. (1997). *The Principles of Representative Government*, Cambridge: Cambridge University Press.

Norton, P. (2000). Reforming Parliament in the United Kingdom: The Report of the Commission to Strengthen Parliament, *Journal of Legislative Studies* 6 (3), 1–14.

Pennings, P. (2000). Parliamentary Control of the Executive in 47 Democracies, Paper presented in the 28th ECPR Joint Sessions Workshops, University of Copenhagen, Copenhagen, 14–19 April.

Russo, F. and Verzichelli, L. (2012). Parliament and Citizens in Italy: An Unfilled Gap, *Journal of Legislative Studies 18* (3–4), 351–367.

Saalfeld, T. and Dobmeier, R. (2012). The Bundestag and German Citizens: More Communication, Growing Distance, *Journal of Legislative Studies* 18 (3–4), 314–333

Schmitt, C. (1998 [1923]). *The Crisis of Parliamentary Democracy*, Cambridge: MIT Press.

Simitis, K. (2007). *I Dimokratia se Krisi?*, Athens: Polis.

TA NEA (2/3/2015) Sakellaridis: "Den tha Feroume ti Symfonia sti Vouli" (Daily newspaper).

Teperoglou, E. and Tsatsanis, E. (2014). Dealignment, De-legitimation and the Implosion of the Two-Party System in Greece: The Earthquake Election of 6 May 2012, *Journal of Elections, Public Opinion and Parties* 24 (2), 222–242.

Acknowledgments

My gratitude goes to all the interviewees who devoted their time to answer my questions, and to the Hellenic Parliament administration for providing me data on the parliament's legislative performance. In addition, I would like to thank Spyros Blavoukos for his comments and support, and Yiannis Panouris for transcribing the interviews.

Spatial Inequalities and the Rise of the Far-right Wing Euroscepticism in Southern Europe: the cases of Greece and France

GEORGE KRITIKOS

The rise of right wing extremism within national electorates in the European Union exemplifies the complexity of defining place, in terms of the nationalization of people, regardless of how institutionalized frontiers in Europe have become. 'Fortress Europe' as a means of restriction to people who want to cross EU's external frontiers means very little, while the presence of hundreds of thousands immigrants—legal or illegal—has a profound impact on the social and political space of the host societies. The economic crisis and the consequent austerity measures have rendered plans of multiculturalism or European unification rather problematic. Universal values and democratic institutions have been put under the scrutiny of populism and extremism in search of enemies and scapegoats. Under this pressure, support for far-right wing parties of Southern Europe—like Le Pen's Front National in France and Chrysi Avgi (Golden Dawn) in Greece- has risen significantly. This study will: 1. explore why the EU is presented as a real threat to the nation-state or to the idea of sovereignty in different electorates; 2. examine the impact of the economic crisis and immigration upon electorates that contribute to the rise of the far-right; 3. analyze the reasons for the rise of the far-right wing in the countries of Southern Europe that are related to their economic and social space; 4. investigate how Euroskepticism drew on different nationalist subcultures and produced governmental policies that aim to control human rights and immigration; 5. assess the effect of various factors on the ideological development of the far-right extremist parties, the nature of extreme right mobilization and its complex relationship with spatial differences.

George Kritikos is an associate professor at the department of Geography of Harokopeio University of Athens

Key Words: Spatial inequalities; Far-Right; Euroskepticism; Golden Dawn; Front National;

Editors' Note

The unfolding of the European crisis brought to the surface another underlying political phenomenon that seems to have deep roots in European societies. Far-right ideologies with all their polemic and xenophobic stance and their radical and violent manners, had started to strengthen during the years of EU normality, preceding the crisis. The Far-right wing parties appealed to the worries and fears of the people, by directly connecting migration with the rise of unemployment and crime rates. And while the rising uncertainty of the crisis started to undermine the EU vision, the far-right, timely played the Euroscepticism hand. People's sentiments of injustice and abandonment led them towards Euroscepticism. Many analysts attempt to ascribe the phenomenon to the EU crisis, claiming that the rise of prosperity will eventually weaken it and redirect people to the EU. However, a closer look would suggest that there is a persistence of certain viewpoints, that horizontally go through the whole political spectrum and are, from time to time, invoked in order to attract their holders to follow extremist and Eurosceptic political forces. Professor George Kritikos, by examining the cases of France and Greece, attempts to approach the issue of Euroscepticism of the Far-right political parties in these countries, by analyzing the routes of the respective parties to their rise and the spatial inequalities that reflect the reality of radicalism.

Introduction

This study will analyze Euroscepticism as expressed through the support of far-right wing ideology in Greece and in France. In specific, it will investigate reasons for the rise of the far right wing related to inequalities produced in their economic and social space.

The term spatial inequality was introduced in the welfare geography of the late 1960s and 1970s to account for the marginalization or subordination of certain groups. It provided insights related to the unequal trajectory of society by adopting a center-periphery approach that drew all its attention to inequality in living standards and elements thereof (Smith 1994). However, preoccupation with these patterns, obscures the notion of inequality by groups such as class or race, and raises the risk of losing sight of the structural basis of inequality. Thus, in this paper I will analyze how the lack of spatial accessibility to need satisfaction resources such as the labor market or housing and property—that construct the image of successful citizen who climbs his way to the top—produced supporters for the respective political parties in Greece and France.

Many studies consider that voting for the extreme right reveals a negative stigmatization that is capable of inspiring action among citizens who collectively feel the negative sentiments of being pariahs, of being excluded from the political arena and are in search of a more resolute, more authoritarian right wing (Lafont 2006: 117–118). Bert Klandermans and Nonna Mayers claim that stigmatization may deter people from activism "but once they are in it, it becomes the cement that holds them together because of the feeling of injustice and discrimination it generates" (2006: 272). Other studies claim that support for the radical right reflects protest politics and derives from dissatisfaction with the political establishment. Broadly speaking, the object of this negative voting is interpreted as dissatisfaction with the function of democracy (Lubbers et al. 2002). They could disagree with the performance of the government over specific issues (such as unemployment, European integration, immigration, etc.), or be socially intolerant citizens lacking interpersonal trust (Norris 2005: 152). Alternatively, they could be unhappy voters, dissatisfied by the work of the political system and with lack of confidence in the representative democracy institutions in their country (Betz 1994).

Adopting a geographical perspective, the present research will explore the areas that produced spatial inequalities and, thus, dissatisfaction with the performance of the government or antiestablishment sentiments. Within this framework, the territoriality of the far-right wing vote could be seen as a need for personal 'defensible' space and for control of mass immigration. The ironclad nation-state implies a sense of belonging and control, relying on the ability to exclude others from that place (Holloway & Hubbard 2001: 96).

The first part will briefly describe the history of the Far Right parties in Greece and France and their connections with voters traditionally supporting the extreme right-wing ideology during the last decades. The second part investigates how the far-right gained support in the space of these two countries based on Euroscepticism sourcing in mass immigration, housing conditions, unemployment and the respective governmental policies. Last but not least, the paper will examine the legislation and naturalization process that control immigration.

History of the Far-Right Wing in post-1974 Greece

Without focusing on the old pre-Second World War Metaxas dictatorship (1936–1940), political commentators tend to date the emergence of contemporary extreme right-wing parties in Greece to the post-1974 period. After the end of the military coup and the 'colonels' regime, the most significant extreme right-wing party was the National Camp (or Camp (EP)) that won 6.8 per cent in the 1977 parliamentary election. In addition, two other, more extreme right wing parties won a seat each in the European Parliament: in 1981 the Progress (Progressive) Party (KP) (2 per cent) and, in 1984, the National Political Union (EPEN) (2.3 per cent) (Hainsworth 2008: 65). EPEN was a fiercely anti-Communist party nominally led by the imprisoned dictator George Papadopoulos that centered its programmatic appeal on his release. Due to its strong sympathies for the colonel's regime and its subsequently imprisoned leaders, EPEN was squeezed by the main-stream 'catchall party', New Democracy (ND). In 1989, mass defections from the party led the formation of the National Party (NP) with a shift of emphasis on nationalism. It was considered as the missing link between the party and society by the leader of EPEN's youth group, Makis Vorides (Ellinas 2010: 132–133). "In 1990, the electoral law passed, brought in a 3 per cent quota for election to parliament. This was designed, with a degree of success, to act as a deterrent to would-be parties on the extreme right and elsewhere" (Hainsworth 2008: 65).

Two more extreme right wing organizations: the small Front Line—a party headed by the Holocaust denier Constantine Plevris—and the Hellenic Front—formed in 1994 by Makis Vorides—did not manage to play any significant role in the Greek politics. Cas Mudde characterized them as tiny (populist) radical right groupuscules that supported alternative plans of EU integration by expressing bizarre ambitions of reshaping its current form (Mudde 2007: 166). In 2003, in his address at the French Front National 12th Convention Makis Vorides rejected the current EU attitude. He proclaimed that "Europe, caged by the false pacifism and the egalitarian ideals of the Left, seems to inescapably fulfill its destiny: equal to Athenians, Roman and Byzantine empire, equal to leaders such as Alexander the Great, Napoleon the Great and Peter the Great" (Mudde 2007: 166). In addition, the Party of Hellenism of Sotiris Sofianopoulos called since 1981 for a return to 'Hellenic roots" and presented "Hellenism" as a substitute of capitalism, socialism, and communism (Ellinas 2010: 134–135).

Since 2000, Georgios Karatzaferis' Popular Orthodox Rally (LAOS), a breakaway faction from the nationalist part of New Democracy, drew personnel and inspiration from the far right wing populist ideology. It was based on religious orthodox support and it articulated a xenophobic, anti-immigrant strict law enforcing, Eurosceptic discourse (Hainsworth 2008: 66). Karatzaferis blended moral traditionalism with anti-Semitism and blamed "World Zionism" for corrupting "Helleno-Christian" traditions (Ellinas 2010: 133). Although he supported the coalition government of Loukas Papademos, LAOS was not elected in the parliament during the last two national elections. Some of his most influential MPs along with the old leader of EPEN youth (Makis Vorides) were incorporated in the parliamentarians of ND.

All these implied far-right wing experiments dominated this political space until the appearance of Golden Dawn which was the third political party in votes in the last European and Greek parliamentary elections of 2014 and 2015. It won 16 seats in the Greek Parliament of 2015 even though its leader Nikos Michaloliakos and several MPs were in pre-trial custody following the murder of an anti-racist musician in September 2013. The victim was Pavlos Fyssas, who was fatally stabbed by a self-confessed member of GD in a working class area of Athens. Members of the GD have been also accused of perpetrating attacks on foreigners or political opponents. They have been seen doing Nazi-style salutes, parading or constructing hierarchies in a militaristic way. Twenty years after the death of Rudolf Walter Richard Hess the newspaper "Golden Dawn" issued in memoriam an article under the title "Rudolf Hess is at last free" (*Golden Dawn* 2007). The newspaper along with the magazine *Antepithesi* (Counterattack) and the magazine or the newspaper *Chrysi Avgi* (Golden Dawn) included past publications of their MPs, expressing their aversion to Communism and their support for Nazism as well as to the Greek Junta of 1967. In its 23rd issue of June 2005, *Antepithesi* published articles that adopt eugenics and ethnobiology that call for the exclusion of homosexuals and immigrants (Chasapopoulos 2013: 115)

The party's support shrunk after the prosecution of its leadership, since the members of the party were rallied around their leader. GD tried to victimize its leader Nikos Michaloliakos in the Greek public opinion. Even the women's 100m hurdles gold medalist in the 1992 Barcelona Olympics, Voula Patoulidou—one of Greece's greatest sporting legends and a former PASOK Social-democrat party candidate—described the ongoing criminal inquiry as politically motivated and based on lies (Smith 2014a). Almost two months after the murder of Pavlos Fyssas two GD members were murdered in a drive-by shooting outside one of GD's Athens office and a third one was severely injured in what the police called a 'terrorist attack' (Smith 2013).

GD used anti-constitutionalist populism and anti-Europeanism to attack the so-called corrupted political establishment. The party promised national regeneration and the punishment of the politicians who tied the country to the EU bailout agreements. It claimed that only GD represented the true feeling and aspirations of the Greek people. Its electoral program did not contain any reference to the prospect of European integration apart from the fact that there is no possibility of a "Grexit" since there is no process of exit from the Eurozone. It also called the heads of the Greek government Antonis Samaras and Evangelos Venizelos as "employees of Berlin" and characterized Brussels "international terrorists" and "ravens of the markets" who speculate at the expense of Front Greece (Political Programme 2015: 2).

History of the Front National

In France, the Front National (FN) was founded in 1972. Rejecting an alliance with established political parties, it occupied a marginal position in the political arena. In the presidential elections of 1974 Jean-Marie Le Pen gathered only 0.8 per cent of votes while in 1981 he did not even obtain the required number of signatures needed to qualify for candidature (Platone 1994: 62–63). The isolated position of the FN was caused by its own policy which was not only anti-communist and anti-socialist but mainly anti-establishment.

Le Pen promoted the image of the anti-systemic political formation and mobilized the people by articulating grievances against the corrupt ruling elite. He used to label the mainstream parties as 'the gang of four' (socialist PS, communist PCF, Gaullist RPR and center-right UDF). The situation changed when in 1983, in a local by-election, a joint UDF-RPR-FN list was formed to defeat the left in the second round of a local by-election. This alliance with the moderate right provided the FN with the political legitimacy and visibility it had longed for (Klandermans & Mayers, 2006: 35).

The use of the proportional representation system both for the European elections of 1984 and for the parliamentary elections of 1986 ensured parliamentarians in Brussels as well as in Paris for Le Pen's party (Mény 1994: 65). In fact, the 1986 parliamentary elections brought the first FN deputies into the National Assembly (9.8 per cent). However, Le Pen continued to denounce the 'gang of four' and many of the party's "militants" took an anti-system line, accepting no alliance with the moderate right. Towards the end of 1998 tension between the two opposing strategies within the party resulted in an open conflict, leading to the split of December 1998–January 1999. Bruno Mégret, the deputy general, favored integration in the political system on the basis of alliances with the other right-wing parties, while Le Pen refused any form of political compromise (Klandermans and Mayer 2006: 36).

This transformation of the FN from a minor party into a major one, within a given context may be seen as a schismatic process. As soon as the minor party had turned into a major party, intergroup conflicts—that until that time were directed outside the party—were likely to rise inside the party itself: inner fights among pre-existing subgroups became so acute that a schism was likely to occur. On the other hand, FN dropped some of the negative features commonly attributed to it—those related to fascism and racism—and placed strong emphasis on immigration, national identity, security and unemployment. The absence of any direct historical link between FN and fascism or Nazism rendered this transformation easier (Castellani, Milesi, Crescentini 2006: 207).

After FN's success, Jean-Marie Le Pen and Bruno Mégret, who until that time had represented two different souls within FN—'heart' and 'reason' respectively—split (Catellani, Milesi and Crescentini 2006: 207). Yet, Le Pen made a decisive breakthrough in the French presidential elections of April 2002. He shocked commentators by coming in second with 17 per cent of the vote, gaining over six million ballots, in the first round (Norris 2005: 60). Since this electoral success the FN established its position as one of the major players in the French political scene.

On 16 January 2011 a change of guard from Le Pen father to Le Pen daughter took place. An article of Paul Bracchi for the *Daily Mail* refers to the rise of the 'Devil's daughter' and analyzes how Marine Le Pen's seduced a quarter of France's voters by presenting herself as the acceptable face of the Far Right. He notes that "she's every bit as extreme as her Holocaust-denying father. The resurgence of the Front National under Marine Le Pen has coincided with a perfect storm of political scandals and economic stagnation. The country is blighted by spiraling unemployment and more days lost through strikes than in any other European country" (Bracchi 2014).

Marine Le Pen has sought to move the FN beyond the status of anti-system or protest party that was formerly embraced by her father and to recast it as a responsible *parti de gouvernment* (Goodliffe 2003:97). In the French local elections of March 2015 Le Pen attracted 25 per cent support of the electorate. FN came in second after the center-right UMP party of Nicolas Sarkozy, whereas President Francois Hollande's socialists trailed in third with 22 per cent.

The next parts of this study will examine the reasons that nurtured the rise of the far in the political, economic and social space of Greece and France.

Spatial Inequalities in Greece

In Greece, the EU austerity programs along with the inability of the Greek governments to eliminate tax-evasion and to protect social welfare, constituted the main motives for voters to support anti-systemic, Eurosceptic parties throughout Greece. After assuming office in October 2009, the response of Giorgos Papandreou to the economic crisis included tough austerity measures such as spending cuts and tax increases. He also vowed to reduce the public sector. In May 2010, European leaders and the International Monetary Fund (IMF) agreed to a three-year, €110 billion bailout for Greece which was tied to additional austerity measures through cuts in the public spending (civil servants' salaries, freezing pensions, raising the retirement age) and hikes in taxes and fuel duty. The general sales tax was raised from 19% to 21%. These moves led to a 4% economic contraction in 2010. In addition, austerity measures and economic crisis had a dramatic impact upon the social and economic web of Greece. Among the EU Member States, the lowest unemployment rates were recorded in Germany (4.8 per cent) and Austria (4.9 per cent) and the highest in Greece (25.8 per cent in October 2014) and Spain (23.7 per cent)[1].

Paul Mason wrote in *The Guardian* on 25 January 2015: "The IMF predicted Greece would grow as the result of its aid package in 2010. Instead the economy has shrunk by 25%. Wages are down by the same amount, whereas youth unemployment stands at 60%—and that is among those who are still in the country" (Mason 2015). The persistence of austerity measures was translated as unwillingness or inefficiency of the political establishment to fight rampant tax evasion, and the rage invoked by the high rate of unemployment or the heavy taxes that destroyed the middle-class led also to the revenge through voting for the GD party. The latter, capitalized on Greek citizens' anxieties brought about by economic crisis, illegal immigration issues, high unemployment rates, increasing crime rates, anti-austerity sentiments, and the uncertainty over the country's future and managed to become, in just a few years, a formidable political party in Greece (Bistis 2013).

Along these lines, in its electoral campaign, GD set the same Eurosceptic targets as other parties; including Syriza that has been in power since February 2015. It promised to "tear up" the requirements of its 240 billion euro bailout, to get rid of the European Commission, ECB and International Monetary Fund "troika" and write off Greece's debt. In the 2015 GD's electoral program there is not even a single line about alternative plans of European Integration. It outlines on its front page: "the thieves in jail and the Greeks in power." It also stresses that "only a nationalist Greece could negotiate with the usurers of Berlin and exploit the natural resources of the country that would lead it to real autarchy and development"(GD Political Programme 2015).

European integration is rejected since it is projected by traditional left wing and extreme right wing parties as an elitist supranational project that weakens national sovereignty, state autonomy and traditional values. Vasilopoulou's typology of the constructed theories against EU integrationist policies identifies three types of Euroscepticism: firstly, the 'rejecting' type, which includes parties that stand wholeheartedly against any multilateral cooperation at the European level; secondly, the 'conditional' type comprising of parties not against the principle of cooperation at the European level but against the EU framework and the future deepening of integration; thirdly, the 'compromising' type, containing parties which accept both the principle and the practice of EU cooperation but oppose future integration and a deeper political union. Extreme right, nationalist parties in various EU member states adopt these three different positions regarding Europe (Vasilopoulou 2009: 18–19). Within this context, GD belongs to the "rejecting type".

The elections of 2015 showed the strength of the GD in the underprivileged areas of the urban centers in Greece. It is worth noticing that in Athens and in the second periphery of Thessaloniki where 87 and 14 of the 300 parliamentary seats are

---

[1] (http://ec.europa.ieu/eurostat/statistics explained/index)

respectively decided, GD received two of its five highest electorate percentages in Greece[2]. Far right wing extremism penetrated deeply into the most disadvantaged social layers; the working-class neighborhoods of these areas. Left wing and far right wing competed for grassroots support at neighborhood level in the suburban and poor areas of Attica (Nikaia, Keratsini, Perama, etc.[3]) and Thessaloniki.

On the one hand, in these urban areas the local middle-class was dissatisfied by the political establishment since it lost much of its wealth by investing in the property market. Before the crisis, property prices were incredibly inflated because most Greeks were able to get a cheap loan after the country's entry into the Eurozone.Today, the prices are falling but the market is not moving after almost six years of recession. In fact, Greece has suffered the second biggest property crash in the EU since the debt crisis began. In 2010, Giorgos Stathakis, the shadow development minister for the opposition Syriza party, said "In Crete, where I am from, a lot of investment went into housing for foreigners, and it was the first to collapse," he continues on to say "Foreigners stopped buying, or started selling off their houses, when the crisis began" (Smith 2014b). The situation is even more serious in the urban areas where property demand remains weak. In Athens, the capital and the country's largest city, the average price of apartments plummeted by 12.91 per cent, whereas in 2013 it plunged by 10.87 per cent, according to the Bank of Greece. The Bank of Greece also found that the number of residential property appraisals-transactions in Greece fell by 23.1 per cent in 2013. The number of building permits dropped 27.7 per cent. In Thessaloniki, the second largest city, house prices dropped 7 per cent (-4.9 per cent inflation-adjusted) in 2013 from the previous year (Delmendo 2014).

Property was traditionally among the most significant mechanisms or symbols of social mobility. Nicos Poulantzas argued that the petty-bourgeoisie consists of small scale production, and ownership, independent craftsmen and traders (1979a: 204). He also stresses that "with the fear of proletarianization below, and the attraction of the bourgeoisie above, the petty bourgeoisie aspires to join the bourgeoisie, by the individual rise of the 'best' and 'most able'" (1974b: 241). However, after the crisis of the economic system which is the central part and the core of its being, there were no social structures according to Poulantzas or instruments of the state according to Miliband (1969) for those who possessed economic power that would enable the underprivileged to act in the interests of the bourgeoisie regardless of their background. The state is able to preserve the political power of the ruling class by offering open avenues of social mobility for the few who advocate the values and the ethos of the elite. One may argue that the supporters of the FN and the GD are those who realized that these avenues through labor or through the acquisition of property were closed and thus they could not have undergone a process of bourgeoisification and could not turn to a proletarianization either. They were disappointed by the unemployment, the falling housing prices, the degradation of their urban areas brought about by the settlement of immigrants, high taxation and loan debts that could not be paid off.

---

[2] http://www.ekloges.ypes.gr/current/more/index.html
[3] Pavlos Fyssas' murder took place in one of these regions of Piraeus (Keratsini)

Moreover, under the control of the EU and the IMF, policy-makers could not create expectations to tie the citizens up with the clientelist political mechanisms. In the past, "Clientelistic voters rationally cast a ballot for concrete material benefits, such as delivery of individual or public goods" (Norris 2005: 150). This was a tradition in Greek political space where highly personalized relations and patronage controlled access to resources, services and social mobility. This system of socialization in the urban centers or in the rural peripheries made people believe that they were not protected by the state, in which impersonal rules for the allocation of resources or public goods were lacking or ignored. One may argue that kinship of the nineteenth century was replaced by party membership in terms of controlling the state from within. State became the main employer and security provider for those who could get access to purely personal clientelistic networks.

In this way, Greece created an overgrown state bureaucracy which became a huge burden. Greece was obliged to reduce the size of its public service to show the European Commission that Greece deserved further tranches of its Cohesion funds. However, the governments never fully implemented their commitments and fell back on traditional forms of patronage to satisfy supporters. The Mitsotakis government in the early 1990s was obliged to adopt a policy of replacing only one out of three civil servants and the Papantoniou budget for 1997 referred to replacing only one in five civil servants (Featherstone 1998: 30).

After the bailout agreements in the early 2010s the Greek political establishment could not promise employment in the public sector or other expenditure, whereas state intervention had to be the order of the day to alleviate the pressure on the working class during the economic crisis. At the same time, middle-class natives became fully dependent on state provisions. They had not only to pay off their rural and housing debts or loans, to support their small business, but also to settle the question of ownership titles of houses which were in danger to put up to auction, while the prices remained extremely low. The real estate crisis also shows that there were no more routes of social mobility for the hard-working people of "humble origin" to climb their way to the top by investing in property.

It should be noted though, that housing prices decreased not only because of the lack of buyers but also because of the degradation provoked by the mass settlement of immigrants and asylum seekers in the urban areas of Greece. GD gained also a lot of support by capitalizing on the rise of immigration, criminality and xenophobia of people who lived in the underprivileged areas of Athens, B' district and Thessaloniki , B' district. GD offered protection to Greeks who were fearful of the presence of immigrants in their urban neighborhoods. It formed militia patrols and ATM escorts for the elderly in a country where state authority was collapsing. Within this framework, its activities received some positive publicity, highlighting the party's 'social work', and helped legitimizing GD's 'cleansing' operations in districts with high immigrant population like Agios Panteleimon in Athens.

After the June election 2012, GD's relatively easy access to both the electronic and print media allowed it to reinforce this favorable 'social' and ethnocentric image of the party. In the next month it continued undertaking community work by donating to blood banks 'only for Greeks' (Ellinas 2013: 559). In addition, it pledged to hold a "Greek only" food handout on the Thursday before Easter, the most important religious festival in the Orthodox calendar (Smith 2014a). These acts, though limited in scale, caught the attention of the media allowing GD to claim a social role at the local level while emphasizing its ethnocentric message.

In addition, the absence of state mechanisms and the penetration of the GD in some police stations, where policemen proved to be supporters of the extreme right wing party, exacerbated the anarchy created by the presence of thousands of immigrants in the center of Athens. The former Commander of the Police Department in *Agios Panteleimonas* (St. Panteleimon) was arrested and suspended, as he was accused of not taking the necessary measures to tackle GD's actions in his jurisdiction. The police's Internal Affairs agency discovered that the former commander had not investigated the allegations of immigrants that they had been attacked and that any reports involving racially-motivated attacks against immigrants were filed away. The result was that local residents were urged to contact the local GD offices to address any problems they might have with immigrants[4].

These areas were transformed into ghettoes within towns and were abandoned by most of their Greek proprietors or tenants. Along the same lines, we investigate the situation of the French urban areas that voted for Le Pen's party.

Spatial Inequalities in France

Nowadays, geographers suggest that ghetto is not a social monolith. Notwithstanding their extreme dilapidation, many inner-city neighborhoods still contain a modicum of familial variety. These areas constituted ghettoes not only in the sense of segregation, exclusion or deprivation and poverty, but also as an institutional form, that is, a distinctive, spatially based concatenation with mechanisms or ethno-racial closure and control. They could be also defined as ethnic ghettoes in residential areas with a concentration of a particular group of people characterized by the different religious and linguistic characteristics of their population (Holloway & Hubbard 2001: 140–143). They can be described ideal-typically as a bounded, ethnically uniform socio-spatial formation born of the forcible relegation of a negatively typed population—such as Jews in the principalities of Renaissance Europe and African Americans in the United States during the age of Fordist consolidation—to a reserved territory within which this population develops an array of specific institutions operate both as a functional substitute for and as a protective buffer against, the dominant institutions of the encompassing society (Wacquant 2008: 49).

In France immigrants from the Maghreb area (Algerians, Tunisians and Marroquin) were admitted to the "cheap housing projects" (HLM). However, their concentration at high percentages provoked hostile reactions by the locals. In municipalities and

---

[4] https://icantrelaxingreece.wordpress.com/2013/10/03/former-commander-of-agios-panteleimonas-pd-arrested

neighborhoods where different life-styles and daily rhythms (e.g. smells and sounds, work, sleep and leisure schedules, family size and so on) were not affordable, racist notions were cited by the natives. When the *bidonvilles* (i.e. impoverished slum housing similar to the kind that surrounds urban centers in the Third World) were gradually destroyed at the end of the 1960s and the beginning of the 1970s, there was not enough cheap housing available for everyone, and many African families were judged to be "unadaptable" to life in modern French dwellings. To accommodate these families (mostly North Africans) the government built the *cités de transit,* (i.e. housing complexes where the immigrants were to live for two or three years to receive education that would facilitate their integration into French society). However, these poor constructions were not at all provisional. Most of the *cités* turned into ghettos, and the children who grew up there posed difficult questions to the French society (Verbunt 1985: 149).

Spatial inequalities are brought to the surface when immigrants claim their emancipation. In the early 1980s' France, immigrants had demonstrated against exploitation and marginalization, years before the uprising in the quartiers of Paris. The natives resented the fact that the 'black' labor market where thousands of immigrants working in small building firms, the textile industry, the confection industry, agriculture or as domestic personnel demanded their social rights and social security. In enterprises like Renault, unskilled workers (mostly immigrants) had gone on strike because after ten or fifteen years they were never promoted and had never had the same opportunity to attend formation as their French colleagues, who did not stay many years at the bottom of the ladder (Verbunt 1986: 152). Immigrants that were accommodated to the *foyers* caused a rent-strike which lasted for several years. These constructions were built as homes for single workers with public funds and forced workers to live like soldiers in barracks or students in a boarding school, with former soldiers as supervisors and many restrictions in personal liberties. Because they represented a concentration of (foreign) men the *foyers* were not appreciated by the neighbors, and this led to segregation (Verbunt 1986: 149).

In modern French urban space, most of the immigrants and Muslim populations are located at the outskirts of Paris, Lyon, and Marseilles in neighborhoods known as *cités* or *banlieues*. Traditionally, these areas are identified as being subject to higher rates of poverty and crime (Marchese 2015: 2). All these neighborhoods were to give birth to the social conflict led by the descendants of immigrants (or third-generation immigrants) in 2005. In French suburbs like Clichy-sous-Bois, Aulnay-sous-Bois, Seine St. Denis, Grigny, descendants of Maghreb immigrants do not live their 'French dream'. Instead, they experience the highest rates of dropouts from school, unemployment, poverty and crime. As a Minister of Interior, Nicolas Sarkozy brought in restrictive immigration rule and tough policing in the *banlieues* that exacerbated youth discontent (Castles and Miller: 2009, 257). In November 2005 one Kurd and two Tunisians juveniles died after a police chase in Chichy-sous-Bois. The overnight clashes left many public and private properties destroyed, policemen as well as civilians injured and the areas more segregated than ever. One may argue that these riots were prophetically presented in the film of Mathieu Kassovitz "*La Heine*" that depicts approximately nineteen consecutive hours in the lives of three friends from immigrant families living in an impoverished multi-ethnic French housing project (a ZUP - *zone d'urbanisation prioritaire*) in the suburbs of Paris. In the film, actors experience the brutalization by the police feeling humiliated and racially as well as physically abused. In real life, the death of those children in the French *banlieues*—provoked by segregation, isolation and lack of social cohesion—led to acts of vengeance from both sides of the society (the French and the immigrants). The official response to the severe rioting was not to question the existing policy approach to these areas or to the minorities residing them, but to call for even tougher law and order measures (Castles and Miller: 2009, 257).

The same areas suffered from high rates of criminality and unemployment. Low levels of unemployment provided a safety valve against extremism for many years in French social space. In the mid-1980s, however, the first breakthrough of the FN in the elections coincided with the rise of poverty in the country. As of March 1986, the two-year cap of jobless persons living on extended unemployment benefits (518.000) was reached while in 1987 it was estimated that 2,500,000 people lived in families receiving less than half the minimum wage. One rough indicator of increasing distress is that from 600,000 to 1,000,000 car owners had allowed their insurance to lapse by 1987 (Freeman 1994: 198).

In the same period, FN voters came mostly from the Right-wing parties, from new voters and previous abstainers as well as, in lesser measure, the non-Communist Left. The FN, at the time, no longer had the activist means to lead, or the institutional power to control (Platone 1994: 64). In 1988 Le Pen secured the votes of 31 per cent of small business owners, 21 per cent of professional people (doctors, lawyers, etc.), 21 per cent of shop workers, 19 per cent of unemployed people, 18 per cent of farmers and agricultural workers and 16 per cent of factory workers. In terms of geographic spectrum, the FN's activities gave the party considerable strength, especially in the south of France (i.e. Perpignan and Marseilles). The FN had also a lot of influence in the police, the judiciary and the armed forces (Ford 1992: 21). Moreover, in the depressed steel and coal-producing areas of northern and eastern France, regions most badly hit by slow de-industrialization, the FN challenged the declining *Parti Communist Français* (PCF) for the working class vote. This challenge even extended into the historic heartland of French communism, Seine-St Denis in the "red belt" around Paris (Ford 1992: 20–21).

The second rise of the FN's electorate percentages came at a time when a socialist government under Laurent Fabius turned decisively towards the liberalization of the domestic market. Government controls over the nationalized industries were loosened so that they could lay off workers, become more profitable, invest abroad, and even sell off some subsidiaries to raise funds, whereas public sector wages were held down so as to enhance corporate profitability (Hall 1994: 178). The FN at its electoral peak (1995–2000) won the votes of 20–25 per cent of the unemployed in France (Ivaldi 2004: 63). Jean Marie Le Pen's victory over the Socialist ex-Prime Minister Lionel Jospin in the first round of the French parliamentary elections held in April 2002, amply demonstrated the inroads that the Far Right has been able to make into mainstream European politics (Singh 2002: 441).

Voters with grievances deriving from the rising unemployment and the austerity-sceptic allied themselves with traditional Euroscepticism in areas spreading from across the Channel up to the edges of Southern European electorates and called for a new EU-led strategy.

The lack of investment or growth and the liberalization of the labor market gave rise to Euroscepticism in 2005. At that time, France became the breeding ground of a dynamic nationalistic far-right wing rhetoric that was developed against the EU constitution. People were called on to decide about the ratification of the European Constitution via a referendum. Euroscepticism was founded on the inequalities existing in the domestic labor market and those attributed to the freedom of labor, people or services within European borders. The native middle-class disliked the liberalization of the economy as well as the lack of protective measures towards the local capital that led to a massive exodus abroad. As a result of this policy, many jobs were lost. Actually, a phrase became the origin of a controversy during the EU Constitution referendum: "Polish plumber" became well known after the Directive of Frits Bolkestein. This *cliché* symbolized the fear of cheap Central and East European labor threatening the jobs of West Europeans in the domestic market.

In the past, FN had also capitalized the liberalization of the labor market and pleaded for the rejection of the European Constitution. In 2005 the rate of unemployment in France had lain at 10 per cent, which supported the negative attitude towards the constitution as well as government policies. The party leader Jean-Marie Le Pen warned that the Constitution would weaken the rights of the workers in all sectors on the one hand and would heighten the rate of unemployment on the other. That was also the left-wing arguments against the ratification of the constitutional treaty. In addition, FN urged the reduction of social equality and the loss of the French sovereignty as the main reasons for his party's attitude. The reasons for the failure of the European Constitution can be detected in the national dissatisfaction concerning social inequality, a high rate of unemployment and a failed tax reform.

So, the referendum concerning the European Constitution was the next possibility to punish the head of state Jacques Chirac and the unpopular government of Jean-Pierre Raffarin (MacCormick 2005: 37–39). This was also a chance for the isolated FN that stood consistently in opposition to public opinion's positive assessment of France membership of the EC / EU and on the issue of the common currency, to identify with the dissatisfaction of the masses. This temporary dip in the public opinion's positive attitude coincided with the referendum on the proposed European Constitutional Treaty (Williams 2013: 143). After its rejection in France, the Dutch people also rejected the European Constitution Treaty on June 1st 2005. The French Prime Minister resigned from office and took the responsibility for the development of the referendum. The results were celebrated by the left and the far right wing voters for different reasons. At that time, Le Pen's anti-systemic and Eurosceptic stance was rewarded.

In this context, the rise of the FN was the reflection of social and economic inequalities at a local level where neighborhoods were transformed into ghettoes. At the local level, it can be expected that lower social strata are more likely to vote for extreme right-wing parties in countries where levels of inter-ethnic competition are higher (Lubbers 2002: 352). However, the present phenomena are a clear reflection of the global economic and political space. Migration along with the rapid process of social modernization, globalization and structural redefinition of the western nation-state, "provided the background to a highly diverse, variable and self-contradictory increase in right-wing extremism and the violence associated with it" (Heitmeyer, 2003: 399).

Violence by and against immigrants in the dilapidated Greek and French suburbs with high concentrations of these people made immigration the most tense political issue. In the next sub-chapter I will examine how the far right wing politicians manipulated the migration issue and set new challenges to the European integration as well as to the traditional understanding of citizenship linked to national belonging.

Migration and Naturalized Space in Greece

Until the 1990s, Greece had never been a country of receiving immigrants. Along with other countries of Southern Europe (Spain, Italy, Portugal) it was considered as a land of emigration and the only immigration involved repatriation of ethnic Greeks from abroad and arrivals of refugees in transit. However, the Dublin II Convention created congestion in the Southern European periphery, which the immigrants use as an entrance to the EU (Aegean Sea or Evros River in Greece, Lampedusa in Italy or Gibraltar). In the post-Cold War period, immigration soared and foreigners constituted 8 per cent of the total population of nearly 11 million and 13 percent of the workforce by 2001. In 2005, 1.1 million foreign-born persons settled and 105,000 foreigners born in Greece were recorded (Castles and Miller: 2009, 113).

The economic crisis and the consequent austerity measures have rendered multicultural or EU integrative plans problematic in Greek society. As in the French foyers and banlieues, the co-existence with Greek citizens is not tolerated when immigrants decide to claim their rights. In these cases, the presence of immigrants is interpreted as a societal threat particularly when they demand their share in accordance with the modern perception of security as freedom from want, freedom from war and freedom from fear (Amouyel, 2006: 13). (Amouyel, 2006: 13). For instance, in Manolada—a rural area of the Ilia region in Greece—some strawberry fields' foremen, faced charges for bodily harm and not for attempted murder despite shooting at their immigrant workers who were demonstrating against inhuman treatment and economic exploitation. Many immigrants were shot and injured by hunting weapons. They were threatened with being burnt alive if they demanded their salaries (Nodaros 2014).

Yves Mény argues that "whether or not they indulge in over racism, extreme right-wing parties reject the idea of a multiracial society and argue that the presence of substantial ethnic minorities constitutes a mortal threat to national identity that should be reversed" (Mény 1994: 12). '*La France aux Francais*' and '*Greece belongs to the Greeks*' are the simplistic slogans of the FN and of GD respectively.

In 2015, GD's electoral programs referred to the need to arrest and evict all illegal immigrants. Moreover, it stressed that they should not be detained in spaces with air-conditions, free lunches and luxuries that native Greek citizens cannot afford (GD electoral program 2015: 10). As we have seen, they exploited the fears of citizens in urban areas facing mass immigration.

Antonis Ellinas notes that repeated Eurobarometer polls of 2003 and 2009 show Greeks to be much more apprehensive of immigration than most Europeans. However, he stresses that according to Human Rights Watch report of 2012, "The latent xenophobia of the Greek electorate remained untapped by mainstream parties and the issue did not become politicized until recently, when immigration flows from Africa and Asia started changing 'the demographics of the entire country" (in Ellinas 2013: 557).

On the other hand, political parties placed immigration high in their political agendas and did not dare to transform jus sanguinis which is traditionally the norm of naturalization. According to law 2910/2001 (articles 58–64) only the immigrants, who live permanently and continuously in the country for ten of the last twelve years, are eligible to apply for citizenship. It is the longest time limit provided by national legislation along with that of Switzerland (Triantafyllides & Gropas 2008: 205).

In 2001 the government issued a three-year program: the Action Plan for the Social integration of immigrants (for the periods 2002–5), while in 2004 decided to issue permits of two-year duration to ease the task of administration and application by immigrants. In an attempt to rationalize policy, a new immigration bill was adopted on entry, stay and integration of third-country nationals in Greece, which was to become effective in January 2006. "*The bill was criticized for ignoring the majority of the illegal migrant population and preventing 70 per cent of the immigrants from obtaining resident permits*" (Arnold 2012: 103).

As we have seen, the spatial inequalities in the urban centers contributed significantly to the marginalization of certain geographical areas in Greece as well as in France. The hitherto marginalized areas had to deal with issues like crime and illegal immigration that pointed to deep-rooted socio-economic problems simmering below the apparently tranquil facade of European society. The humanistic theoretical approach of the left wing parties was not enough to convince the natives who were looking for scapegoats enraged by the inefficient protection measures by the state authorities during the crisis.

These constituencies confirm Alan Milward's argument about the two main social foundations of fascist mass movements: "The first, was urban, and either middle class or with middle-class attributes, shopkeepers, and shop-workers, minor bureaucrats and officials, professional people, students, unemployed personnel from the armed forces, and handicraft workers. The other was rural, peasant landowners, sharecroppers and occasionally larger landowners" (1982: 420). Since the inter-war years in Europe, the economic degradation of this middle-class signifies the rise of xenophobia and racism.

Jef Huysmans explored the links between the European integration process and the securitization of immigration, describing the latter as a parallel internal security project legitimating the exclusion of certain categories of people from the benefits of the European integration project by 'reifying them as dangers' (Huysmans 2000: 771). Huysmans claims that two images linked to one another are evident in the western European media: one is the growing feeling of insecurity (e.g. the image of big cities as places full of criminals and violence); the other is that Europe seems to be full of acts of violence against migrants and refugees and an escalating discourse of 'they are not welcome', or, 'they do not belong here'. In this construction of xenophobia and racism the security tale also speaks about 'us' (expressed in slogans such as 'we Austrians', 'own people first', etc.) who are threatened by the foreigners. "So the image seems to be not only one of insecure individuals threatened by 'foreigners', but also one of an insecure collective identity which unites the insecure individuals" (Huysmans 1995: 53). Huysmans, among others, has drawn attention to the defining role of language as an integrating or exclusionary force in social relations. He also outlines its role in naming threats and constituting a link between migration and security problems—such as drug trafficking, terrorism, and fundamentalism (Huysmans, 2002: 44–45).

The findings of an empirical research study conducted in 2000 by Panteion University in Athens on members of the judiciary and district attorneys of Athens show that "86 per cent of Greek judges consider immigrants to be responsible for the increase in Greece of criminal behavior, even though 50 per cent of those interviewed stated their 'affinity' for immigrants. One in four judges expressed a feeling of fear regarding the trend of migration" (Stangos 2006: 171).

GD effectively manipulated the rise of xenophobia and put the blame on European and Greek policies.

Migration and Naturalized Space in France

Rogers Brubaker (1992) argues that there are two legal grounds on which citizenship is attributed to immigrants: either a descent-based citizenship (*jus sanguinis*) or a place of birth (*jus solis*) regime—as happens in USA and Great Britain. It is noteworthy that in both France and Germany, as throughout Continental Europe, citizenship is ascribed to children of citizens, following the principle of *jus sanguinis*. Nonetheless, only French citizenship law incorporates substantial elements of *jus solis* (citizenship through birth in France) by attributing it at birth to a child born in France if at least one parent was born in France—including Algeria and other colonies and territories before their independence. In this context, citizenship is acquired automatically at the age 18 by all children born in France of foreign parents, provided they have resided in France for the last five years and have not been the object of certain criminal condemnations (Brubaker 1992: 81).

It could be argued that under circumstances of economic crisis even in a liberal state like France, *jus sanguinis* is the rule of naturalization of foreigners. As long as the economy is prosperous, plans of integration and multiculturalism have been largely workable. Under conditions of economic instability and fluidity however, migrants are seen even more as alien and their presence as an unwanted and intimidating disruption of the daily lives of native populations. In the early 1970s, labor shortages in France disappeared, and the first important decision to stem immigration was taken in July 1974 (Anderson 1997: 139). During the same period of time, the first world oil crisis also produced a lot of instability and inequalities in the domestic socio-economic space that had an impact on immigration policy.

In the mid-1970s, 32 Algerians were murdered in Marseilles, Toulon and Nice (Mousourou 1991: 157). In 1979 the attempts of President Giscard d'Estaing to repatriate almost 500,000 Algerians failed due to the resistance of the left-wing parties. In 1981, the election of a new President introduced a more integrative policy toward immigrants for a few years. Nevertheless, after 1981, the failure of the left to deliver, once in power, and to end the economic crisis through a structural break with capitalism dictated a new political agenda that offered the opportunity to Le Pen's populism. His electorate was held together by fear of immigration and immigrants—"it is relatively small, for example, in conservative areas of western France with low immigrant populations" (Mény 1994: 65).

In the 1990s, the country returned to tolerance and solidarity towards the needs of immigrants. The acceptance of multiculturalism is illustrated by a court rule of November 1989. The French *Conseil d'Etat* decided that Muslim Moroccan girls had the right to wear a veil in school, as long as this was the expression of their religious identity, they did not disrupt school activities and they abstained from proselytizing fellow students (Jopke 1996: 275). The compromise in the *chador* controversy has a symbolic importance for the government of Michel Rocard and the ongoing European integration and the redrawing of Europe after the collapse of the Soviet Union and the end of the Cold War. The decision endorsed by the Council of State balanced between the universalistic (human and civil rights) dimension of French republicanism and its particularistic (nationalist) dimension and received criticism from the right and the left wing parties (Hollified 1994: 166).

Economic development did not allow extreme right wing fears to be spread in the society. For instance, despite the aroused fears about fundamentalism, especially after violence in Algeria spilled over into bomb attacks on the Paris Metro in 1995, and some deportations of immigrants a year after, the republican principle of *ius soli* was not essentially undermined.

The Socialist government of 1997–2002 reinstated it for descendants of immigrants and liberalized rules of entry and residence" (Castles and Miller: 2009, 257). The same unresolved tension is also found with respect to the existence of a European citizenship, particularly where it involves the granting of voting rights in local and European elections to EU nationals living in other member-states. In the 1990s, European member-states introduced a concept of EU citizenship in Maastricht and confirmed it in Amsterdam linking it to *a priori* belonging of the individual to one of the member-states national communities. In practice, these treaties abolished internal borders for the EU citizens and at the same time raised walls to non-European citizens who tried to cross the external ones. "This implied a renewal of nationalism under the form of a European supranationalism that accounts for the exclusion of third-country nationals legally residing in Europe from the benefits of EU citizenship" (Martiniello 2000: 354).

The French government was under pressure by the Schengen Group and the Maastricht Treaty model that promoted citizenship for EU nationals and vote to EU nationals in local elections. In essence, these adoptions of citizenship implied that France had to renegotiate visa restrictions with its former colonies (Hollified 1994: 166–167). The paradox of a different reading of Euroskepticism can be traced here. The French government desired the unification of internal European borders but was skeptical about the adoption of treaties that constructed external ones challenging her republican model.

FN adopted a different reading of the treaties and since 1997 it called for a 'renegotiation' and for a rejection of Maastricht and Schengen. Yet, given that the role of Schengen is also to provide European borders, FN liked the fact that this treaty called for 'reinforcement of European borders against third world immigration'. In this context, the FN and socialist audiences agreed on a Euroskeptic approach of the treaties for different reasons. Even though immigration control and citizenship issues were not the Maastricht Treaty's primary objectives, they were hotly debated during the referendum over the creation of a single European market and currency, which passed in September 1992 by the narrowest of margins (Hollified 1994: 166–167).

After the Asiatic and later the world economic crisis, however, French governments started taking up the FN's agenda that reinforced anti-immigration rhetoric: the manifesto for the 2004 European election strongly opposed the concept of European citizenship, not only because of the perceived outcome of the erosion of the primacy of French sovereignty and citizenship, but also because according to the FN, that was becoming a major political force, it would lead to the naturalization of immigration (Williams 2013: 140). In the event, immigration and racial purity became a focal point of campaign debates of the right wing politician scrambling to avoid losing votes to Le Pen. When France lost the World Cup final in 2006, Le Pen complained that the team fielded too many players 'of color'. As Bracchi (2014) has successfully observed "*He has a string of convictions for inciting racial hatred*". He renewed his call for abolishing *jus soli*, ending immigrant family reunifications and giving a preference to French employees over foreigners (Ellinas 2010: 193).

One year after the severe rioting in the autumn of 2005, Sarkozy enacted his Immigration and Integration Law which introduced three new elements: an immigration policy based on selection according to economic criteria, mandatory 'integration contracts' for long-term residents and policies of 'co-development' to link migration, return and development of countries of origin. It has been argued that the law was popular and appears to have helped Sarkozy become President of France in April 2007 (Castles and Miller: 2009, 257). It should be noted though that he triumphed by enlisting the support of many former Le Pen voters and by placing immigration high on his political agenda. The FN continued to account for roughly four million votes and "some of its ideas, particularly the conflation of immigration, criminality, and Islam, remained broadly accepted beyond its own electorate" (Goodliffe 2013: 95).

The FN exploited confusion surrounding laïcité in French social and public space. It was a policy implemented since 1905 to eliminate the influence of religious authorities from any prominence within the state as well as to assimilate Jewish population who were the 'foreigners' at that time in France. Although the first official citing of laïcité was in the constitutional document that crafted the Fourth Republic in 1947 there is still a confusion of how tolerance or communication among those with and without faith can be guaranteed in this type of modernity. To acquire electoral support the FN painted a picture of the Republic as being outmaneuvered by an international schema of highly organized Islamist militants that brought the issue of immigration to the forefront of public concern (Marchese 2015: 2).

Chirac and Sarkozy, have tapped into the centre-right electorate by a hardline policy on immigration and adopting some of the extremist rhetoric of the FN. The latter put forward the idea of selective immigration of young and skillful immigrant workers to combat against racism. Moreover, the creation of the French Council of the Muslim Religion (CFCM) was perceived as a visible hand of the state in Muslim affairs frustrating purist defenders of laïcité, who claimed that the CFCM violated laïcité by blurring the dividing line between church and state (Marchese 2015: 2). In addition, Sarkozy took initiatives to crack down on this issue—such as the attempt to introduce DNA test as a precondition for reuniting immigrant families; the inauguration of a 'debate' on immigration and nationality; proposals to strip immigrants who are convicted of certain crimes of the French nationality and to create a probationary period during which the nationality of naturalized immigrants could be revoked; the banning of burqa and *niqab* in public spaces; the stepping up of deportations of *sans papiers*— were always to drive a rift between the most liberal and repressive wings of Sarkozy's electorate (Goodliffe 2013: 95). All French consulates were expected to be equipped with a biometrics system by the end of 2008. To control family reunification the law of 2007 required the applicant to earn the minimum wage and the law of 2006 extended the period of residence in France before becoming eligible to apply for permanent visa from twelve to eighteen months.

Moreover, the government was criticized for the policy involving the use of DNA test for family reunification mostly by far-left organizations within the *Unis Contre une Immigration Jetable* (UCIJ). While the Socialist Party leaders signed a collective petition of organizations in fierce disagreement with DNA tests introduction, none of them had attended the UCIJ meetings. This proved, not only that the party was ideologically divided, but also that most members publicly agreed with the idea of regulations to migration. This division gave power to Sarkozy's ethnocentric policy of 'chosen migration' for which his opponents claimed that it implies a utilitarian stance linking entry and stay to an economic interest (Coste 2008: 75–77).

However, the attribution of French citizenship was not enough to bring about the kind of social advancement and political integration of Muslim immigrants that had been accomplished by French Jews in the previous century. Spatial and economic conditions of the Muslim immigrants are quite different in modern France. "Compounded by the growing discontent among the Muslim population within the *banlieues*, one would be hard-pressed to contend that Sarkozy's integration strategy has been effective" (Marchese 2015: 3).

On the other hand, Marine Le Pen's far-right National Front (FN) adopted a more republican line by opposing euthanasia or speaking about reduction of immigration, while her father wanted to abolish it. However, as Gabriel Goodliffe stresses, the extent of the FN transformation into a systemic political party should not be exaggerated. "Anti-immigrant and particularly anti-Islamic racism and xenophobia still occasionally show through the new FN chief's rhetoric" (2003: 100). More effective than her father in media marketing, Marine Le Pen effectively promoted an unabashedly nationalist, populist, Islamophobic, xenophobic, and Eurosceptic ideology among the 'native' French citizens. In an article in 'Daily Telegraph' she heavily criticized Muslims praying outdoors, equalizing their action to Nazi occupiers. She noted that though there are no tanks and there are no soldiers "it is nevertheless an occupation and it weighs heavily on local residents" (Le Pen 2010).

In particular, after 9/11 a negative connotation was attributed to immigration. The challenge for Europe though, is how to manage the potential security implications of immigration—such as trafficking, large-scale unwanted immigration and criminal or terrorist links to migrant networks—without undermining those core 'European values' such as the commitment to freedom, human rights and justice, which are at the heart of the European liberal project (Dannreuther 2010: 111). Immigration followed the same path with state securitization where security is elevated over freedom and liberty (Bigo 2001: 123)[5].

Under the circumstances of economic crisis, democratic principles of egalitarianism, reciprocity, solidarity or integration on the basis of European democratic tradition become increasingly challenged and Euroscepticism, as it is expressed by GD and FN towards these values, is on the rise. As the Procurer of France and the Director of the French Institute in Thessalonica (Christophe Le Rigoleur) notes after Charlie Hebdo and the terrorist attack at the Jewish super-market in Paris, French people demanded with their demonstrations to pronounce the unity, solidarity and progress of the French democracy and the neutrality of the state towards religion (Le Rigoleur 2015). It is questionable whether Laïcité will be interpreted as an expression of co-existence, dialogue and toleration and whether respect will prevail.

Conclusions

Under conditions of economic instability and fluidity, democratic principles of egalitarianism, reciprocity, solidarity and integration on the basis of equality for all within open European societies, are challenged by far right wing parties in Greece and in France. In the economic crisis environment both GD and FN flourished by capitalizing on populist, nationalistic and xenophobic arguments. High unemployment rates along with the failure of the political parties in power to deliver their promises

---

[5] The UN estimates that 2.5 million people are in forced labor (including sexual exploitation) at any time, as a result of trafficking (Goldin, Cameron and Balarajan 2010: 207).

about development within the tight constraints of the European economy led to a search for scapegoats or for solutions against the established political system. The spatial inequalities produced in this environment nurtured far right wing electorates and played a very important part in tightening immigration rules and treatment of asylum seekers within the country.

Both FN and GD applied populism, xenophobic arguments and anti-Europeanism to contrast the political establishment. Both parties promoted the image of anti-systemic and anti-European political formation to challenge governments and enlist the grassroots support of electorates. However, GD has a distance to cover in order to promote itself as a non-antiestablishment party with a rejecting Euroscepticism, as the father of Marine Le Pen used to do. Marine Le Pen managed to convince French electorate that she has adopted Conditional Euroscepticism in Vassilopoulou's terms (2009: 7).

On the other hand, the defection from the traditional governmental parties and the support for far right wing parties indicates how powerful the spatial inequalities in both states are. The economic crisis, the high rates of unemployment and high taxation along with the falling housing prices accentuated socio-economic differences and destroyed the middle class. The presence of immigrants creating ghettoes and offering cheap labour ready to be exploited increased the fears of citizens for the preservation of their standards of living.

In addition, due to the economic crisis the hopes of the petty-bourgeoisies in underprivileged areas ('natives' or descendants of immigrants) of social mobility were shattered. In this space, it was clear that welfare provisions or property were not to be the great equalizers of men and social mobility could not be attained. Inequalities were worsening and dependency on state intervention was even greater in France and Greece. Both states could not prevent universal values and democratic institutions from being put under the scrutiny of populism and extremism that search for enemies and scapegoats.

Although voting for the far-right wing could be considered an action of revenge against the traditional political order rather than as a conscious identification with an extreme ideology that promised a brave new world, it threatened the rulers of states. During economic crisis and being unable to tap their electorates many of the traditional political parties in Greece as well as in France adopted some of the rhetoric of the extreme right wing and progressively pushed immigrants into the periphery of public life through a procrustean idea of what it means to be French or Greek. As in every society in Greek and French cultural and social space, two types of nationalism co-existed: the civic and the ethnic sphere. 'Civic nationalism is regarded by many scholars as having derived from the rationalism of the eighteenth-century Enlightenment, whereas ethnic nationalism emerged from organic notions of identity associated with the Romantic Movement' (Ignatieff 1993: 6). The latter looked mostly to the German ideal of ethnic nationalism appropriated and focused selectively on glorified notions of their remote past in order to achieve national assertion and to unite their people with false traditions in a 'homogeneous' society.

This stands opposed to approaches of Enlightenment philosophers like Descartes, Leibniz and Spinoza, who emphasized the universality of reason and the systematic justification as the template of a rationalist epistemology and denied the enslavement of people to passionate, imaginary or emotional interpretation (Ignatieff 1993: 7). It is the responsibility of the authorities to educate citizens to adopt the civic approach and not the ethnic one that expresses itself as a collective xenophobic grievance against the 'Others' (immigrants or European supranational policy-makers) even when these citizens see their wealth or their hopes of gaining access to the upper strata of the society being evaporated.

Since the political establishment eroded during economic crisis, the far right wing parties in Greece and France as an alternative proposed the organic category of a homogenous xenophobic, racist nation for those people who did want to vote for the political establishment or to adopt a value system in a left wing environment. They also proposed a positivist system of ethnic values for the creation of a 'homogenous' society at the time when the traditional political parties had difficulty in consolidating and defending a modern European society under the conditions of relativism prevailed in their economic or cultural space. They expressed a Euroscepticism that was a reflection of the inequalities in the economic and social web of the respective countries and created a polarized vertical division in their political space. GD and FN provided the nexus for those who could not adapt themselves in a multicultural, civic and open European society and viewed the latter as the source of spatial inequalities, either by flattering their primordial identities or by manipulating their financial and cultural insecurities.

References

Amouyel, A. (2006). What is Human Security? *Human Security Journal*, Issue 1, April, 10–23.

Anderson, M. (1997). *Frontiers, Territory and State Formation in the Modern World*, Oxford: Blackwell.

Arendt, H. (1958). *The origins of Totalitarianism*, Cleveland and New York: Meridian Books.

Arnold, G. (2012). *Migration. Changing the World*, London: Pluto Press.

Barnes, I.R. (2000). Antisemitic Europe and the 'Third Way': The Ideas of Maurice Bardèche, *Patterns of Prejudice*, 34:2, 57–73.

Betz, HG. (1994). *Radicalism and Right Wing Populism in Western Europe*, New York: St. Martin's Press.

Bigo, D. (2001). Migration and Security. In Guiraudon, V. and Joppke, Ch. (Eds.), *Controlling a New Migration World*, New York: Routledge, 121–149.

Bistis G. (2013), Golden Dawn or Democratic Sunset: The Rise of the Far Right in Greece, *Mediterranean Quarterly*, 24(3): 35–55.

Bracchi, P. (2014). The rise of the 'Devil's daughter', *The Daily Mail*, 30 May, published online in: http://www.dailymail.co.uk/news/article

Brubaker, R. (1992). *Citizenship and Nationhood in France and Germany*, Cambridge Massachusetts: Harvard University Press.

Chasapopoulos, N. (2013). *Chysi Avgi. Hi Istoria, Ta Prosopa kai hi Alithia* (Golden Dawn. History, Persons and Truth, Athens: Livanis.

Castles, S. and Miller, M.J. (2009). *The Age of Migration. International Population Movements in the Modern World*, New York: Palgrave Macmillan, 4th Edition.

Coste, F. (2008). Report from France. In Doomernik Jeroen & Jandl Michael (Eds), *Modes of Migration Regulation and Control in Europe*, IMISCOE Reports: Amsterdam University Press.

Catellani, P., Milesi P. and Crescentini A. (2006). One root, different branches. Identity, injustice and schism. In Klandermans, B. and Mayer, N. (Eds), *Extreme Right Activists in Europe. Through the Magnifying Glass*, London and New York: Routledge, 2006, 204–223.

Dannreuther, R. (2010). *International Security. The Contemporary Agenda*, Cambridge: Polity.

Delmendo, L.C. (2014). Greece's housing market remains depressed, published online in: http://www.globalpropertyguide.com/Europe/Greece/Price-History

Ellinas, A.A. (2010). *The Media and the Far Right in Western Europe: Playing the Nationalistic Card*, New York, NY: Cambridge University Press.

Ellinas, A.A. (2013). The Rise of Golden Dawn: The New Face of the Far Right in Greece, *South European Society and Politics*, 18:4, 543–565.

Featherstone, K (1998). Europeanization' and the Centre Periphery: The Case of Greece in the 1990s, *South European Society & Politics*, Vol. 3 (1), 23–39.

Freeman, G.P. (1994). Financial Crisis and Policy Continuity in the Welfare State. In Hall, P. A., Hayward, J. and Machin, H., *Developments in French Politics*, London: Macmillan, 188–200.

Ford, G. (1992) *Fascist Europe. The Rise of Racism and Xenophobia* (London – Colorado: Pluto Press).

Golden Dawn Political Programme 2015, (included in the newspaper *Chrysi Avgi* 14 January 2015, No, 911).

Goldin, I., Cameron, G. and Balarajan, M. (2010). *Exceptional People: How Migration Shaped Our World and Will Define Our Future*, Princeton and Oxford: Princeton University Press.

Goodlife, C. (2013). Globalization, class crisis and the extreme right in France in the new Century. In Andrea Mammone, Emmanuel Godin and Brian Jenkins, *Varieties of right-wing extremism in Europe*, London – New York: Routledge, 85–103.

Hainsworth, P. (2008). *The Extreme Right in Western Europe*, London and New York: Routledge.

Heitmeyer, W. (2003). Right Wing Extremist Violence. In Heitmeyer W & Hagan J. (Eds), *International Handbook of Violent Research*, Norwell: Kluwer Academic Publishers, 399–458.

Hollifield, J.F. (1994). Reconsidering the Republican Model. In Cornelius W.A., Martin P.L. Hollified J.F., *Controlling Immigration. A Global Perspective*, Standford: Standford University Press, 143–175.

Holloway, L. & Hubbard, P. (2001), *People and place: the extraordinary geographies of everyday life*, Harlow: Prentice Hall.

Huysmans, J. (1995). Migrants as a security problem: dangers of 'securitizing' societal issues. In Thranhardt, D. and Miles R. (Eds), *Migration and European Integration: the dynamics of inclusion and exclusion*, London.

Huysmans, J. (2000). The European Union and the securitization of migration, *Journal of Common Market Studies*, 38(5): 751–77.

Huysmans, J. (2002), Defining Social Constructivism in Security Studies. The Normative Dilemma of Writing Security, *Alternatives*, 27(suppl.),41–42

Ignatieff, M., Blood and Belonging: Journeys into the New Nationalism, New York: Farar, Strauss and Giroux, 1993.

'Internal Affairs charged former police commander with not taking necessary actions to stop Golden Dawn', Wednesday, October 02, 2013, published online in: https://icantrelaxingreece.wordpress.com/2013/10/03/former-commander-of-agios-panteleimonas-pd-arrested/

Ivaldi, G. (2004). *Droites populistes et extrêmes en Europe occidentale*, Paris: La documentation Francaise. In Hainsworth P. (2008), *The Extreme Right in Western Europe*, London and New York: Routledge.

Klandermans, B. and Mayers, N. (2006). Context, alliances and conflict. In Klandermans B. and Mayers N. (Eds.), *Extreme Right Activists in Europe. Through the magnifying* glass London – New York: Routledge, 28–41.

Kopecky, P. and Mudde, C. (2002). The two sides of Euroscepticism: Party positions on European Integration to East Central Europe, *European Union Politics* 3 (3), 297–326. Quoted in Williams B. (2013). *Right Wing Extremism and the Integration of the European Union. Electorate strategy trumps political ideology*. In Andrea Mammone, Emmanuel Godin and Brian Jenkins, London – New York: Routledge.

Lafont, V. (2006). France: A two-centuries-old galaxy. In Klandermans B. and Mayers N. (Eds.), *Extreme Right Activists in Europe. Through the magnifying* glass, London – New York: Routledge, 93–126.

Le Pen, M. (2010). Muslims in France 'like Nazi occupation, *The Telegraph*, UK, 12 December.

Le Rigoleur, C. (2015). Pos Antilamvanomaste tin enoia tis laïcité meta tis tromokratikes epithesis sto Parisi [How we conceive the meaning of laïcité after the terrorist attacks in Paris], published on line: http://www.ambafrance-gr.org/

Lubbers, M., Gijsberts, M. and Scheepers, P. (2002). Extreme right wing voting in Western Europe, *European Journal of Political Research* 41(3): 345–378

MacCormick, N. (2005). Who's Afraid of a European Constitution?, Exeter, Charlottesville: Imprint Academic Publisher.

Marchese, A. (2015). *Redefining laïcité: French integration and the radical right*, 24 January, published online in: https://www.opendemocracy.net/can-europe-make-it/anna-marchese/redefining- laïcité/

Margaronis, M. (2012). Fear and loathing Athens: the rise of Golden Dawn and the far right, *The Guardian*, 26 October.

Martiniello, M. (2000). Citizenship in the European Union. In Aleinikoff, A. T. and Klusmeyer, D. (Eds.), *From Migrants to Citizens: Membership in a Changing World*, Washington DC: Tarnegies Endowment for International Peace.

Mény, Y. (1994). *Government and Politics in Western Europe: Britain, France, Italy, Germany* [revised by Andrew Knapp and translated by Janet Lloyd], Oxford: Oxford University Press.

Miliband, R. (1969). *The State in Capitalist Society*, London: Weidenfeld & Nicolson.

Mousourou, L.M. (1991). *Metanasteusi kai metanasteutike politike stin Ellada kai tin Europi* [Mirgration and migratory policy in Greece and in Europe], Athens: Gutenberg.

Mudde, C. (2007). *Populist Radical Right Parties in Europe*, Cambridge: Cambridge University Press.

Nodaros, M. (02 August, 2014). *We will burn you alive if you ask for your accruals*, published online in: https://icantrelaxingreece.wordpress.com/author/icantrelaxingreece/

Norris, P. (2005). *Radical Right. Voters and Parties in the Electorate Market*, Cambridge: Cambridge University Press.

Platone, F. (1994). Public Opinion and Electorate Change, In P.A. Hall, J. Hayward & H. Machin (Eds), *Developments in French Politics*, London: McMillan, 55–76.

Poulantzas, N. (1979a). *Classes in Contemporary Capitalism*, London: Verso Editions.

Poulantzas, N. (1979b). *Fascism and Dictatorship*, London: Verso Editions.

Renton, D. (1999). *Fascism. Theory and Practice*, London: Pluto Press.

Sprague-Jones, J. (2011). Extreme right-wing vote and support for multiculturalism in Europe, *Ethnic and Racial Studies*, 34:4, 535–555.

Singh, P. (2002). The return of the extreme right in Europe, *Strategic Analysis*, 26:3, 441–446.

Smith, D.M. (1994). *Geography and Social Change*, Oxford: Blackwell.

Smith, H. (2013). Two Golden Dawn members killed in drive-by shooting outside Athens office, *The Guardian*, Friday 1 November, published online in: http://www.theguardian.com/world/2013/nov/01/golden-dawn-killed-shooting-athens

Smith, H. (2014a). Greece's Golden Dawn party describes Hitler as 'great personality', *The Guardian*, Wednesday 16 April, published online in: http://www.theguardian.com/world/2014/apr/16/greece-golden-dawn-hitler

Smith, H. (2014b). Home ownership in Greece 'a sick joke' as property market collapses, *The Guardian*, Friday 28 February, published online in: http://www.theguardian.com/world/2014/feb/28/home-ownership-greece-property-market

Stangos, P (2006). The Fight Against Racism, Xenophobia and Discrimination in Greece Today. The Normative Framework, Public Actions, and the European Challenge. In Papademetriou, D. G. and Gavounidis, J. (Eds), *Managing Migration: The Greek, EU, and the International Contexts*, Athens: IMEPO, 157–175.

Triantafyllidou, A. and Gropas, R. (2009). *Metanasteusi stin Enomeni Europi* [Immigration in United Europe], Athens: Kritiki.

Vasilopoulou, S. (2009). Varieties of Euroscepticism: The Case of the European Extreme Right, I *Journal of Contemporary European Research* (JCER), *Vol. 5* (1), 3- 23.

Verbunt, G. (1985), France. In Hammar, T., *European immigration policy. A comparative study*, Cambridge – New York: Cambridge University Press, 127–164.

Wacquant, L. (2002). Cutting the Ghetto: Political Censorship and Conceptual Retrenchment in the American Debate on Urban Destitution. In Cross, M. and Moore, R. (Eds), *Globalization and the New City*, Basingstoke and New York: Palgrave, 32–49.

Wacquant, L. (2008). *Urban Outcasts. A Comparative Sociology of Advanced Marginality* Cambridge: Cambridge University Press.

Waever, O., Buzan, B., Kelstrup, M. and Lemaitre, P. (1993). *Identity, Migration and the New Security Agenda in Europe*, London: Pinter.

Williams, B. (2013). Right Wing Extremism and the Integration of the European Union. Electorate strategy trumps political ideology. In Mammone, A., Godin, E. and Jenkins, B., *Varieties of right-wing extremism in Europe*, London – New York: Routledge, 134–148.

The Emergence of the ECB as a Political Actor

MAX LÜGGERT

The spread of the crisis across several states of the Euro area has seen a reconfiguration of one of Europe's most crucial institutions, the European Central Bank (ECB). Since its inception, the Bank has served a fairly conventional purpose, albeit on a different scale. However, as the sustainability of the public debt of several Euro zone countries was questioned, financial support became necessary. Additionally, in order to lower interest rates on government bonds, the ECB has announced to purchase sovereign bonds on the secondary market. This is a promising, but legally questionable affair, since the ECB is prohibited by statute to take part in the direct financing of government debt. All support is connected to the implementation of certain political measures. Apart from the economic considerations, the effects of the ECB's engagement on democratic responsiveness loom even larger. Countries such as Greece or Spain have to implement austerity policies which limit the options which are available to lawmakers and which have caused significant public backlash. My contribution seeks to understand how the ECB has evolved from a managing to a more political entity in recent years, and what effects this has on fundamental issues of liberal democracy.

Max Lüggert is PhD candidate at the Institute of Political Science and Sociology at Bonn University.

Keywords: ECB; Troika; Austerity; Crisis

Editors' Note

The role that the European Central Bank has perfomed during the crisis, highlights a seemingly apparent but, in fact, particularly valuable conceptual contribution: when in crisis, a system transforms. When socioeconomic systems transform, authority is transposed and new actors emerge in order to take up roles and mandates of their obsolete predecessors. In this framework, the paper of Max Lüggert discusses how and why the ECB is becoming a political player. The new role taken up by the ECB in the context of the crisis, to a certain point, sums up the process of EU's institutional progress that is balancing between political choices and organic evolution. It also indicates the disproportionally strong impact of the period of the crisis on EU integration. On a different level, the author cautiously refers to the unclear dividing lines between economic forces and political decision making both in the EU model of governance and beyond. The article reminds that authority comes with responsibility and that, if the

ECB is to sidestep its original institutional and legal mandate in the future, it needs to build its capacities and instruments for doing it more successfully.

Introduction

The consequences of the financial and economic crisis still pose a significant challenge to the European Union (EU). It is no exaggeration that the current crisis can be seen as the most severe one since the inception of the EU and that it has exposed several institutional flaws of the EU. All of this has caused discord about the further path of European integration, especially regarding the design of financial aid (Pacheco Pardo 2012: 78–80).

After the financial crisis escalated in the United States following the bankruptcy of Lehman Brothers in September 2008, it spread over Europe the following year. A key event was the announcement of an unexpectedly high budget deficit by the Greek government. This initiated a vicious cycle which has been observed several times in other Euro countries in the following years: investors losing trust because of high deficits, subsequently rating agencies downgrading sovereign bonds leading to the most critical development: higher interest rates on sovereign bonds (Petrakis, Kostis and Valsamis 2013: 13). This was a significant shock, especially for the southern countries of the Euro zone. Prior to the introduction of the common currency, those countries had fairly high interest rates, also due to their tendency to devaluate their currencies. However, once the Euro was introduced, the interest rates of all sovereign bonds in the Euro zone converged to a much lower level, closer to the rates that were demanded for German sovereign bonds (Geeroms, Ide and Naert 2014: 154). As governments of the southern Euro countries had grown accustomed to the new low rates, those sudden hikes in interest rates had a severe impact on the public finances of the most affected countries.

The initial response to the crisis in Greece was an assistance programme, but once other countries such as Ireland and Portugal had to face similar issues, the decision was made to institutionalise financial aid at the European level. As a result, bodies such as the European Financial Stability Facility (EFSF) and later the European Stability Mechanism (ESM) were established (Petrakis, Kostis and Valsamis 2013: 13–14). However, any financial support is subject to the implementation of austerity policies, which are mostly characterized by cuts in public spending. The implementation of such policies also led to some political anomalies; in both Greece and Italy, extraordinary government changes occurred, as two technocrats—Loukas Papadimos and Mario Monti—assumed the office of Prime Minister with no election taking place. These policy changes did not take place without criticism or opposition, as social unrest arose in several crisis countries; and conversely, the crisis proved to be an unprecedented test of solidarity for those countries which were contributing the most to the financial aid (Antentas and Vivas 2014: 15; Tosun, Wetzel and Zapryanova 2014: 196).

From a very critical point of view, the influence of European political bodies could be viewed as an exercise of "neo-colonial power" (Antentas and Vivas 2014: 15), but even a more level-headed assessment should come to the conclusion that the present crisis poses a significant challenge to the European social model (Pacheco Pardo 2012: 80).

As a consequence, one institution was put into the spotlight of the crisis reactions, the European Central Bank (ECB). This appears to be a logical development; many of the problems the EU faces are related to liquidity and solvency issues—due to its nature and instruments at hand, an institution with "unlimited firing power" (de Grauwe 2013: 529) such as the ECB is well suited to assist in solving said issues.

However, this new role also comes with several institutional shifts and developments, which I will address in this contribution. The ECB is able and willing to assist in the solvency and liquidity problems of the crisis countries, but the bank does not provide this support out of sheer altruism and goodwill. It expects certain policy conditions to be met. This influence becomes visible in two activities the ECB has undertaken, which are different from the measures and tools it used before the crisis. One activity is the ECB's participation in the so called Troika, alongside the European Commission and the International Monetary Fund (IMF). This arrangement undertakes the task of monitoring the implementation of policy reforms in the countries which ask for assistance, and furthermore the Troika can decide to withhold further financial support, if it deems that the requested reforms are being insufficiently implemented.

The second new tool used by the ECB is the announcement of the purchase of sovereign bonds in the secondary market. Two programmes are being used by the ECB for this purpose, the Securities Markets Programme (SMP) and the Outright Monetary Transactions (OMT)[1]. This measure is intended to lower interest rates on sovereign bonds in order to alleviate the debt situation of crisis countries; but just as is the case with the support by the Troika, all bond purchases are contingent on policy conditionality.

Both those interventions pose the question whether or not the ECB is emerging as an actor that not only has a clear role in the economic system, but that also shapes the political landscape in the crisis countries and the EU at large. I intend to answer this question by initially explaining how an organisation outside the political sphere (narrowly speaking) can wield political influence. Afterwards, I will explain the nature and the rationale behind the ECB's new instruments which were just mentioned. And finally, I will transpose the theoretical and institutional arguments upon two countries—Spain and Greece—in order to assess the actual change in the political influence of the ECB.

The Political Influence of Central Banks

Even though central banks are—from a strict point of view—not political institutions, they possess a certain political influence. Before explaining this influence later in this article, I intend to give a short theoretical overview about how political influence of central banks can be conceptualized.

---

[1] This programme is supposed to create market incentives that make sovereign bonds of the crisis countries appear as a less risky investment. More on that below.

One theory dealing with the standing of non-political institutions is multi-level governance, developed among others by Marks, Hooghe and Blank (1996). This theory deals with two developments: the increasing interdependence between several political levels—such as the national and the European level—as well as the less distinct difference between public and private institutions, which leads to the involvement of non-political institutions in decision-making (Piattoni 2010: 28). Even though the value and utility of this theory does not go unchallenged,[2] I find it useful because it focuses on two issues which converge into a distinct phenomenon: the influence that a non-political institution on the European level can impose on political institutions at the national level.

But even if one acknowledges the fact that institutions such as central banks *can* exercise political influence, one still has to consider *how* this influence can be gauged. Referring to the theory of social systems, several components of political influence can be identified. Generally speaking, power exists where someone in power is able to control the choice among several alternative actions of someone who is subordinate to power. From a classic political science perspective this can be done by hierarchies, which in turn can be clarified and legally institutionalized—for example through a constitution. But even without that, power can manifest itself in relations, where such a control of alternative actions takes place. This situation can be amplified when there is a certain event or a certain sanction the subordinate seeks to avoid; in such a case the actor in power is able to influence the decision of the subordinate to reach a certain result, regardless of whether the subordinate likes this result or not (Luhmann 2012: 16–19, 30–31).

Exceptional circumstances, such as the crisis that has been unfolding for several years now, can also lead to a situation where political options are being curtailed because of presumed or manifest necessities. In the crisis situation at hand, central banks can take over a more important and determining role in the affairs of a state. One crucial aspect shared by all crisis countries is the dire need for refinancing means, since their access to refinancing via bond markets is partially or completely restricted. Like I said in the introduction, the ECB can provide liquidity at will since it is one of the few actors in the financial sphere that can create liquidity *all by itself*. Applying the constellations of power mentioned earlier, this can create a situation where central banks can gain a powerful position.

Crisis countries in the Euro area identify a scenario they seek to avoid, namely the uncontrolled sovereign default and the exit from the common currency area; in order to prevent this from happening they can turn to the support of the ECB. From this pattern, the ECB can exercise influence if it receives agreement to a (politically speaking) disadvantageous result from its counterparts: the acceptance of a narrowed margin for

---

[2] Knodt and Große Hüttmann (2006: 235–236) mention the criticism that multi-level governance does not really constitute a new theory, but rather an amalgamation of hypotheses from existing theories. Piattoni (2010: 91) however offers a convincing rebuttal to this. Additionally, the criticism that multi-level governance suffers from a problem solution bias that neglects the political nature of questions such as legitimacy, hierarchy and accountability (Teßmer 2012: 79–83) has likewise been addressed by several authors (for an example, see Papadopoulos 2008: 38).

political action. If this conditional support is also planned out to a certain timetable, another condition of power is met: the initial acceptance of conditionality would be motivated from the desire to not declare sovereign default, while the repeated acceptance and implementation of conditionality would be motivated from the desire to avoid sanctions, namely the withdrawal of financial support.

Departing from this model situation, I will turn to explaining it in two steps. Initially I will focus on two of the new instruments used by the ECB in crisis reactions—its participation in the Troika and its bond purchase programmes—before turning to Greece and Spain, which serve as case studies for the analysis of the implementation of the aforementioned new instruments.

The New Instruments of the ECB

Prior to the crisis, many central banks—including the ECB—were following the conventional wisdom of proper central bank conduct, which had established itself since the 1970s. Price stability and central bank independence were put forward as the pillars of any sound model of monetary governance. The main instrument of monetary policy was the adjustment of interest rates, while the task of supervising and ensuring financial systemic stability was often delegated to separate organizations, assuming that the maintenance of a certain inflation target would by itself already defuse the threat of bubbles in the financial sector (Cukierman 2013: 374).

The escalation of the crisis led to a complete turn in the ECB's monetary policy and to a historic loosening regarding liquidity provision. In a climate of uncertainty and extreme caution in the financial markets, the ECB was put into the position of acting as a lender of last resort (Cukierman 2013: 379–380), which it never had to do before. For the purpose of this article—assessing the political influence of the ECB—I look at two measures[3] fully or partially initiated by the ECB: its participation in the Troika and its role as a purchasing agent of sovereign bonds.

The ECB as Part of the Troika

As a response to the needs of the most critically affected countries, support mechanisms were implemented in order to provide funding to those countries which could not expect to refinance themselves in the open market. In this regard Greece, Portugal, Ireland, Cyprus and Spain received financial assistance in various forms. After the first financial support for Greece had been conducted on a bilateral and somewhat provisional basis, the need for assistance in other countries prompted policy-makers throughout Europe to reach an institutionalization of financial support. This institutionalization materialized in the establishment of different bodies such as the European Financial Stabilisation Mechanism (EFSM), the European Financial

---

[3] Another important instrument of the ECB is the provision of liquidity through long-term refinancing operations (LTROs). The objective of these operations is to alleviate liquidity problems in the banking sector (Buiter and Rahbari 2012: 1); because this constitutes actions between banks, rather than actions between a central bank and governments, I refrain from addressing LTROs in further detail.

Stabilisation Facility and the European Stability Mechanism, which now serves as a permanent framework for financial assistance within the EU. While the ECB itself does not make any financial contributions, it is a part of the so called Troika, which is a crucial actor in this setting. The Troika is composed of representatives of the ECB, the European Commission and the IMF; it is charged with monitoring the implementation of adjustment policies, which form the precondition for any sort of financial assistance (Geeroms, Ide and Naert 2014: 180–185).

The focus on low levels of budget deficits and sovereign debt levels, also represented by the Troika, follows a certain line of thought. The 3% threshold on deficits is intended to secure the functioning of the common monetary policy of the Euro area, and the limit on the ratio of sovereign debt and GDP is designed to prevent private investments being crowded out by debt-financed public spending. The vicious cycle of rising interest rates which reinforce the critical debt position of states has been mentioned in the introduction, but also serves as a rationale for restricting sovereign debt levels (Geeroms, Ide and Naert 2014: 249). In theory, these guidelines should ensure a steadily prosperous economic development. The actual effects of the adjustments set forth in accordance with these premises will be addressed later in this article.

In the context of the implementation of adjustment policies, the ECB takes a swift turn into the political sphere. As a part of the Troika it is not directly involved by issuing any financial support, as this is done through the several European crisis institutions, such as the EFSM, the EFSF or the ESM and the IMF; the funding is therefore primarily provided by countries and not by the central bank itself. Nonetheless, the ECB is part of a body that can predetermine political decision-making and can issue a stoppage in financial assistance if the predetermined political path is not followed in a satisfactory manner.

Notwithstanding the actual implementation of the assistance-adjustment nexus in the different countries, this basic situation puts the Troika—and therefore to some extent the ECB—into a position where it can exercise political influence.

Bond Purchasing Programmes

A critical aspect of the crisis developments were the hikes in interest rates for sovereign bonds, which magnified the burden of debt that some countries had to deal with. While the adjustment and monitoring under the guidance of the Troika has the general objective of improving the economic situation in a certain country, the bond purchases are a specific response of the ECB to these volatilities in the bond markets.

The main premise of bond purchases is to signify confidence in the countries' ability to repay their debt. Additionally, investors may take a chance on investing in certain countries if they know that they can shift possible losses to another institution. This measure carries a legal uncertainty though; according to Article 123 of the Treaty on the Functioning of the European Union (TFEU) the ECB is not permitted to purchase debt instruments such as sovereign bonds directly from EU member countries. Therefore, the ECB does not purchase those bonds directly, but rather on the secondary market from other investors. Whether this also constitutes a breach of the provision of Art. 123 TFEU is a matter of legal debate[4], and this uncertainty can cause a loss of confidence in the ECB's integrity (Duncan 2013: 197–207).

Two bond purchasing programmes have been conducted by the ECB to date. The first programme was the SMP, introduced in 2010. In 2010 and 2011, sovereign bonds were purchased in two phases: Greek, Irish and Portuguese bonds in the first and Italian and Spanish bonds in the second phase (Malo de Molina 2014: 53).

In 2012, with SMP well underway, there was still a fluctuation of interest rates which could not be explained by substantial shifts in the macroeconomic environment, but was rather the consequence of a diffuse loss in confidence. The response to this was a shift to the Outright Monetary Transactions programme, which was designed as a more aggressive variation of the earlier SMP and was supposed to act as a clear signal[5] to deter any doubts in the ECB's willingness to engage in the secondary bond markets. Two main aspects are different from the SMP: first of all, there are no limitations in the duration or the volume of bond purchases and secondly, countries who seek assistance through bond purchases now have to subject themselves to political conditionality, similar to the Troika support. In practice, this should be realized by making the activation of an adjustment programme according to the ESM a precondition for OMT support (Geeroms, Ide and Naert 2014: 234; Duncan 2013: 199).

These measures also constitute a drastic departure from what is considered as sound monetary policy by an independent central bank; however, just the announcement of the OMT led to lower interest rates, as the programme itself has not been invoked thus far (de Grauwe 2013: 520; Duncan 2013: 199). And since the shift to OMT introduced the aspect of conditionality, the ECB once again widened its range into the political sphere, providing another instrument of support that depends on the fulfilment of certain political targets.

A preliminary view of the ECB's new instruments shows that the ECB has put itself in a position of political influence. In dealing with the crisis, it interacts with the countries affected by the crisis; providing support, but at the same time expecting a certain behavior in policy. To assess the actual scope of influence, it is advisable to look at the situation in certain countries in more detail. I shall do so in the following section by examining the developments in Greece and Spain.

---

[4] Duncan (2013: 206) espouses a critical view of the ECB's bond purchases, stating that even though those purchases occur on the secondary market "the ECB is ultimately financing government debt, but is simply doing so using third party intermediaries." Additionally, the ECB's bond purchasing programmes are still subject to legal review. Recently, a case against the OMT programme was brought forward to the German Constitutional Court, which deferred the final judgment on the matter to the European Court of Justice; see Wendel (2014). In its judgment, the European Court of Justice finally declared the bond purchases under the OMT programme as in line with the ECB's mandate.

[5] In this regard, the introduction of OMT is often linked to the promise, that "the ECB is ready to do whatever it takes to preserve the Euro", made by ECB chief Mario Draghi in London, on a conference in July 2012. The full transcript of said speech is available at www.ecb.europa.eu/press/key/date/2012/html/sp120726.en.html (last checked December 17th 2014).

The Presence of the ECB in Crisis Countries

Before explaining the ECB's activities in two crisis countries—Greece and Spain—in further detail, I will quickly explain why I chose to look at these countries more closely. Apart from the fact that a contribution within a volume cannot run to an unlimited length, which naturally constrains the number of cases which can be observed, I find the chosen countries to represent some critical junctures within the crisis development. Greece stands for the escalation of what was primarily a disorder in the financial sphere into a matter of serious doubts in the viability of the very economic and social foundations of a state; and furthermore the Greek case made the deficiencies of the single European monetary regime apparent to observers inside and outside Europe.

While the Spanish case has different features, it still constitutes a major aspect of the crisis because of the country's standing in the political and economic framework of Europe. While other crisis countries such as Ireland, Portugal or Cyprus were also severely affected, none of these countries represented such a sizeable part of the European economy and population as Spain does. The support for Ireland, Portugal and Cyprus was (among other assumptions) based on the thought that because of those countries' smaller sizes, their problems would not pose an insurmountable challenge to the capabilities of the other European countries. With Spain struggling though, the result is that a larger economic entity draws on the support of a smaller number of partners within the EU. This can contribute to a development where fewer countries have to participate in increasingly large support schemes.

Greece: Exploring the Path

As mentioned earlier, the announcement of an unexpectedly high budget deficit by the Greek government in October 2009 led to the escalation of the sovereign debt crisis in Europe (Petrakis, Kostis and Valsamis 2013: 13). But from a Greek perspective, this was the consequence of developments that had started a long time before.

The Greek political setting had been characterized by a political-administrative sphere with significant influence in the economic affairs. Additionally, the existence of a large group of civil servants with strict political loyalty and the high juridification of all sorts of public affairs led to a situation where the administrative system was equally extensive and unorganized; resulting in inefficiency, especially in the welfare sector. One also has to note that this does not signify a quasi-socialist setting, where the state dictates all matters; it could rather be read as a legacy of the weakness of the Greek bourgeois class of entrepreneurs, which has always sought good relations to those in power due to its inability to act as an autonomous agent on its own (Katrougalos 2013: 94–96).

The specific economic issues were preceded by two developments. In the eighties and nineties, the socialist governments led by Andreas Papandreou followed a policy intended to raise private income and state expenditure; an understandable reaction given the era of instability and political violence that preceded this time. Since no substantial productivity growth materialized, higher debts and deficits were the consequence of this approach. The introduction of the common currency[6] intensified this development as it lowered the interest rates on bonds for all Euro countries, down towards the level of German bonds. As a consequence, more lending took place in Greece which raised consumption and investments, but also came with higher wage costs, which hampered Greece's competitiveness.[7] The already mentioned deficiencies of the state did not help solving the problem either. State expenses were coordinated, organized and controlled poorly and the tax system was hamstrung by a lack of technical capabilities and political will, leading to a suboptimal state income situation.

After the announcement of the high deficit, credit downgrades raised the interest rates on sovereign bonds, which further deteriorated the general economic situation. As a result, the sovereign debt quota which had been floating around 105% for several years skyrocketed to 165% in 2011 (Blyth 2014: 96–97). It should be noted that other governments after Papandreou played a role in critical developments as well. Greece's accession to the Euro, which was finalized in 2001 during the government of Kostas Simitis was based on inaccurate budget data.[8] Additionally, Simitis and his successor Kostas Karamanlis oversaw a significant rise in loans issued for house purchases. The widespread collapse of loans in this sector was one of the main reasons for the severe problems banks were facing at the beginning of the crisis and in Greece, this problem was more pronounced than anywhere else in the Eurozone[9] (Geeroms, Ide and Nart 2014: 155, 159).

The decision to support Greece in this situation was partly founded in political and symbolic motives, looking to prevent the disintegration of one of the youngest, albeit most manifest symbols of political unity in Europe—the common currency. The economic rationale was just as important though; coming off the Lehman bankruptcy shock, many European banks faced a critical situation in which one of their biggest debtors—the Greek state—could default, rendering significant parts of their assets worthless (Geeroms, Ide and Naert 2014: 178). As a response, Greece had to be supported financially twice; an aspect which also signifies the development of the crisis architecture in the meantime. The initial support started in 2010 and was conducted on a bilateral basis, with support from the IMF, in order to reduce the financial commitment

---

[6] In this context it should be noted that in the year preceding Greece's accession to the Euro, the deficit was reported to be 1,8% - so within the Maastricht threshold of 3% - but actually was 3,7%. And even though the European statistical agency Eurostat had suspicions about the validity of the Greek data, the ECOFIN decided not to halt Greece's accession to the Euro (Geeroms, Ide and Naert 2014: 159). This shows that only blaming Greek representatives for enabling Greece to join the Euro under false premises is inaccurate; representatives of the other Euro countries could have decided to pay closer attention to the doubts which were put forward—they decided not to, and thus have their own share of the responsibility.

[7] For instance, the average annual change of unit labor costs in Greece was at the third-highest level in the Euro area, only surpassed by Luxembourg and Cyprus (Geerome, Ide and Naert 2014: 161).

[8] Once again, the negligence of other European actors—as mentioned in the endnote 5—should be kept in mind.

[9] From 1999 to 2008, the annual increase in loans for house purchases amounts to more than 30% in Greece. In comparison, Ireland and Spain—two countries which are widely associated with having suffered from a similar housing bubbles—have much lower figures in this regard, at 23 and 20%, respectively (Geeroms, Ide and Naert 2014: 155).

of the EU and to receive expertise from an institution that has dealt with similar support in times past. By 2011 though, the previous assistance proved to be insufficient, despite a haircut having been agreed upon. By that time, financial support had already been somewhat institutionalized in the framework of the EFSF; this facility was then the main source of support in the second programme. The two programmes had a volume of 110 and 164 billion Euros, respectively (Geeroms, Ide and Naert 2014: 180–184).

As mentioned above, any kind of financial support is subject to policy conditionality, which comes with regular supervision by the Troika, including the ECB. The background to the development of this conditionality mirrors the unexpected nature of this crisis, though. The MoU, which fixes both the support payments and the political conditions attached to those payments had to be put together quite rapidly and its wording relied heavily on earlier agreements between the IMF and Turkey or Mexico. Because of this, the MoU could not really address the specific deficiencies of the Greek economy; instead, the main pillars of the political conditionality were a reduction of public expenses in all fields, deregulations in the labor market and privatization of public corporations and other assets. In many cases, these measures have little impact concerning financial utility and are rather following a neo-liberal orientation, which is regularly espoused by the ECB and the IMF alike. Despite the difficult situation in key social services such as education and healthcare, strict personnel reduction targets had to be met.[10] Keeping in mind the tremendous social costs associated with this policy shift, one also has to remember that none of the support is designated to provide additional state funding, it is rather supposed to provide the Greek state with sufficient liquidity to meet its repayment and refinancing needs. Thus, ultimately, the main financial burden of the crisis adjustments lies with the population at large (Katrougalos 2013: 97–100).

Apart from the economic and social fallout, the implementation of the adjustment policies is debatable from a legal and institutional standpoint. Several legal acts which have been enacted in fulfilling policy targets determined by the Troika have lowered wages, even for employees outside the public sector. This constitutes a severe violation of the right to collective bargaining; a basic social right, not only protected by the Greek constitution, but also reaffirmed by several international treaties, such as the European Social Charter. Furthermore, the policy measures are designed to circumvent parliamentary participation. One law specifically states that economic agreements conducted in the context of crisis are presented to the parliament only for discussion and information and not for ratification, since those agreements shall be valid upon signature. The Greek constitution declares that international treaties dealing with economic cooperation which may burden Greek citizens have to be ratified by parliament (Katrougalos 2013: 102–103). It is very hard to argue that the Memorandum

---

[10] One example of this approach is the reduction of expenses for hospitals and primary care by 25% since the onset of the crisis. This step has already yielded dramatic consequences: between 2009 and 2013, Greece has reported a 32-fold rise in HIV infections, a rise in child mortality of 43% and its first case of Malaria since 1974 (Blyth 2014: 331–332).

between Greece and the Troika by nature does not constitute such a kind of treaty, which would require full parliamentary consent.

After assessing the enormous social consequences of the adjustments, it is necessary to gauge whether the ECB as part of the Troika has been able to maintain a position of power vis-à-vis the Greek government. Despite the shaky constitutionality of several central adjustment policies, most of those measures up until now have withstood judicial review. And even though some tranches of the support were suspended because of delays in the reports from the Greek government, regular disbursements have taken place since May 2010, with the Directorate General for Economic and Financial Affairs of the European Commission (DG ECFIN) noting that as of April 2014 all 49 major political objectives agreed upon in the MoU have been met. The "reward" for this compliance has been a total financial support of nearly 215 billion Euros, provided between May 2010 and December 2013 (DG ECFIN 2014: 69–70, 75–78; Katrougalos 2013: 103).

The continuous implementation of the adjustment measures shows that the Greek government is willing to subject itself to a policy predetermination by the Troika, only to ensure the continued financial assistance. Since the Greek government is dependent on the provision of financial support, it is in a structurally weaker and powerless position. And while the Troika itself has to be cautious not to put forward completely destructive policy proposals, it could notice that the Greek government is willing to accept provisions which violate fundamental social and constitutional principles, only to keep its part of the deal. In post-crisis-Greece, the ECB—as part of the Troika—has been able to establish itself as an agenda-setting, predetermining and evaluating agent that holds significant power and has shaped most of the country's (economic) policy in the last few years.

Spain: Continuing the Routine

In Spain, the conditions prior to the crisis were somewhat different to those in Greece. In fact, during the first years of the Euro, Spain experienced general economic success and profited from the expansive effects of the new common currency. By introducing the Euro, Spain followed the common credibly low inflation target put forth by the ECB; this way an expansive development in demand helped Spain get closer to European standards of economic progress, stability and welfare (Malo de Molina 2014: 43). On the other hand, several critical developments also took place, which helped set up the enormous economic collapse after the crisis.

In the previous decades the composition of Spain's economic output has taken a turn away from industry and more towards services. This can also constitute a viable economic strategy, however it comes at a cost, which is the higher dependence on (foreign) income. In turn this means that once credit flows subside, as in crisis times, those economic sectors face problems (Blyth 2014: 101). The economic expansion in Spain also caused a rise in credit availability, and foreign lenders were willing to borrow to Spain at a low rate. This pattern was also visible in Greece (see the previous subsection) and showed that the market reacted to the common currency area differently than envisaged.[11] The vast amounts of available credit were channelled into the construction and real estate sectors, two sectors which are most vulnerable to swift changes in interest rates. Furthermore, an entire branch of the Spanish financial sector, the so called *cajas de ahorros*, was exposed the most in this credit expansion. The credit expansion led to oversized balance sheets for many cajas, and additionally their local or regional foundation caused a business behaviour which was more focused on pleasing local political authorities than making sound investment decisions.[12] The danger of this development did not go unnoticed to Spanish monetary authorities, as a report of the *Banco de España* from 2006 already notes that the steadily rising need for refinancing signalled a growth pattern which cannot be upheld indefinitely (Malo de Molina 2014: 44; Neal and García-Iglesias 2013: 341).

What has to be mentioned is that the public finances of Spain were very solid prior to the crisis. Unlike Greece, which had to deal with a difficult financial situation well before the crisis, the Spanish public debt rate was 26% in 2007, almost half of Germany's rate at the time (50%). The escalation of the Spanish crisis completely evaporated this position, as the burst of the real estate bubble triggered a severe debilitation of the entire Spanish banking system. Massive losses in existing assets were combined with a sudden cutback in refinancing, and the support for financial institutions undertaken by the state led to a rise in public debt (Blyth 2014: 99; Malo de Molina: 48–49).

Keeping this in mind one popular crisis narrative—attributing financial problems to inflated and overspending government structures—does not hold true for Spain. Spain had to ask for support because it was confronted with a sudden rise of public debt to a critical level. The reasons for this were completely different from the Greek case though. While Spanish public finances were solid compared to other European countries, it was the real estate and construction sectors which grew unsustainably to enormous sizes, meaning that the crisis in those sectors pulled the rest of the Spanish economy down as well. In this context, Spanish government authorities could (and should) be blamed for turning a blind eye on the excessive developments in key economic sectors, but they cannot be blamed for continuous and excessive spending habits.

Despite these structural differences, the Troika's response for Spain seems awfully similar. Spain was provided with support from the EFSF in order to help recapitalize and restructure the Spanish banking sector (Geeroms, Ide and Naert 2014: 184). Just like Greece, Spain had to sign a Memorandum of Understanding and obliged itself to

---

[11] There were two assumptions which considered how to avoid excessive macroeconomic imbalances: 1. markets being assumed to be efficient, the hope was that countries deviating from the common path of stability would have to pay higher risk premia, which should make refinancing more difficult and work as an incentive to undertake the necessary adjustments; 2. governments were considered capable of leaving a risky economic path in time. As Malo de Molina (2014: 46) simply puts: "None of this happened." (orig: "Nada de esto occurió.")

[12] This is true especially for the Spanish coastal regions, where the real estate boom provided ample opportunity for engagement by the cajas (Neal and García-Iglesias 2013: 340–341). Not all political involvement in the cajas fuelled the calamitous engagement in the real estate sector, though. In the Basque country for instance, political involvement determined that real estate investments had to be limited; in turn, more investments were diverted to manufacturing industries instead (Blyth 2014: 103).

policies, which were predetermined by the Troika and subject to its review. Unlike Greece, where many specific general economic policies were set forth in the MoU, the bulk of the conditionality in the MoU with Spain is centred on issues relating to banking and the financial sector at large (DG ECFIN 2012: 65–66).

Nonetheless, the adjustment which was to be implemented in Spain also carried several neoliberal economic policy proposals. Deregulation of the labour market was another element of the adjustment in Spain, containing several steps already undertaken in Greece, such as the decentralization of wage-setting—i.e. a step back from the principle of collective bargaining—and the shift from rigid full-time to more flexible part-time contracts (Neal and García-Iglesias 2013: 342). Even though the MoU does not explicitly state these steps as political conditions, it includes a general provision of opening the Spanish economy to new funding sources,[13] under which policies aimed at improving competitiveness can be grossly subsumed.

Spain was also one of the main participants in the ECB's bond purchases, at the time of writing (as of February 2015) only under the umbrella of the SMP. This first programme, not yet associated with conditionality was somewhat successful in reducing the general interest rates on Spanish sovereign bonds, thus relieving some of the refinancing burden for the Spanish state. However, the macroeconomic effect within Spain has been rather limited, as families and companies still face difficulties in access to credit. Credit conditions so far have not loosened substantially, thus credit flows to families and corporations are still far from reaching normal patterns (Malo de Molina 2014: 54–55). It is therefore not unlikely for Spain to apply for support from the OMT programme at some point; in that case Spain would once again be faced with policy conditionality.

The social fallout of the adjustment in Spain proves to be equally dramatic as in Greece. The most glaring figure in this context is a 52% youth unemployment rate, as of mid-2012 (Blyth 2014: 102). Additionally, Spain was the third EU member country to introduce a cap on public debt and deficits in its constitution; this change in 2011 carried a solid parliamentary majority but had to face stiff criticism. One channel of this criticism against this new regime of austerity was the movement of the *indignados*, who became famous for occupying large public places such as the Puerta del Sol in Madrid or the Plaza Catalunya in Barcelona (Antentas and Vivas 2014: 47; Bar Cendón 2012: 66–67).

The Spanish case proves that the path of adjustment initially devised in the Greek case, with a large focus on austerity measures such as cutting public spending, initiating wage reductions, deregulating labour markets etc., was followed in similar fashion in Spain as well. Notwithstanding fundamental differences, such as the fairly good budgetary position of Spain prior to the crisis, one of the main rationales of the Troika measures was to reduce public spending, which did nothing to subside the downturn of the Spanish economy. In assessing the influence of the ECB, one has to acknowledge that its influence in Spain cannot be compared to the Greek case.

---

[13] Point 17 of the MoU's Annex regarding conditionality: "Prepare proposals for the strengthening of non-bank financial intermediation including capital market funding and venture capital." (DG ECFIN 2012: 65).

The strict conditionality that was put forth covered a much smaller area of politics. Austerity measures were taken nonetheless, and the elevation of the duty to keep deficits in line with European guidelines to a constitutional norm surely please representatives of the ECB, but there were no sanctions attached to not doing so, at least not in the framework of the MoU for Spain. Conditionality and political influence of the ECB could return once Spain has to enter the OMT programme, but until now, while the results in Spain and Greece have been equally disruptive, the ECB's political influence in Spain has been much more subdued and limited.

I shall now conclude my contribution, joining a recap of my findings with a critical assessment of the implications of the crisis reactions put forth under the auspices of the ECB.

Conclusions

The aim of this article was to analyze whether the European Central Bank has gained more political influence as a consequence of the crisis. Understanding political influence broadly, that is to say as the ability to significantly influence the choice of alternative actions, coupled with the credible threat of significant sanctions, it can be said that the ECB has gained political influence—especially as a part of the Troika.

In Greece, and to a lesser extent in Spain, the respective governments receive financial support, but had to bind themselves to political conditionality and supervision by the Troika. While in Spain's case, most of the required political adjustments have a focus on the restructuring of the local banking sector, the Greek government faces a wide array of measures to implement. Public downsizing affects all aspects of the state infrastructure, including massive cuts in the welfare system. Furthermore, several measures in Greece are highly questionable since they breach social rights such as collective bargaining or constitutional principles such as the principle of ratification.

While the integrity of the Euro area has been maintained up until the time of writing, the social fallout is immense. Economic recession, rising unemployment and a partial collapse of welfare state systems represent the price that has been paid in order to save the common currency area. This redistribution of hardships at the expense of the working populace is difficult to legitimize, let alone explain in a regular setting. The fact that these measures are implemented under the threat of a withdrawal of financial support, puts governments in a quagmire: giving in to the demands of the population to ease austerity measures means a higher possibility of default as a consequence of a funding stop; going forward with austerity measures means continued financial support, but generally comes with widespread and understandable discontent.

The political influence of non-political actors such as the ECB (and the IMF in the Troika setting) poses a serious problem of legitimacy. In the crisis cases, the Troika virtually dictates the course of action in several policy areas which deal with the redistribution of the economic outputs within a country. To have organizations with shaky democratic legitimacy such as the ECB in such a position of political predetermination and supervision can erode the trust in the fundamental workings of representative democracy.

Discontent with political results can still be expressed by voting the opposition into power, but if an opposition accepts the predetermined policies as well, the population loses its main instrument of enabling political change. And furthermore, decision-makers within organizations such as the ECB cannot be held accountable the same way as ministers or members of parliament. If low interest rates provide a moral hazard for irresponsible public spending; is it not possible that an absence of accountability provides a moral hazard leading to reckless austerity policies?

Some things can be brought forward to mitigate the criticisms of the actions of the ECB and the Troika. If this crisis remains an extraordinary event, if the crisis countries are able to get back on a path of prosperity and general well-being and if the new institutions and rules at the European level prove to be sound enough to withstand further shocks, the argument can be made that the Troika arrangement and the austerity measures were a painful, arguably unjust but ultimately necessary and successful response to a sudden and unexpected crisis. And when analyzing the working of the Troika, the blame cannot be put entirely on the ECB. First of all, the European Commission and the IMF are equally responsible for the effects of the Troika's policies as they are all part of it. And up until now, the Troika arrangement could always rely at least on the tacit consent of the other governments of the EU, expressed in the European Council and the Council.

Nonetheless, the Troika arrangement is a risky bet on the effectiveness of austerity policies. Should there not be a long-term socioeconomic improvement, the entire crisis response arrangement will be put into question by several sides. People in the crisis countries at some point will be fed up with carrying the burden of economic restructuring, and people in the "donor" countries will no longer see the use in providing taxpayers' funds for an unsuccessful economic adjustment. A possible consequence of this could be further mistrust in politicians and the workings of representative democracy, leading at best to political apathy or at worst to a turn towards extremist groups. Such a development would constitute a major crisis of society, a crisis which the ECB could no longer be able to manage and contain.

However, the recent developments in Greece should be taken into account for any outlook on the Troika. This contribution was written just days after Alexis Tsipras of the left-wing SYRIZA party assumed office as the Prime Minister of Greece. The pillar of his election manifesto was to dispose of the Troika, a commitment that has been reaffirmed by Tsipras several times after SYRIZA's victory. Assuming that Greece ceases to cooperate with the Troika and still receives some sort of financial support, this would alter the findings of this article significantly. Until Tsipras came into power, the Greek government obliged to the vast majority of the political conditions set forth by the Troika. If the Tsipras government can successfully leave the Troika arrangement, the political influence of the ECB, channelled through the Troika, would be vastly diminished, while democratically legitimized government would have a firmer hold on the design and execution of policy.

As this development is still subject to the consent of other European political actors—among those the member states, the Commission or the Eurogroup—any final verdict on the rearrangements put forward by the Tsipras government would be premature.

References

Antentas, J. M. and Vivas, E. (2014). Planeta indignado. Die Welt der Empörten. Ursachen und Perspektiven der Rebellion, Cologne: ISP.

Bar, C. A. (2012). La reforma constitucional y la gobernanza económica de la Unión Europea, *Teoría y realidad constitucional, No. 30*, pp. 59–88.

Blyth, M. (2014). *Wie Europa sich kaputtspart. Die gescheiterte Idee der Austeritätspolitik*, Bonn: J. H. W. Dietz Nachfolger.

Buiter, W. H. and Rahbari, E. (2012). *The ECB as Lender of Last Resort for Sovereigns in the Euro Area*, Technical report, No. 8974, London: Centre for Economic Policy Research.

Cukierman, A. (2013). Monetary policy and institutions before, during, and after the global financial crisis, *Journal of Financial Stability, Vol. 9* (3), 373–384.

de Grauwe, P. (2013). The European Central Bank as Lender of Last Resort in the Government Bond Markets, *CESifo Economic Studies, Vol. 59* (3), 520–535.

Duncan, E. (2013). Legalizing European Central Bank bond purchases: how the ECB can protect its own legitimacy and the future of the Euro, *George Washington International Law Review, Vol. 45* (1), 183–213.

European Commission, Directorate General for Economic and Financial Affairs (2012), *The Financial Sector Adjustment Programme for Spain*, Brussels, European Union.

European Commission, Directorate General for Economic and Financial Affairs (2014). *The Second Economic Adjustment Programme for Greece*. Fourth Review – April 2014, Brussels: European Union.

Geeroms, H., Ide, S. and Naert, F. (2014). *The European Union and the Euro. How to Deal with a Currency Built on Dreams*, Cambridge: Intersentia.

Katrougalos, G. (2013). 'Memoranda': Greek Exceptionalism or the Mirror of Europe's Future?" In Triandafyllidou, A., Gropas, R., Kouki, H. (eds), *The Greek Crisis and European Modernity*, Houndmills Basingstoke: Palgrave Macmillan, 89–109.

Knodt, M. and Große Hüttmann, M. (2006). Der Multi-Level Governance-Ansatz. In Bieling, H. - J., Lerch, M. (eds), *Theorien der europäischen Integration*, Wiesbaden: VS Verlag für Sozialwissenschaften, 223–247.

Luhmann, N. (2012). *Macht*, Konstanz, Munich: UVK.

Marks, G., Liesbet, H., and Blank, K. (1996). European Integration from the 1980s: State-Centric v. Multi-level Governance, *Journal of Common Market Studies, Vol. 34* (3), 341–378.

Malo de Molina, J. L. (2014). La acción del BCE y la economía española en los quince primeros años del euro, *Banco de España, Boletín Económico, Vol. 2014* (2), 43–56.

Neal, L. & Iglesias, G., Concepción, M. (2013). The economy of Spain in the euro-zone before and after the crisis of 2008, *The Quarterly Review of Economics and Finance, Vol. 53* (4), 36–344.

Pacheco Pardo, R. (2012). Leadership, decision-making and governance in the EU and East Asia: crisis and post-crisis, *Asia Europe Journal, Vol. 9* (2–4), 77–90.

Papadopoulos, Y. (2008). Problems of Democratic Accountability in Network and Multi-level Governance. In Conzelmann, T., Smith, R. (eds), *Multi-level Governance in the European Union: Taking Stock and Looking Ahead*, Baden-Baden: Nomos, 31–52.

Petrakis, P. E., Pantelis, K. and Valsamis, D. G. (2013). *European Economics and Politics in the Midst of the Crisis. From the Outbreak of the Crisis to the Fragmented European Federation*. Berlin, Heidelberg: Springer.

Piattoni, S. (2010). *The Theory of Multi-level Governance. Conceptual, Empirical and Normative Challenges*, Oxford: Oxford University Press.

Teßmer, H. G. (2012). *Governancistische Demokratie. Zur Balance von Vollmacht und Misstrauen im heutigen Europa*, Berlin: Lit.

Tosun, J., Wetzel, A. and Zapryanova, G. (2014). The EU in Crisis: Advancing the Debate, *Journal of European Integration, Vol. 36* (3), 195–211.

Wendel, M. (2014). Exceeding Judicial Competence in the Name of Democracy: The German Federal Constitutional Court's OMT Reference, *European Constitutional Law Review, Vol. 10* (2), 263–307

The Principle of Subsidiarity after Lisbon: Towards a Sustainable System of EU Multi-Level Governance?

ANNA-LENA HÖGENAUER

Since the Treaty of Maastricht, the formal powers of regional actors in EU policy-making have been strengthened in successive rounds of treaty reform. In the process, the European Union has turned into a system of multi-level governance. However, in the case of legislative regions, the question is whether these participation rights offset the centralizing tendencies of integration and are sufficient to re-establish the balance between the member states and their regions. In addition, for a long time, European integration has had the effect of strengthening national and regional governments over national and regional parliaments, thereby risking the creation of a system of multi-level governance without multi-level parliamentarism. This chapter will therefore analyze the powers of both the governments and parliaments of strong legislative regions in four member states. It finds that regional governments have become active players, but also that regional parliaments are still largely excluded from EU decision-making and that the eurozone crisis has further exacerbated these trends.

Dr. Anna-Lena Högenauer is Adjoint de Recherche at the University of Luxemburg.

Key words: Multi-level governance; Subsidiarity; Multi-level parliamentarism; Legislative regions

Editors' Note

The limitations of the Lisbon Treaty in containing the growing demand for more representation and participation of Europeans in the EU decision-making process, has been questioned since its inception. The crisis has intensified and diversified these concerns. Dr. Anna-Lena Hogenauer analyzes the capacity of the EU to function and to inspire confidence as a sustainable system of multi-level governance. Setting off from questions that recent developments, such as the referendum on the question of independence in Scotland and the unofficial plebiscite in Cataluña have raised about the viability of the EU's institutional structure, the author examines the role of regional governments and legislative regions in the decision making process. She associates this role to the everlasting crisis of legitimacy and representation of the EU on the one end, and the capacity of the EU to promote itself as an effective player for European citizens after the Lisbon treaty, on the other. While seemingly technical, this paper handsomely fits the collection on both counts of the EU crisis and integrationism. It problematizes on the present and the future of European integration in the framework set by the EU's crisis and identifies challenges, requirements and fields of priority for the EU's political and institutional adjustment and adaptation. Besides, the paper touches upon a central aspect of the crisis that is the capacity of the EU to institutionalize the involvement of instruments that are legitimized and closer to the public. All in all, Högenauer's research signifies in a practical way just how easy it would be for the whole EU edifice in its current form to fall apart if the existing institutions did not function and if an ineffective confrontation of the crisis enhanced the disintegrative forces and institutional maladies.

Introduction

The principle of subsidiarity has been strengthened in successive rounds of Treaty reform, a process that has gone hand in hand with the recognition of the political legitimacy of regions in the decision-making of the European Union. While the Treaty of Maastricht first accorded subnational actors a formal role in EU decision-making through the creation of the consultative Committee of the Regions and officially allowed regional representatives to be involved in the Council of Ministers, the Treaty of Lisbon has now allocated the role of "watchdog of subsidiarity" to various subnational actors. The Committee of the Regions can bring cases on grounds of a breach of subsidiarity before the European Court of Justice, while regional parliaments with legislative powers can participate in subsidiarity control via the national parliaments and the Early Warning System.

The increasing recognition of subnational actors has been the result of pressures from subnational actors themselves. Legislative regions, i.e. the regions of federal or strongly decentralized states, have played a leading role in this context, as European integration involved a transfer of competences from the regional to the European level (Große Hüttmann and Knodt 2006: 595). However, as channels for subnational participation in EU policy-making are mostly consultative or indirect even today, the central question of this paper is whether the Lisbon reforms with their emphasis on subsidiarity have been able to re-empower strong legislative regions in EU decision-making, thereby creating a sustainable system of multi-level governance?

This question is all the more important in the light of the two consultations on independence that took place in 2014. The officially recognized referendum for Scottish independence was narrowly lost by the "yes"-side (44.7 per cent), but also saw a record-breaking voter turn-out of 84.6 percent—the highest in the UK for an election or referendum since the introduction of universal suffrage (Koplowitz 2014). On 9 November 2014, the Catalan government held a popular consultation on Catalan independence in defiance of the Spanish Constitutional Court, after the Constitutional Court suspended plans for a referendum on independence and a also a consultation on independence. The population registered an overwhelming support for independence (around 80 percent), but with a turn out that was below 50 percent (BBC 2014). The Catalan results are also difficult to interpret because of an anti-independence boycott of the consultation (Gyldenkerne and Sanz 2014). Nevertheless, both the hotly contested referendum in Scotland and the acrimonious political battle in Catalonia raise the question of whether European multi-level governance provides a satisfactory setting for strong legislative regions. Neither of the two independence movements is anti-European—in fact both would like to see their regions become EU member states. Thus, are Europe's legislative regions getting enough decision-making powers *as regions* in the current Treaty framework? There is a risk that the EU will have to seriously confront the question whether or not former regions can be admitted as newly-formed member states—and it will have to face the consequence of far-reaching institutional reforms due to the changing number and size of member states.

Taking into account the legal and political science literatures and drawing on past research into the regions of federal and strongly decentralized states, notably Germany, Belgium, Austria and the UK, the chapter will assess this question from a comparative perspective, taking into account both regional governments and regional parliaments as actors. The analysis will be based on a discussion of the formal (constitutional) powers of these actors, of their actual capacity to act, as well as on the use that they make of these powers in practice. It argues that both regional governments and parliaments have been strengthened in terms of formal powers, but that only regional governments have reached a level of activity that allows them to have an impact. Regional parliaments in general still have few powers and lack the capacity to use those powers effectively in practice. As a result, the system of multi-level governance is sustainable on the level of the executives, but the EU has not managed to stop the trend of deparliamentarization and a truly multi-level system of parliamentarism has failed to emerge despite the greater emphasis on parliaments in the Lisbon Treaty. Policy-making during the eurozone crisis has further exacerbated the trend toward executive governance beyond the control of parliaments. If policy-making by means of intergovernmental negotiations becomes the norm, there is a risk that the democratic credibility of the EU will in fact further decrease despite the attempts of the Lisbon Treaty to involve parliaments on all levels more systematically.

Multi-level Governance and European Regions in the Literature

The multi-level governance (MLG) literature fosters the dominant approaches to regional interest representation in European policy-making. The conceptualization of the EU as a multi-level system became particularly prominent through the writings of Gary Marks and Liesbeth Hooghe. According to Hooghe (1995: 178), MLG 'is the only model where regions would be a governmental level of importance next to national, European and local arenas. This Europe cannot be one of the national states, nor of regions, but only a Europe with the Regions'. The approach argues that the EU is 'a system of continuous negotiation among nested governments at several territorial tiers—supranational, national, regional and local—as the result of a broad process of institutional creation and decisional reallocation that has pulled some previously centralized functions of the state up to the supranational level and some down to the local/regional level' (Marks 1993: 392; Hooghe and Marks 2001: 12).

In the 1990s, the MLG approach embodied an optimistic outlook on the evolving role of regions in EU policy-making. Inspired by the increasing recognition of regions in the Treaty of Maastricht (cf. next section), authors argued that the EU was moving towards being a "Europe of the Regions" or "Europe with the Regions" (e.g. Hooghe 1995; Hooghe and Marks 1996). The European Parliament and the European Commission were seen as actors with their own agendas, who would try to mobilize regions as part of an alliance that would allow the supranational and subnational level to strengthen their negotiating position vis-à-vis the member states (Benz and Eberlein 1999: 331; McCarthy 1997: 443; Tömmel 1998: 72). However, the enthusiasm of the mid-1990s soon ebbed and was replaced by the recognition that central governments were still the strongest actors while the precise level of influence of regions in European policy-making became something of an open question (cf. Hooghe and Marks 2001; Jeffery 2000).

Part of the disillusionment stemmed from the realization that Europe's regions are not uniform entities, but very diverse in terms of size, wealth, strength of identity and—most importantly—in terms of their position within the political system of their member state. Consequently they have different levels of resources, different patterns of mobilization and are affected by integration in different ways (e.g. Tatham 2010; Marks, Haesly and Mbaye 2001; Nielsen and Salk 1998). Thus, while traditionally weak regions stand to benefit from EU integration in the form of funding (e.g. Structural Funds) and consultation practices, constitutionally strong regions have seen some of their competences shift to the European level—with the risk of (co-)decision powers being replaced by mere consultation. As a result, strong legislative regions have in the past been pushing for a greater role in EU decision-making. In addition, there are a number of cases where legislative regions felt constrained by EU policy-making (cf. Jeffery 1998; Streb 2007: 222–3).

According to Jeffery, strong legislative regions—and the German regions in particular—have adopted a strategy whereby they try to protect the nation-state and its competences and even attempt to roll-back European integration, as a strong nation-state is seen as the best guarantor of regional authority (Jeffery 2005; GroßeHüttmann and Knodt 2006: 596–7). According to this view, the regions would prefer separate competences—in contrast to the Commission's emphasis in its White Paper on European Governance on sharing competences (European Commission Communication 2001: 35). Indeed, looking at the European Constitutional debate and the Treaty of Lisbon, the focus was no longer on *sharing* powers, but on *defining* the EU's competences more clearly. Thus, one of the questions is whether Lisbon has reinforced the role of strong legislative regions in EU policy-making, thereby creating a satisfactory balance of power that makes EU integration sustainable in the long term? After all, one of the risks of permanently frustrated regions is that they may eventually wish to become full member states rather than regions, thereby threatening the internal stability of the EU.

Another concern is the state of multi-level parliamentarism in the European Union. In the past, European integration has generally been seen as carrying the risk of de-parliamentarization for the member states. The European Parliament does of course provide parliamentary control over decision-making at the European level but national interests are represented in the Council of Ministers by *national governments*. If the national parliaments are unwilling or unable to scrutinize closely how those interests are represented by their governments, there is a risk of deparliamentarization (O'Brennan 2007).

For the parliaments of legislative regions, the challenge is even greater, as they are moved one step further from EU policy-making. There are nowadays eight member states with regions with legislative competences: Germany, Austria, Belgium, the United Kingdom, Spain, Italy, Portugal and Finland. Yet, until the Treaty of Lisbon, regional parliaments had practically no formal role to play in EU policy-making. They had at best one or two representatives in the consultative Committee of the Regions. Domestically, their control function was limited by the fact that they would have to scrutinize what their regional government negotiated with the national government and other regional governments, which would then be represented—usually by the national government—in the Council of Ministers. At the same time, they could not directly scrutinize the actions of the national government, as the national government is only accountable to the national parliament. As a result, the emerging multi-level system of inter*governmenta*l negotiation in the EU has—in the past—not been accompanied by a comparable system of multi-level *parliamentarism*.

The Treaty of Lisbon has, however, recognized regional parliaments for the first time and created new mechanisms of consultation for national and regional parliaments. It is thus worth investigating to what extent the current system of multi-level governance involves a balanced representation of regional governments and parliaments.

EU Treaties: Multi-level Governance through the Ages

The European Treaties had a regional dimension from the start. However, in the Treaties of Rome of 1957, regions were seen purely as an object of policy-making, not as one of the potential policy makers. Thus, the preamble of these treaties emphasized the objective of economic integration, including the aim to reduce the gap between regions and to help weaker regions catch up. This objective was a recurrent theme that was picked up again in the context of agricultural policy (art. 39), the free movement of workers (art. 49), transport policy (art. 75) and the principles guiding the work of the Commission (art. 80), to name but a few examples. The Treaties also created the European Investment Bank that could now grant loans on a non-profit basis to stimulate the development of economically weaker regions (Art. 129).

The regional dimension of EU policy-making was further strengthened through the creation of the European Regional Development Fund in 1975 and its recognition in the Single European Act in 1986 (art. 130b, art. 130c). However, at this stage regions were still not recognized as policy-makers in the Treaties, except in the framework of the Structural Funds as stakeholders.

The first change in that regard took place in the Treaty of Maastricht in 1993. This Treaty gave regions for the first time a formal role in EU policy-making, in the form of the new Committee of the Regions (Chapter 4, TEC). This advisory body was to consist of representatives of regional and local authorities and had to be consulted on a range of policies before the Council of Ministers and the European Parliament reached their conclusions. It could also adopt opinions on its own initiative. Regional and local actors were thus recognized for the first time in the Treaties as potential policy-makers.

The Treaty of Maastricht also introduced for the first time the principle of subsidiarity. The aim of this principle is to take decisions on the most appropriate level, while trying to take them as closely as possible to the citizens. It would thus later help regions defend their competences. However, in the Treaty of Maastricht, subsidiarity was defined as follows:

> "In areas which do not fall within its exclusive competence, the Community shall take action, in accordance with the principle of subsidiarity, only if and in so far as the objectives of the proposed action cannot be sufficiently achieved by the Member states and can therefore, by reason of the scale or effects of the proposed action, be better achieved by the Community. Any action by the Community shall not go beyond what is necessary to achieve the objectives of this Treaty."
>
> (art. 3b TEU)

Subsidiarity was therefore still defined as a question of competence between the member states and the European Union, and regions were not explicitly mentioned at that point in time.

In addition, Art. 146 (TEC) of the Treaty of Maastricht made it possible for member states to be represented by the member of a regional government. The formulation "The Council shall consist of a representative of each Member State at ministerial level, authorized to commit the government of that Member State" allows any minister—including a regional minister—to speak for the member states provided that that person can represent the position of the member state as a whole. This change was particularly important for strong legislative regions, as it meant that they could potentially represent their country in the Council of Ministers in those cases where their exclusive competences were affected. Belgium, for example, is usually represented by a minister from the Flemish, Walloon or Brussels regional governments on matters related to environment policy, fisheries, agriculture and many more. Germany is represented by a regional minister on issues related to education, culture and broadcasting.

The Treaty of Amsterdam and the Treaty of Nice made only incremental changes to the position of regional governments, for example by extending the powers of the Committee of the Regions and by defining the principle of subsidiarity in more detail in the *Protocol on the application of the principles of subsidiarity and proportionality*. This protocol also mentions the need for the Commission to consider the cost impact on the subnational level, and thus officially recognizes the existence of multiple levels of government within member states.

Most recently, the Treaty of Lisbon introduced three changes that could have an impact on the ability of legislative regions to represent their interests on the European level. Firstly, the subsidiarity clause was reworded, with article 5(3) of the TEU now referring explicitly to the regional level in the definition of the principle of subsidiarity:

"Under the principle of subsidiarity, in areas which do not fall within its exclusive competence, the Union shall act only if and in so far as the objectives of the proposed action cannot be sufficiently achieved by the Member States, either at central level or at regional and local level, but can rather, by reason of the scale or effects of the proposed action, be better achieved at Union level."

(Art. 5(3) TEU)

Secondly, while the rewording of the subsidiarity principle could be seen as being merely a symbolic concession, the Treaty of Lisbon also introduces two new procedures for the monitoring of the implementation of the principle. The Committee of the Regions was given the right to appeal to the European Court of Justice on grounds of a breach of the subsidiarity principle or to defend its consultation rights. In addition, the consultation of the CoR is now also mandatory for the European Parliament in certain areas. While the Opinions of the CoR are non-binding, it is worth remembering that the European Parliament's rise to power went through the same stage (Stahl 2009: 138–9; McCown 2003: 974, 977). As the breach of the principle of subsidiarity or failure to consult the CoR may lead to the annulment of EU legislation, regions have now, for the first time, gained 'hard' powers at the European level. A clever use of the threat of an appeal could force the Commission and Council to take subsidiarity seriously and to give it a broad definition and might even serve as a bargaining chip on points of substance. One promising step towards the effective use of the new rights is the Subsidiarity Monitoring Network that the CoR has developed with a variety of regional and local partners (subsidiarity.cor.europa.eu/objreseau/tabid/81/Default.aspx). However, the effectiveness of this tool will also depend on the ECJ's view on the matter (Högenauer 2008: 548–554).

The third change gives national parliaments more influence in European policy-making in two instances. On the one hand, any national parliament can veto a decision of the European Council to move from unanimity to qualified majority voting in a policy area (Art. 48(7) TEU). On the other hand, the *Protocol on the Role of National Parliaments in the EU* and the *Protocol on the Application of the Principles of Subsidiarity and Proportionality* assign national parliaments a role in monitoring subsidiarity through an 'early warning system' (EWS). This affects strong legislative regions in two ways: in the case of bicameral systems, the EWS includes a chamber representing regional governments, such as the German Bundesrat. In addition, national parliaments are asked to consult regional parliaments where appropriate.

The basis of the new procedure is that national legislatures now obtain all documents of legislative planning and draft legislation. Then, parliaments have eight weeks during which any national parliament or chamber of a national parliament can submit a reasoned opinion to the presidents of the European Parliament, the Commission and the Council of Ministers if it finds the draft to be in breach of the principle of subsidiarity. If reasoned opinions amounting to at least one third of the total number of votes find the legislation in breach of the principle of subsidiarity, the draft must be reviewed (at least a quarter of votes in the case of issues in the area of freedom, security and justice). The initiator of the draft may then decide to confirm, amend or withdraw the draft. If objections amount to at least a simple majority of the votes allocated to national parliaments (28 out of 54), the Commission has to decide whether to confirm, amend or withdraw the draft. If it decides to confirm it, it has to issue a reasoned opinion on the matter. If 55 per cent of the members of the Council or a simple majority of votes cast in the EP decide that the proposal is not in line with subsidiarity, it shall not be further considered.

However, while Cooper sees the early warning system as potentially leading to a "virtual third chamber" of national legislatures, the impact is likely to be very limited for regions (Cooper 2006: 283). Most importantly, few regions will be represented at the national level in an upper chamber like the Bundesrat. All other regions have to rely on the consultation of the regional parliaments by the national parliament. Secondly, the system is still mainly advisory. Only the Council of Ministers or the European Parliament can force the Commission to withdraw a proposal. Finally, in order for the procedure to work, a large number of parliaments have to follow European affairs actively and invest resources into the monitoring and evaluation of proposed legislation. Parliaments also regret the fact that they can only block a European proposal, but there is no formal mechanism that allows them to have a more positive and constructive impact on EU policy-making. For example, they cannot ask for a new European proposal, if they feel that there is *more* need for cooperation in a policy area.

On the whole, the Treaty of Lisbon is thus unlikely to have much impact on the regions' policy-shaping rights on the European level, but it does provide them with a new opportunity to block legislation and challenge the Commission's interpretation of the principle of subsidiarity (Sturm 2009: 17). As previously, the Committee of the Regions is the only formal representation of regions on the European level, a role that has been emphasized by the fact that most changes affected its role and powers (16–17). At the same time, any real improvement in the unmediated influence of regions is likely to depend on the extent and quality of coordination of parliaments across member states (Chardon and Eppler 2009: 28).

Regional Governments as Multi-level Players

Regional governments were recognized as stakeholders in EU policy-making almost two decades before the Lisbon Treaty. The governments of legislative regions in particular started to lobby for the European recognition of their status in the late 1980s, including the creation of the Committee of the Regions. In the process, they carved out a role for themselves in EU policy-making. They were also among the first regions to establish offices in Brussels that would help them to gather information and devise lobbying strategies (Hüttmann and Knodt 2006: 595). The 1990s then saw an exponential rise in the number of regional offices in Brussels, going hand-in-hand with demands for a "Europe of the Regions" (Ruge 2003). Even though the optimism soon abated, this extended period of activism meant that the governments of strong legislative regions had established ways of contributing to EU policy-making long before the Lisbon Treaty.

On the European level, the main channels of interest representation for regional governments are the Council of Ministers, the Committee of the Regions, the lobbying of MEPs from the region, regional offices for lobbying and regional networks on the European level. The Council of Ministers theoretically provides regions with the most formal and substantial means to influence EU policy-making. In those cases where regional ministers attend the Council, they become part of the key legislator at the EU level and—in some cases—can cast a vote. There are, however, some drawbacks: firstly, whoever sits in the Council has to be able 'to commit the government of that member state' (Art. 203 TEC), which means that regional ministers cannot represent purely regional concerns. Instead, a common, national position has to be agreed prior to the Council meeting. Secondly, only strong legislative regions have the opportunity to send ministers, and even in that case there are differences between member states depending on whether regional officials can be present as observers, as speakers or even as chairs.

The Belgian regions have the most extensive representation rights in the Council of Ministers, in line with the Belgian constitutional principle (art. 167) that each part of the state (the central state, the regions and the communities) has foreign policy competences in the policy areas that fall under its domestic competences (Hogwood et al. 2003: 3). Based on the Cooperation Agreement Act of 8 March 1994 and the Lambermont Agreement, regional ministers sit in the Council in the case of exclusive regional competences. When predominantly central competences are concerned, a national minister is being assisted by a regional representative and, for predominantly regional matters, a regional minister is assisted by a representative of the national level (Kovziridze 2002: 149). By comparison, the German regions can only represent Germany in the Council in education, culture and broadcasting policy, i.e. a much narrower range of policies (Chardon and Eppler 2009: 29–30). The regional representation in Austria is even more limited: a regions-nominated representative can participate in the Council, if the domestic legislative competences of the regions are concerned, but only if the national government agrees (Art. 23d Federal Constitution). While ministerial participation in the Council is relatively rare, the option to include a representative of the regions in the Austrian delegation to Council working groups under article 8 of the Federal-Regional Agreement has been frequently used (Bußjäger and Djanani 2009: 64). The situation in the UK is somewhat similar to the Austrian case, in that the decision on whether or not to include a Scottish minister or expert in the UK delegation rests with the UK leads. Once they are part of the delegation, Scottish ministers and officials require the permission of the UK lead before they can take the floor (Swenden 2009). Thus, while there are differences in the extent of participation of strong legislative regions in the Council of Ministers, most of them have some level of access to it.

All of the regions have access to the Committee of the Regions, which is the most institutionalized channel of regional interest representation. However, after lobbying for its creation, the legislative regions—with the possible exception of the Austrian regions—soon lost interest in it as it contained too many representatives from weak regions or local authorities (McCarthy 1997; Nergelius 2005: 126). There is also an ideological element to this: Scotland under the government of the Scottish National

Party, for example, sees itself as a nation, not as a region, and therefore feels that the CoR is not the right channel for it. It even stopped sending ministers to the CoR and instead now only sends Members of the Scottish Parliament and local councilors.[1] Similarly, the Belgian regions feel that their presence in the Council is more important than the work of the CoR.[2] Some of the German regions also do not send a representative—Mecklenburg-West Pomerania, for example, because they feel that the Committee of the Regions is too weak to have a real impact.[3]

Instead of using the CoR, regional governments often resort to lobbying strategies. One of the main targets are MEPs from the country or region. The advantage of this type of lobbying are the low costs involved—all it takes is a letter or phone call. Even if the MEPs are not directly involved in the workings of a key committee, they may be able to introduce amendments that reflect the region's concerns (cf. Tatham 2008: 504–6). However, one of the problems with this channel is that some regions have very few MEPs in the European parliament, especially where country-wide lists are used for the elections. The East German regions are currently in that position and therefore organize coordination meetings between all East German regional offices in Brussels and the MEPs.[4]

Finally, almost all legislative regions—with the exception of the Austrian region of Vorarlberg—have a Brussels office that helps with the direct lobbying of the European Commission and the organization of events. The most important functions of these offices include information gathering for the regional government at home, networking, assisting private actors at home (e.g. in applications for funding), active attempts to influence policies and the general improvement of relations with other tiers of governments (Moore 2006). Moore furthermore distinguishes a 'promotional' role, where regions serve as showcases for economic and cultural elements of the region (Moore 2006). The offices also help with the creation and organization of regional networks on priority issues, such as the VANGUARD network on economic and industrial policy that brings together around 20 regions.[5]

In addition, federal and strongly devolved member states have developed coordination mechanisms that allow regional governments to contribute to the formulation of the national position. As in the case of representation in the Council, there are substantial differences in the consultation or co-decision rights of regions in the negotiation of member state positions.

The Belgian regions are again in the most advantageous position. On the one hand, there are only three regions, which facilitates coordination and makes it easier for individual voices to be heard. On the other hand, they have obtained veto rights over the national position (Lambertz and Förster 2009: 24). The central coordinating role for

---

[1] Interview with the Head of the SGOEU and a policy officer of the SGOEU, Brussels, 8/04/2014.
[2] Interview with an attaché Wallon in the Permanent Representation of Belgium in Brussels, 7/04/2014.
[3] Interview with the Director of the Brussels Office of Mecklenburg-West Pomerania, Brussels, 2/04/2014.
[4] Interview with the Director of the Brussels Office of Mecklenburg-West Pomerania, Brussels, 2/04/2014.
[5] Interview with an attaché Wallon in the Permanent Representation of Belgium in Brussels, 7/04/2014.

Belgium's official position in the European Union is played by the Directorate for European Affairs of the Federal Public Service of Foreign Affairs (DEA). It is an administrative body composed of representatives of the federal, regional and community ministries and headed by a federal representative. Decisions are taken by consensus, which gives each entity veto powers.

By contrast, the German regions do not have an individual voice in the coordination process, but instead have to formulate a collective regional position in the Bundesrat (Art. 23 of the Basic Law (BL) and the Law on Cooperation (LC) between the Bund and the regions Concerning European Matters of 12 March 1993). In addition, the Bundesrat does not have genuine veto powers over the national position: if the European measure predominantly concerns the legislative and administrative competences of the regions, the position of the Bundesrat has to be decisively taken into account ("massgeblichzuberücksichtigen") by the federal government. In case of disagreement, the Bundesratcan ultimately confirms its original opinion with a two-thirds majority ("Beharrungsbeschluss") and appeal to the Federal Constitutional Court, but it rarely fully exploits these options. In the case of legislative projects that touch upon predominantly federal competences or concurrent federal-regional competences when the federal government has already previously legislated in the area, the federal government has to take the position of the Bundesrat into account, but is not obliged to incorporate it into the national position (see Müller-Graff 2005; Art.23 BL and §5(2) LC). Overall, this means that the input of each individual region into European policy-making is thus diluted at three stages: twice internally, during the negotiations among regions and during the negotiations with the central government, and again at the European level in negotiations with other member states and European institutions. In fact, the greatest risk for a Land is to become isolated (and outvoted) at an early stage.

The Austrian system is similar to the German system (see Art. 23d of the federal constitution and the Vereinbarung zwischen dem Bund und den regionsn gemäss Art. 15a B-VG über die Mitwirkungsrechte der regions und Gemeinden in Angelegenheiten der europäischen Integration, 1992). In cases of European legislation that affect their exclusive competences, the regions can adopt a 'unified position' that binds the federal government except if there are compelling reasons of integration or foreign policy that require adaptation. As the definition of this exception is rather vague, the federal government has some leeway in practice.[6] Unified positions have to be adopted by a majority of regions (at least five) with no opposition from the remaining regions. As the Austrian regions have only few exclusive competences, only 75 unified positions were adopted between 1993 and 2008, an average of about five a year (Bußjäger and Djanani 2009: 61). In all other policy areas, the regions can adopt 'simple positions' individually or coordinate horizontally to achieve a common position—but these are not binding.

Finally, in the UK, Scotland, Wales and Northern Ireland the regions have even less formal powers. They benefit from the fact that there are only three devolved governments and thus relatively few regions need to be consulted. However, the UK government retains the responsibility for EU policy and thus only has to consult the

---

[6] Interview with an official, Liaison Office of the Austrian Länder, Vienna, 2/04/2009.

regions—even in policy areas that are otherwise completely devolved (Cairney 2006: 439). The consultation generally takes place on the level of civil servants, through letters between ministers or in Joint Ministerial Committees (Swenden 2009).

Thus, overall, the governments of legislative regions managed to develop a variety of ways of influencing EU policy-making long before the Treaty of Lisbon. While the formal powers of regions vary considerable between member states even for strong legislative regions, they all have multiple mechanisms of consultation and lobbying in place. The Treaty of Lisbon has therefore had practically no effect on multi-level governance in that regard. The regions seem to generally welcome the new focus of the CoR on subsidiarity, but even the new powers have not fundamentally changed their sceptical perception of this body. They also feel the need to engage more with their regional parliaments, which have been empowered somewhat by Lisbon. But the general impression is that their approach to EU policy-making has not been changed by the Treaty. [7] One could generally argue that multi-level governance on the level of the executives works well. Where it needs strengthening, this is not so much a task for the European level, but for the member states, as some national coordination procedures do not yet adequately reflect the power that regions would have in purely domestic policy-making.

Regional Parliaments Struggling to Keep up

While the governments of strong legislative regions have thus managed to carve out a role for themselves in EU policy-making—be it through formal mechanisms of intra-state coordination or through investments in lobbying—regional parliaments have gained official recognition in EU policy-making only recently. It is here that the greatest problems with multi-level governance arise.

While many regional parliaments tried to adapt to the new opportunities offered by the Lisbon Treaty, their level of activity remains modest. We can measure the mobilization of regional parliaments on EU issues by counting the number of opinions / reasoned opinions that they upload into databases such as REGPEX, which is used by regional parliaments and governments to collect and exchange their positions on subsidiarity. According to Fleischer's analysis of the REGPEX database, only 34 reasoned opinions (EWS) and 44 opinions (political dialogue) were recorded by regional parliaments between 2008 and 2013. However, as regional parliaments do not always upload their documents, this data probably somewhat underestimates the real level of activity (Fleischer 2014). The numbers are, however, an indication of the fact that regional parliaments have used the Early Warning System only to a very limited extent. By comparison, national parliaments submitted 2431 opinions under the political dialogue and 319 reasoned opinions between 2008 and 2013.

---

[7] Interview with an attaché Wallon in the Permanent Representation of Belgium in Brussels, 7/04/2014.Interview with the Director of the Brussels Office of Mecklenburg-West Pomerania, Brussels, 2/04/2014.Interview with the Head of the SGOEU and a policy officer of the SGOEU, Brussels, 8/04/2014.

Part of this problem may be the very short deadline under the EWS combined with a lack of resources. In order for regional parliaments to use the EWS, they have to forward their opinion to the national parliament within six to seven weeks after receiving the legislative proposal, in order to give the national parliament enough time to take their position on board. They thus have to work faster than national parliaments. At the same time, they have much lower staff levels. The average regional parliament has about 1.7 members of staff working on EU affairs, whereas the average national parliament has almost ten (Christiansen et al. 2015). Furthermore, if a regional parliament has objections on grounds of subsidiarity, but the national parliament of the member state is happy with the legislative proposal of the Commission, there will most likely not be a reasoned opinion, which means that the position of the regional parliament may in fact not be passed on.

An example of how difficult it is for the position of a regional parliament to reach the European level is the legislative initiative on e-invoicing. It was one of the priorities identified by the CoR for subsidiarity monitoring in 2013 and should thus have received special attention by regional parliaments. Furthermore, in order to facilitate scrutiny, the CoR launched a consultation through its REGPEX website. In parallel, at the 16th Plenary Assembly of the Conference of European Regional Legislative Assemblies (CALRE) in 2012, a working group on subsidiarity was set up to monitor subsidiarity compliance on the priorities of the CoR, including the proposal on e-invoicing.

As Vara Arribas and Högenauer (2015) note, the consultation received critical replies for the Austrian regions, the legislative assembly of Emilia Romagna and the Abruzzo regional government. The level of activity of regional parliaments was again limited to a few active voices. However, Italy and Austria did not adopt a reasoned opinion. Spain adopted an opinion confirming the *conformity* of the proposal with the principle of subsidiarity. Thus, none of the national parliaments followed the views of the regional parliaments. The Assembly of Emilia Romagna also addressed its opinion to its members of the European Parliament, and may thus have gained visibility by way of lobbying efforts. But in general the case illustrates that there is a great risk that the opinions of regional assemblies will not reach the Commission under the EWS.

In addition to the EWS, a number of regional parliaments are also directly represented in the Committee of the Regions. However, apart from being a purely consultative assembly, the Committee of Regions has also a number of other drawbacks. Due to regressive proportionality larger member states, which are more likely to have legislative regions, are underrepresented. Furthermore, some of its members represent local authorities rather than regions. Thus, in May 2013, only about 10 per cent of the CoR's members represented legislative assemblies. That makes it difficult for legislative regions to build majorities (Nergelius 2005: 126; Müller-Graff 2005: 110). That said after the Lisbon Treaty, the Committee of the Regions appears to have found a new focus in the protection and promotion of the principle of subsidiarity. Already in 2005, the Committee of the Regions created a Subsidiarity Monitoring Network (SMN) that ran a number of subsidiarity tests starting in 2006. The SMN tests allowed regional actors to build capacity and expertise and start the process of reform and adaptation. The

Committee of the Regions also developed REGPEX as a database of documents relating to legislative scrutiny. It is connected to OEIL and PreLex, thus allowing members to check the current state of legislation (Stahl 2009: 139–40). Regional parliaments can upload their documents and can sign up for thematic updates. More than half of the regional parliaments with legislative competences of the EU currently participate in these activities (extranet.cor.europa.eu/subsidiarity/regpex/Pages/partners.aspx).

In addition, the Conference of European Regional Legislative Assemblies (CALRE), which represents 74 regions from all eight member states with legislative regions, aims to protect the subsidiarity principle and foster cooperation between the regional and national parliaments and the European parliament (www.calrenet.irisnet.be/index.php/what-is-calre/history). Like the CoR, it has also made subsidiarity monitoring and the political dialogue with the European Commission its priority (CALRE 2011).

Apart from these organs and networks, regional parliaments could also follow the example of regional governments and set up offices in Brussels in order to lobby the EU institutions. In practice, few regional parliaments have chosen this path—probably, in part, due to their comparatively low staffing levels. The responses to a recent survey showed that out of 23 regional parliaments with legislative powers from 6 member states only two currently have a representative or office in Brussels. Many regional parliaments appear to receive at least some information from the office of the regional executive in Brussels, but this usually does not involve active lobbying on their behalf (Christiansen et al. 2015).

Overall, it seems that the Treaty of Lisbon has failed to substantially empower regional parliaments in EU policy-making. On the one hand, regional parliaments appear to lack the capacity to become systematically active across a large number of issues. On the other hand, even when they do use the new mechanisms, such as the EWS, it is far from certain that their opinions will have any impact on outcomes. Nevertheless, the Lisbon changes do seem to have motivated regional parliaments to adapt their procedures and to try and become more active. This can best be seen in the revival of the CoR and of CALRE, which have found a new purpose in the monitoring of subsidiarity. If regional parliaments were to be given more substantial formal powers in the future, we might indeed see the development of genuine multi-level parliamentarism to match the multi-level governance on the level of executives. However, the resource limitations of regional parliaments would still have to be overcome.

Outlook: The Return of Executive Dominance in Times of Crisis?

As we have seen, during the first decades of European integration, the effect of integration was a centralizing one, especially for federal and decentralized states. Competences that had been regional competences or shared competences were increasingly pulled up the European level, where regions could no longer participate in decision-making. In addition, only governments had a place in EU decision-making. Parliamentarism, on the other hand, only existed in the form of a fledgling European

Parliament. This trend risked creating a European political system that de facto reformed member state constitutions from above—shifting the power balance between executives and legislatures and between governments and regions in the absence of conscious deliberation. However, with the increasing activism of legislative regions in the 1980s, the role of regions started to be recognized and regional governments were increasingly given a role in EU policy-making and in the coordination of national positions. While legislative regions are still weaker in EU policy-making than in domestic policy-making, some member states—like Belgium or Germany—created systems of internal coordination of national positions that reflected the process of domestic policy-making. However, in other member states, like the UK, it is still the case that a region that has exclusive competences in domestic policy-making is only consulted in EU policy-making. As a result, for some legislative regions, such as Scotland, the status of a *region* is very disadvantageous in EU policy-making and has the potential to breed resentment.

Nevertheless, legislative regions have by and large started to adapt to European integration, have developed channels of participation and are actively mobilizing when policies affect them. By contrast, regional parliaments were only recognized as relevant actors in EU policy-making in the Treaty of Lisbon. Even then, their role in the Early Warning System is weak and it is extremely difficult for their opinions to become visible.

However, not only is multi-level parliamentarism still underdeveloped, but the eurozone crisis has set-off a new trend towards intergovernmental agreements and executive policy-making that largely bypasses parliaments. Many of the crisis-related mechanisms are almost completely beyond the formal control powers of parliaments. For instance, the European Central Bank has assumed an increasingly important role in the management of the debt crisis, especially since its controversial decision to purchase bonds to provide more liquidity to the markets (especially of countries in crisis). Yet, while the European Central Bank was designed to be politically neutral, parliaments—regional, national and European—have few means to control or influence these decisions, despite the fact that they are very political and widely debated in the media. Similarly, the creation of the new banking union provides little room for maneuver for parliaments. The European Parliament did not have to approve the Framework Regulation for the Single Supervisory Mechanism (Regulation No 468/2014 of the Central Bank).

Similarly, the famous "Troika", the cooperation of European Commission, European Central Bank and International Monetary Fund that negotiates with Eurozone states in crisis—like Greece—about reform programs, is notoriously difficult to subject to parliamentary scrutiny due to the fact that it is composed of different organizations. The Treaty on Stability, Coordination and Governance in the Economic and Monetary Union (TSCG), one of the central pillars of crisis management in the EU, was also the result of negotiation between governments. Parliaments were only involved in its ratification, but even then there was no room for the regional level, despite the fact that the treaty substantially reduces the ability of member states to decide independently on spending policies.

The crisis has thus triggered a new trend towards de-parliamentarization, despite the attempts of the Lisbon Treaty to involve parliaments on all levels of EU policy-making more systematically. This trend is particularly difficult for regions, as they are not perceived as key actors in these times of crisis. However, regions do in fact play an important role in the implementation of the European growth objectives. They are often responsible for innovation, the promotion of small and medium size enterprises, training and education, employment etc. (Stahl and Kuby 2015). Yet, while member states are expected to involve regional authorities in the preparation of national documents in relation to the European Semester, which involves the checking of national budgets by the European Commission, the regional level has so far been consulted only sporadically (ibid.).

If the European Union wishes to maintain a healthy balance between different levels of government and between governments and parliaments, it is therefore important that it revises its approach to policy-making once again after the crisis to address some of these democratic short-comings. Otherwise, there is a risk that the EU will drift ever further away from its citizens.

References

BBC, Catalonia vote: 80% back independence-officials, http://www.bbc.co.uk/news/world-europe-29982960, 10 November 2014.

Benz A. and Eberlein B. (1999). The Europeanization of regional policies: patterns of multi-level governance, *Journal of European Public Policy*, Vol. 6(2), 329–48.

Bußjäger, P. (2010). The Austrian Länder: The Relationship of Regional Parliaments to the Executive Power against the Background of Europeanisation. In R. Hrbek (ed.), *Legislatures in Federal Systems and Multi-Level Governance*. Nomos: Baden-Baden, 105–120.

Bussjäger, P. and Djanani, A. (2009). Europapolitik und Europafähigkeit der Länder in Österreich. In Lambertz, K.-H., Grosse Hüttmann, M. (eds.), *Europapolitik und Europafähigkeit von Regionen*, Nomos, Baden-Baden, 58–70.

Cairney, P. (2006). Venue Shift Following Devolution: When Reserved Meets Devolved in Scotland, *Regional and Federal Studies*, Vol. 16(4), 429–446.

CALRE (2011) Working Group on the Principle of Subsidiarity – Working Plan 2010, http://archive.scottish.parliament.uk/business/committees/europe/norpec.htm, viewed 1 November 2012.

Chardon, M. and Eppler, A. (2009). Mehr europapolitische Handlungsspielräume für die deutschen Länder? Die Auswirkungen der Föderalismusreform I und des Vertrags von Lissabon". In: Lambertz, K.-H. and Grosse Hüttmann, M. (eds.), *Europapolitik und Europafähigkeit von Regionen*, Baden-Baden, Nomos, 25–41.

Christiansen, T., Högenauer, A.L. and Neuhold, C. (under contract 2015). *Parliamentary Administrations in the European Union*, London: Palgrave.

Cooper, I. (2006). The Watchdogs of Subsidiarity: National Parliaments and the Logic of Arguing in the EU, *Journal of Common Market Studies, Vol. 44*(2), 281–304.

European Commission, Communication, European Governance—*A White Paper, Brussels*, 25.7.2001, COM(2001) 428 final.

Fleischer, J. (2014). More scrutiny, more harmony? The Early Warning System and executive-legislative relations at subnational level?, 21st International Conference of Europeanists, Washington D.C. 14–16 March 2014.

Große Hüttmann M., Knodt, M. (2006), 'Diplomatie mit Lokalkolorit': Die Vertretungen der deutschen Länder in Brüssel und ihre Aufgaben im EU-Entscheidungsprozess", *Jahrbuch des Föderalismus, Vol. 7*, 595–605.

Gyldenkerne, E. and Sanz, I., Spain, Catalonia to try dialogue after acrimonious independence vote, Reuters, http://www.reuters.com/article/2014/11/10/us-spain-catalonia-future-idUSKCN0IU1LN20141110, 10 November 2014.

Hogwood, P., Gomez, R., Bulmer, S., Burch, M., Carter, C., Scott, A. (2003). Regional actors and European policy making: lessons for the UK?, *Manchester Papers in Politics: Devolution and European Policy Series*, 8/2003, www.socialsciences.manchester.ac.uk/disciplines/politics/publications/workingpapers/documents/manchester_working_papers/MPP082003.pdf.

Hooghe, L. (1995). Subnational Mobilization in the European Union, *West European Politics, Vol. 18*(3), 175–198.

Hooghe, L. and Marks, G. (1996). 'Europe with the Regions': Channels of Regional Representation in the European Union, *Publius, Vol. 26*(1), pp. 73–92.

Hooghe, L. and Marks, G. (2001). *Multi-Level Governance and European Integration*, Oxford, Rowman & Littlefield Publishers, Inc.

Jeffery, C. (1998). Les Länder allemands et l'Europe: intérêts, stratégies et influence dans les politiques communautaires, in: Négrier, E. et Jouve, B. (eds.), *Que gouvernent les régions d'Europe?*, Paris, L'Harmattan, 55–84.

Jeffery, C. (2000). Subnational Mobilization and European Integration: Does it Make any Difference?, *Journal of Common Market Studies, Vol. 38*(1), 1–23.

Jeffery, C. (2005). Regions and the European Union: Letting them In, and Leaving them Alone. In: Weatherill, S., Bernitz, U. (eds.), *The role of Regions and Sub-National Actors in Europe*, Oxford, Hart Publishing.

Koplowitz, H.: Scottish Independence Voter Turnout Breaks UK Records, International Business Times, http://www.ibtimes.com/scottish-independence-voter-turnout-breaks-uk-records-1691834, 19 September 2014.

Kovziridze, T. (2002). Europeanization of Federal Institutional Relationships: Hierarchical and Interdependent Institutional Relationship Structures in Belgium, Germany and Austria, *Regional and Federal Studies, Vol. 12*(3), 128–155.

Lambertz K.-H., Förster S. (2009). Die belgischen Gemeinschaften und Regionen im europäsichen Rechtsetzungsprozess. In Lambertz, K.-H. and Grosse Hüttmann, M. (eds.), *Europapolitik und Europafähigkeit von Regionen*, Baden-Baden, Nomos, 21–24.

Marks, G. (1993). Structural Policy and Multilevel Governance in the EU. In Cafruny, A. and Rosenthal, G. (eds.), *The State of the European Community*, New York, Lynne Rienner, 164–92.

Marks, G., Haesly, R., Mbaye, H.A.D. (2002). What Do Subnational Offices Think They Are Doing in Brussels?, *Regional and Federal Studies, Vol. 12*(3), pp. 1–23.

McCarthy, R. (1997). The Committee of the Regions: An Advisory Body's Tortuous Path to Influence, *Journal of European Public Policy, Vol. 4*(3), 439–54.

McCown, M. (2003). The European Parliament Before the Bench: ECJ Precedent and EP Litigation Strategies, *JEPP, Vol. 10*(6), 974–95.

Moore, C. (2006). 'Schloss Neuwahnstein'? Why the Länder Continue to Strengthen Their Representations in Brussels, *German Politics, Vol. 15*(2), 192–205.

Müller-Graff, P.C. (2005). The German Länder: Involvement in EC / EU Law and Policy-Making. In Weatherill, S. and Bernitz, U. (eds.), *The role of Regions and Sub-National Actors in Europe*, Oxford, Hart Publishing.

Nergelius, J. (2005). The Committee of the Regions Today and in the Future—A Critical Overview. In Weatherill, S. and Bernitz, U. (eds.), *The role of Regions and Sub-National Actors in Europe*, Oxford, Hart Publishing.

Nielsen F. and Salk, J. (1998). The Ecology of Collective Action and Regional Representation in the European Union, *European Sociological Review, Vol. 14*(3), 231–254.

O'Brennan, J. (2007). Introduction: Deparliamentarization through European Integration? In *National Parliaments within the Enlarged European Union: from 'Victims' of Integration to Competitive Actors?* Routledge advances in European politics (47). Routledge, Abingdon, 1–19.

Ruge, U. (2003). *Die Erfindung des "Europa der Regionen": Kritische Ideengeschichte eines konservativen Konzepts*, Frankfurt, Campus Verlag.

Stahl, G. (2009). Die Rolle des AdR bei der regional Interessenvertretung. In Lambertz, K.-H. and Große Hüttmann, M. (eds.). *Europapolitik und Europafähigkeit von Regionen*. Nomos: Baden Baden, 136–140.

Stahl, G. and Kuby, B. (2015). The Growing Role and Responsibility of Parliaments in European Integration and Economic Governance—A View from the Committee of the Region. In: Abels, G. and Eppler, A. (eds.). *Subnational Parliaments in an EU Multi-level Parliamentary System: Taking Stock of the Post-Lisbon Era*, Studienverlag Innsbruck und

Transaction Publishers New Jersey, USA, Foster Europe International Studies Series vol. 3.

Streb, H. (2007). *Supranational Integration, National Federalism and Subnational States: A Constitutional Approach to the Impact of European Integration on Territorial Relations in Federal Member States*, Thesis for the University of London Degree of Doctor of Philosophy in Politics.

Sturm, R. (2009). Die "Europafähigkeit der Regionen, in: K.-H. Lambertz, M. Grosse Hüttmann (eds.), *Europapolitik und Europafähigkeit von Regionen*, Baden-Baden, Nomos, 11–20.

Swenden, W. (2009), Schottland in Europa: Mit oder ohne Vereinigtes Königreich?, in: Lambertz, K.-H. and Große Hüttmann, M. (eds.), *Europapolitik und Europafähigkeit von Regionen*, Baden-Baden, Nomos, 101–122.

Tatham, M. (2008), Going Solo: Direct Regional Representation in the European Union, *Regional and Federal Studies, Vol. 18*(5), 493–515.

Tatham, M. (2010), With or Without You? Revisiting Territorial State-Bypassing in EU Interest Representation, *Journal of European Public Policy, Vol. 17*(1), 76–99.

VaraArribas, G., Högenauer, A.L. (2015). Legislative Regions after Lisbon: A New Role for Regional Assemblies? In Heffler, C., Neuhold, C., Rozenberg, O., Smith, J. and Wessels, W., *The Palgrave Handbook on National Parliaments and the European Union*, Palgrave.

The Challenges of the European Social Model—Economic & Political Cohesion in Post-Economic Crisis Eurozone

ASIMAKIS TAMOURANTZIS

The deepening of the economic crisis in the Eurozone poses serious threats to the European venture. This was made evident by the emergence and widening of economic imbalances in the north / south divide that highlighted existing institutional weaknesses. The heterogeneity between the Member States hinders the development of coordinated policies and challenges their economic and social structures. Consequently, the confrontation of economic imbalances, especially in Southern Europe, has raised serious doubts about the sustainability of the European Social Model. The leaning towards economic effectiveness contributes substantially to the increase of social injustice, hence divisiveness among Member States. This study is based on the analysis and processing of statistical data and recent reports from institutes and international organizations. Analyzing the determinative factors and challenges which call the sustainability of the European Social Model into question, the developing tendencies are outlined within the frame of post-economic crisis Eurozone.

Asimakis Tamourantzis is a PhD Candidate in Economics at Panteion University of Athens.

Keywords: European Social Model; Eurozone crisis; International institutions; North-South divide.

Editors' Note

The discourse on the role of international institutions in an increasingly globalized economy has developed parallel to the mainstream debate on the economic crisis. The transposition of decision making discretion from the nation-state to international institutions and the reversibility of this process, carries both theoretical and practical interest and implications. To that end, the European Social Model in the frame of the Eurozone crisis constitutes a promising analytical choice. The author describes Eurozone member states, as being on a crossroad between the "determinism" of global economic integration and the traditional role of the state as a welfare provider. The objectives of economic growth and competitiveness, on the one hand, and enhanced social welfare, on the other, are difficult to meet simultaneously even more so in the context of a crisis. However, the current economic predicament in the Eurozone can reveal a lot. Structural deficiencies surface quickly and violently in a period of crisis thus rendering them easier to observe. Inherent limitations deriving from political oversights and the multifaceted diversity of Eurozone's members pose a great challenge to the viability of the Eurozone and the European Social Model. The quality of Eurozone's structure and its capacity to adapt will largely define Europe's economic competitiveness and social viability as well as the future of the ESM as a constitutive part of Europe.

Introduction

The Eurozone faces transformation. The economic crisis has wiped out years of economic and social progress and exposed structural weaknesses in the Eurozone's economy. Meanwhile, the world is moving fast and long-term challenges such as economic globalization, pressure on resources and ageing, have intensified. Within this framework the welfare state, competitiveness and employment in the Eurozone are at the heart of public debate and reform. Consequently, the effects of the crisis on the European Social Model create a field of intense research interest.

The key aims of the European Social Model are to maintain social cohesion to ensure protection from poverty and social exclusion and to promote the common values of democracy, social justice, social welfare, solidarity, individual rights and market economy between Member States; it is a dynamic productive model integrated into economies and societies which aspires to foster economic competition, social security, solidarity and cohesion (European Commission, 1994). The model purports the parallel development of economic and social prosperity and relies on the interdependence between economic effectiveness and social justice.

In the context of the Lisbon Strategy (2000), the European Social Model is based on a dynamic society focusing on competitiveness, research, innovation, sustainable development and social cohesion (European Council, March 2000). The Lisbon Strategy includes a broader content of policies related to economic and social activity. In particular it recommends reforms in the field of labor markets, tax policies, social security systems etc. aiming at a competitive and dynamic Europe with emphasis on employment based on innovation, entrepreneurship, the information society and the fight against poverty and social exclusion. However, the failure to reach the goals of the Lisbon Strategy led to the leaders of European Union to adopt a program, (European Council, June of 2010), which is a continuation of the Lisbon Strategy. The main purposes of Europe 2020 are to produce a development strategy for the European Union and to improve the functions of the Eurozone and the European economy. The Europe 2020 puts forward three mutually reinforcing priorities:

- Smart growth; developing an economy based on knowledge and innovation.
- Sustainable growth; promoting a more resource efficient, greener and more competitive economy.
- Inclusive growth; fostering a high-employment economy which delivers social and territorial cohesion (European Commission, 2010). Finally, recent ILO research (2014) identifies the following key features of the European Social Model:
- Increased minimum rights on working conditions.
- Universal and sustainable social protection systems.

- Inclusive labor markets.
- Strong and well-functioning social dialogue.
- Public services and services of general interest.
- Social inclusion and social cohesion (Vaughan-Whitehead, 2013).

According to the above mentioned outline there is no denying that the European Social Model continues to face pressure from a range of factors such as economic globalization, enhanced economic competition, different structures of labor markets and population ageing. On the positive side, common pressures on Member States should produce economic and social policy convergence. On the negative side, the heterogeneity of Member States complicates the coordination of policies and challenges existing economic and social structures. Different national economic and social conditions ensure that common measures produce different responses, even when goals are similar. In the Eurozone, this was made evident by the emergence and widening of north / south economic imbalances which in turn reflected existing institutional weaknesses[1]. Whilst trying to regain competitiveness, these imbalances have raised serious doubts about the sustainability of the European Social Model, especially in Southern Europe. However, demographic change is one of the most pressing challenges common to all Eurozone countries. Low birth rate and the increased aging of the population pose a significant challenge to economic sustainability. The deepening of the economic crisis in the Eurozone undoubtedly poses the most serious threat to the European venture.

This study is based on the processing and analysis of statistical data including recent reports of institutes and international organizations. It investigates the factors and challenges which call the sustainability of the European Social Model into question. The developing tendencies are outlined within the frame of the post-economic crisis Eurozone. The structure of the paper is as follows. In Section 2 a theoretical framework is presented. Section 3 examines the determinants of economic and social structural transformation in the Eurozone. Section 4 discusses the trends and inclinations at the formation of the European Social Model. Section 5 analyzes the challenges and prospects of the European Social Model in the frame of economic effectiveness and social justice. The orientation towards economic effectiveness contributes substantially to the increase of social injustice and, by extension, the social division amongst Member States.

Theoretical Framework

The acceleration of economic globalization has had a vast impact on social and economic developments in the 21st century. During the last three decades the flow of goods, services and capital has increased substantially on an international scale. This has caused economic, political and social changes that state intervention alone cannot address adequately. The pressure resulting from the acceleration of economic globalization causes transformations as the economic, political, social and demographic

---

[1] For further analysis, see Section 3, "Determinants of Economic and Social Structural Transformation in the Eurozone"

factors as those of previous decades are significantly different. Therefore, due to the failure of the Nation States to conquer the transnational problems the diffusion of power to international institutions is deemed necessary. The intensity of international competition and the technological advances necessitate reforms with the aim of adapting the states to the new era. As a result the social structure is transformed (Prats-Monne, 2009).

Map 1: Globalization Index, (2011)

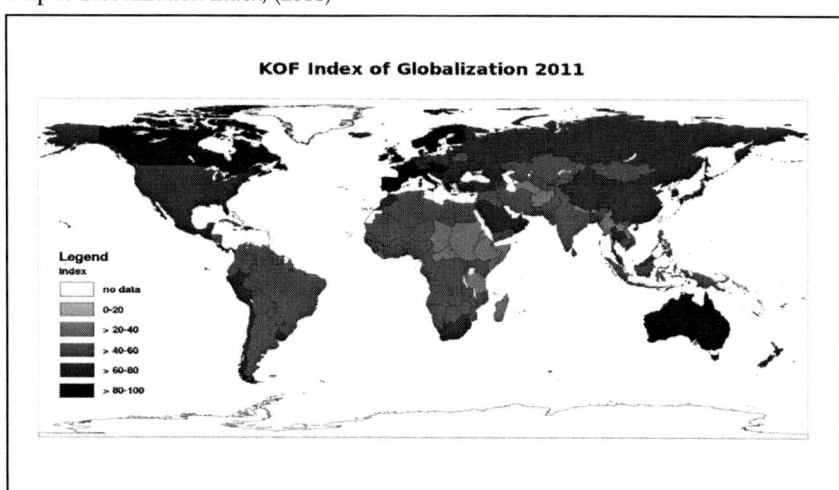

Source: Globalization Index 2011

In this new context Nation states gradually transform from welfare states to competition states driven by international institutions in order to adapt to the new conditions of economic globalization (Cerny, 1997). The dominant position of the state is weakened whilst the internal institutional configuration and the implementation of economic policy are internationalized (Chossudovsky, 1997). The 'Battle for Competitiveness' leads to deregulation policies by undermining the fiscal capacity of supporting welfare policies whilst the intensity of international competition triggers the economic transformation of the states[2]. The restructuring of global economy under the guidance of international institutions[3] turns states into open economy fields thus downgrading the role of the state apparatus.

These changes reflect the intensifying process of international economic integration and prioritize monetary over fiscal policy[4]. Moreover, the achievement of monetary stability via the reduction of fiscal deficits precedes the targets of employment levels and demand management (Pagoulatos, 1999). The rise of Liberal standards and

---

[2] The rise of the Liberal model and of Monetarism was accompanied by economic policies which imposed the deregulation process of capital mobility, the financialization, privatizations e.t.c.

[3] Such as, International Monetary Fund (IMF), World Bank, OECD e.t.c.

[4] The priority of Monetary policy is closely connected with the pursuit of a Monetary stability and the avoidance of fiscal deficits.

Monetarism as the dominant ideologies in a constantly changing environment[5] reflects the strengthening of coalitions of interests[6] which are better served through the adoption of those policies and unsettle the national institutional systems, rules and processes (Pagoulatos, 1999).

This facet of the liberal standard, where International Organizations manage the Global Economy based on the laissez-faire doctrine, has become more obvious during the last decades. This is a field of high research interest. Not only economic, social and cultural relations between states but also the increased influence of the financial system on the real economy of the states. It should be noted that institutional and structural transformations result from a new type of supranational sovereign interventionism which encompasses all sectors of the economic and political system under the supervision of international organizations[7]. At the same time, as neoclassical economics aim at a controlled management of national cases, the social fabric is transformed.

Determinants of Economic and Social Structural Transformation in the Eurozone

The exposure of structural weaknesses and deficiencies of the European Monetary Union as a result of the Economic crisis has caused a widespread debate on the viability of the European Social Model. Inherent weaknesses of the institutional structure, the heterogeneity of Member States and the diversity of the European systems of political economy have hampered the development of harmonized policies. It is clear that the structural achievements of the Eurozone as regards speed and consistency, did neither meet the requirements imposed by the intensity of economic globalization nor did those deriving from technological change. These deficiencies are the result, on the one hand, of adverse economic and demographic factors and, on the other, of international challenges in the fields of labor market, social dangers and competitiveness. Thus, the Eurozone's structural achievements appear weak when confronted with the challenges of international competition (Sapir, 2006).

Many scientific papers and policy reports investigate the impact of institutions and labor markets on economic performance (e.g. OECD Jobs Study, OECD social insurance strategy) aiming at providing insights on the low performance of the Eurozone in terms of employment. Especially in Southern countries, the deepening of the economic crisis in the Eurozone has strongly affected social cohesion and has caused an explosive rise of unemployment and economic and social inequalities. This in turn, has revealed the

---

[5] From the early 1970s till nowadays

[6] The alignment of Central Banks' monetary policy with the demand of the International Financial markets has led to the weakening of the State strength, resulting in the transfer of power from the Governments to Financial markets.

[7] For instance, IMF Conditionality, see https://www.imf.org/external/np/exr/facts/conditio.html OECD Toolkit etc.

inability of the Lisbon Strategy[8] and the European Employment Strategy[9] to achieve their targets. The relative decline in the working age population in the Eurozone forces governments to seek new ways to increase employment levels.

For instance, the emerging consensus on the labor market policy in the Eurozone is that national governments need to promote higher skill levels, higher levels of skill and workforce participation and greater labor market flexibility in order to enhance economic competitiveness and tackle problems of poverty and social exclusion. However, the European systems of political economy have different structures and this has had an impact on the way the European Labor Markets of the Member States function. As a result, those divergences have led to periods of intense shocks.

Imperfect Monetary Union and the Imbalances of the European Labour Markets; The Case of Germany and Greece

In order to explain further how the divergences of the European Labor Markets have related to the different institutional structures among Member States. Figure 1 uses the McDonald-Solow Model (1981). In Figure 1, it has been assumed that the two countries that are depicted in the graph, Germany and Greece, are not members of the Eurozone and follow independent economic policies. The vertical axis of each graph corresponds to the real wage levels whilst the horizontal one depicts the employment levels. It is being assumed that there is only one labor union in each country. The convex curves are the indifference curves of each labor union. The union's usefulness is maximized as a function related to both the levels of wages and employment of its members. The curve DD' which has a negative slope, is the labor demand curve of the economy. Points a and b correspond to the maximum usefulness of the labor unions in the two countries.

Figure 1: McDonald - Solow Model

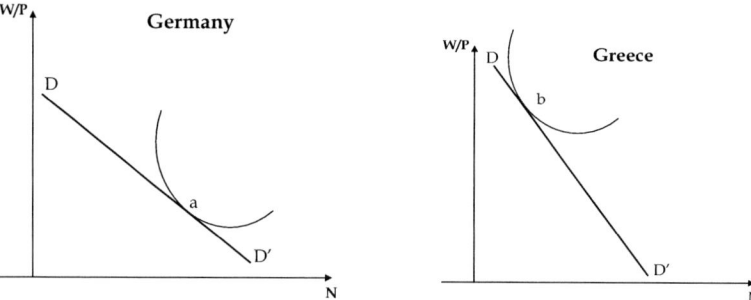

A rise in wages in Germany can create unemployment; therefore, an expansive fiscal and monetary policy will be applied by the government in order to maintain the current

---

[8] For further information, see: European Parliament, (2010), *The Lisbon Strategy 2000–2010. An analysis and evaluation of the methods used and results achieved*, Brussels: European Parliament's Committee on Employment and Social Affairs

[9] For further information, see: De la Porte, C. Ph. Pochet. 2004. The European Employment Strategy: existing research and remaining questions. Journal of European Social Policy 14/1, 71–78.

level of employment. In the case of Greece, the labor demand curve is steeper compared to that of Germany. This is because the government is more determined to apply policies that aim at absorbing unemployment and increasing employment levels. However, in a case where both countries are part of a Monetary Union, the monetary policy is exerted by a central body which is common to all Member States. Consequently, the slope of the labor demand curves converge. The different economic policies and the different institutions of labor markets will make Member States follow divergent trends and this will not make it possible for them to adjust in cases of shocks.

Figure 2: Asymmetric demand shock in a Monetary Union

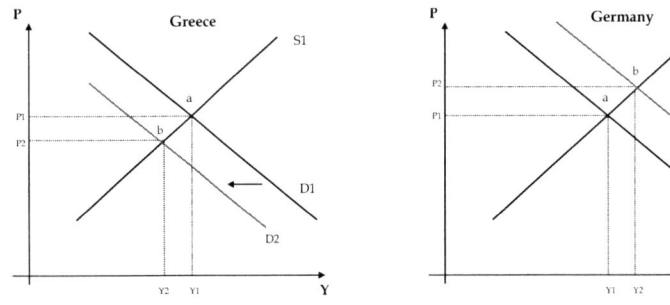

Source: De Grauwe, 2012

Therefore, a permanent asymmetric demand shock in a Monetary Union, as depicted in Figure 2, occurs when the demand curve of Germany is displaced upwards and that of Greece downwards. These displacements cause changes at the level of product equilibrium in the two countries and a simultaneous reduction / increase of unemployment. When the Central Bank aims at achieving a low level of inflation and a monetary union is not an Optimal Currency Area (Mundell, 1961, McKinnon, 1963, Kenen, 1969, Krugman, 1991, 1993, Melitz, 1995, 1996), then these two countries (Germany and Greece) develop an adjustment problem, the system paralyses and the Monetary Union appears imperfect (De Grauwe, 2012).

Figure 3: Balance of inflation rates

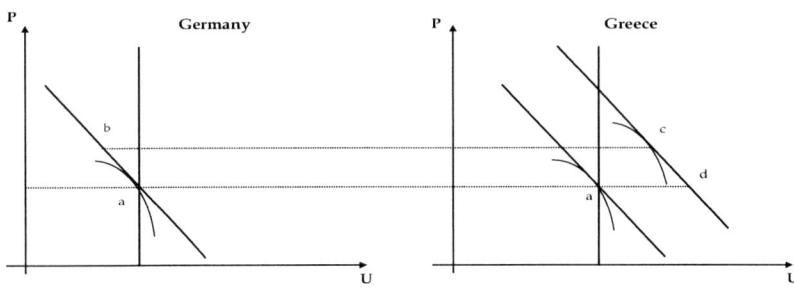

Source: De Grauwe, 1996

In case of the aforementioned asymmetric shock, the short term Phillips curve of Greece is displaced to the right while that of Germany remains steady[10] (Figure 3). If Greece was not a member of the Monetary Union, it would follow an independent monetary policy (Expansive Monetary Policy) in order to enhance its economic activity. As a result the economy would be transferred to point c. However, in a fixed exchange rate system or a system of common currency, when the Central Bank aims at containing the inflation and the Monetary Policy (n-1) is applied from a leader country (Germany), the mitigation of the consequences of an asymmetric shock is difficult. This forces the economic authorities of the weak country (Greece) to transfer the economy to point d thus increasing the unemployment, reducing products and worsening the imbalances (De Grauwe, 1996).

The Implications of the Different Structures in the Eurozone Member States

The above asymmetric shocks would cause intense confrontation between the participating countries; undermining the system's reliability. The problem of 'hysteresis in unemployment'[11], (Blanchard – Summers, 1986) is of major importance as it is a consequence of the increased heterogeneity of Member States. Therefore in cases of asymmetric shocks where there is no economic harmonization, the Central Bank faces extreme difficulty when aiming to stabilize the GDP and employment so it consequently "paralyzes". At the same time, the recovery of the lost competitiveness creates an obsession with anti-inflation policy, which in turn condemns the Monetary Union to economic hardship, uncertainty, high unemployment, recession and economic and social instability.

Europeanization has its own inherent limitations and the introduction of rules from Brussels is not an automatic process. Internal resistance is often intense and effective in its own national way (Tsoukalis, 2012). In Europe there are institutional constraints which obstruct the harmonization of economic policy. For instance, the effective adjustment in the field of the European Labor Markets in times of economic recession can be achieved with part-time employment and temporary unemployment policies (Flexicurity) (Matsaganis, 2011). This means that the reduction of working hours will be combined with monitoring training programs for employees. The countries of Northern Europe that adopted such policies in the period of economic crisis had a smaller decrease in GDP in contrast to those of Southern Europe where the drastic reduction of the number of employees has exacerbated unemployment, poverty and social exclusion leading to the deepening of the recession (Matsaganis, 2013).

---

[10] We assume that in the short run the indifference curves, the inflation rate and the natural rate of unemployment are identical

[11] "Hysteresis in unemployment" means that a temporary disturbance in unemployment, which is due to a temporary recession, becomes a permanent shock because of the rigid forms of the labour markets. In the case which the Central Bank of the system behaves conservatively (i.e. exerting stabilizing policies), the problem of "Hysteresis of unemployment" will be worst. This development will lead to inability to adapt and higher unemployment rates

In fact, the adaptability in the workplace that requires a technological development is important. Equally important is the combination of work and family life. However, the adoption of flexible employment policies does not mean that labor rights are lost. For example, the representation to justice, the employment conditions of supervision and control mechanisms etc. (Giddens, 2006). Additionally, the combination of education, training and retraining programs are active policies that improve adaptability. The low Macroeconomic results of South Europe have resulted in a slow and inefficient adaptation of enterprises to the new international environment. The difference in the effectiveness of response reveals the difference in the institutional environment operating (Sutton, 2006).

The Weaknesses of the Eurozone Institutions

The structural and institutional weaknesses and deficiencies which were revealed through the surfacing of economic imbalances (especially in the southern European countries) made the need for direct institutional changes imperative. The fact that the Eurozone had not adopted mechanisms for income redistribution, for creating a European Monetary Fund and operating 'Lender of last resort' by the European Central Bank (ECB) caused asymmetric consequences for the Member States. The failure of the institutions to prevent the swelling of asymmetries between Member States became apparent at the dawn of the Global Economic Crisis (2007–2008) that particularly affected the South European countries.

Inevitably, the contribution of the International Monetary Fund (IMF) was requested. It was the first time that the IMF offered economic and technical assistance to developed countries of the EMU. In addition, it was the first time that the IMF was collaborating so closely with European institutions. Under the terms of bailout agreements, the governments of Greece, Portugal and Ireland signed Memoranda of Understanding with the IMF, the European Commission (EC) and the ECB (EC-IMF-ECB), known collectively as the 'Troika' of lenders. As in other so-called 'Program Countries', access to credit has been dependent upon satisfactory progress on a detailed program of fiscal consolidation and structural reforms through policy of Internal Devaluation[12] (Matsaganis, 2015).

This new model of cooperation (EC-IMF-ECB), which includes processes of revision, change, complementation and modification of perceptions, is based on the guidelines that international institutions provided during the 1990s (Washington Consensus, World Bank-market friendly strategy, OECD - social insurance strategy, OECD - Jobs strategy). These guidelines affected the architecture of European integration. The new model of cooperation was established with the aim of safeguarding the viability of the (Economic)-Monetary Union (E-MU), correcting the imbalances, restoring the trust and achieving financial stability. This would form the basis of the future relations between international and regional institutions and would impact on

---

[12] For relevant analysis see sub-chapter 3.4

the mutation of the European models (Pisany-Ferry, Sapir & Wolff – Bruegel, 2013). This conclusion is also drawn at the new economic governance framework of E-MU[13].

In order to achieve economic effectiveness, international organizations negotiated with the ultimate goal of economic convergence and harmonization. At the same time, economic powers[14] influenced the modification of structural and business practices of the states (Gilpin, 2002). The achievement of convergence and harmonization is a process of increased interdependence and interaction between national economies which spans across the whole economic activity of each country. This process contributes to the creation of an external environment which influences the application of the economic policy.

The increasing exposure of the Member States of the Eurozone to the international competition is mostly the result of the European economic integration (Begg, Draxter, Mortensen, 2008). The transition from Custom Union to the European Single Market, the Maastricht Treaty criteria, the provisions of Stability and Growth Pact (SGP) as well as the transition to E-MU, were based on the guidelines and notions of the international organizations. This triggered an initial transformation from the early 1990s. However, the fact that the Eurozone is not just a system of rules and political institutions should not be overlooked. The Eurozone is a space where different political traditions, experiences, practices and cultural memories coexist.

The Recovery of Eurozone Competitiveness and the Policy of Internal Devaluation

In order to recover the lost competitiveness in the Southern European countries, the launching of a process of internal devaluation was deemed necessary (Argeitis, 2012). This process targeted the restoration of lost competitiveness and followed the guidelines of the new model of cooperation. The principal aims of this process are the following:

- Reduction of deficits and public debt in sustainable levels.
- The adoption of structural reforms in order to make the economies more efficient and competitive.
- The achievement of financial stability in order to make the southern European countries return to the financial markets (Parliament Budget Office, 4th Quarter Report, 2013).

However, the economic policies of internal devaluation gave priority to economic effectiveness over social justice by adopting policies which undermined the demand and employment, the income redistribution and the social safety net, as they aimed to eradicate the social dangers in order to support the development process. Thus, we can conclude that the European Social model faces increased uncertainty and challenges as

---

[13] See the new framework of economic governance in EZ such as European Semester, The Strategy of 2020, Euro Plus Pact, Fiscal Compact, Macroeconomic Imbalances Procedure etc.
[14] Such as Financial Market forces

many Member States (especially in Southern Europe) face the danger of social aberrance.

The policies that cause the shrinkage of welfare result from the growing number of citizens of the Eurozone that face poverty and social exclusion, as noted in the recent report of the International Labour Organization (ILO, 2014). The erosion of the European Social Model is worsened as the deepening of economic crisis continues. The Gini Index (Figures 4 & 6) and S80 / S2O[15] Index (Figure 5) (especially in the southern European Member States) have proved that the increase of income inequality alters the terms of "Social Contract".

Essentially, the reduction of a range of social protection benefits, the limited access to quality public services, along with persistent unemployment, lower wages and higher taxes, have contributed to increases in poverty and social exclusion. The cost of adjustment has been passed on to populations who have been coping with fewer jobs and lower income for more than five years. Depressed household income levels are leading to lower domestic consumption and lower demand, slowing down recovery. Higher poverty and inequality are the results not only of the severity of the global recession, but also of specific policy decisions curtailing social transfers and limiting access to quality public services. The achievements of the European Social Model, which dramatically reduced poverty and promoted prosperity in the period following the Second World War have been eroded by short-term adjustment reforms. Fiscal consolidation focused on deep cutbacks to public policies and shrinkage of the state as the main way to fix the deficit, calm the markets and revitalize the economy. Following this logic, the European Social Model was depicted as unaffordable and burdensome, which ultimately reduced competitiveness and discouraged growth (ILO, 2014).

---

[15] The most widespread income inequality indicators are the indicator S80 / S20, which measures the ratio of the income of the richest quintile of the population to the income of the poorest quintile and the Gini index which ranges between 0, when all individuals have the same income (complete equality) and 1, when the total disposable income held by one person (maximum inequality). The sensitivity of the Gini index is greater in the middle of income distribution, than towards to the end of it

Figure 4: Gini Index, 2008 & 2013 in the Eurozone (EZ)

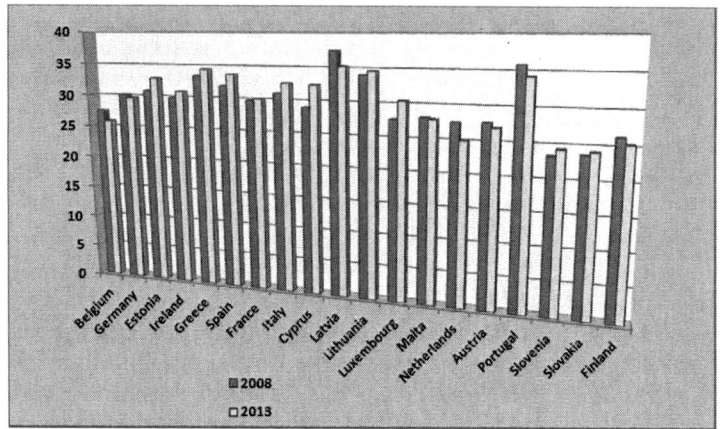

Source: Eurostat

Figure 5: S80 / S20 Index, 2008 & 2013 in the Eurozone

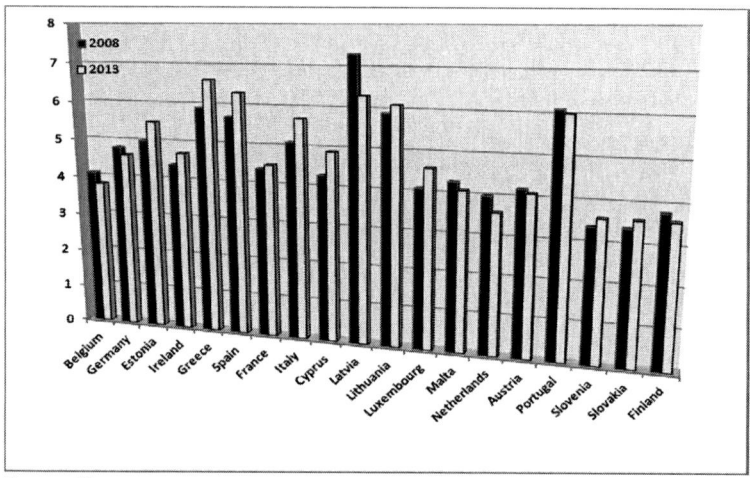

Source: Eurostat

Figure 6: Gini Index, 2008–2013 in selected Eurozone countries[16]

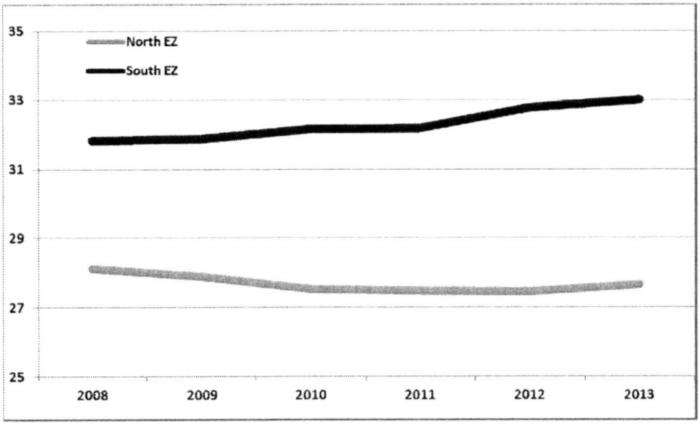

[Line chart showing Gini Index from 2008 to 2013 for North EZ (around 28, slightly declining then flat) and South EZ (rising from ~32 to ~33)]

Source: Eurostat

Trends and Inclinations at the Formation of the European Social Model

In the Eurozone, the reduction in social allowances, health expenses and fundamental social services in the frame of the fiscal rules (Fiscal Compact, SGP) threaten the most sensitive social groups. This 'explosive mix' is further reinforced by the rise of unemployment, low salaries and rising taxes that results in increasing poverty and social marginalization. The achievements of the European Social Model have been eroded and have changed the terms of the Social Contract which were formed on the basis of a social Europe. Social inequalities as a consequence of the current economic crisis threaten social cohesion and have a negative impact on social well-being. The rise of these inequalities challenges the ability of national and European political systems, to limit the imbalances and strengthen the social cohesion in accordance to the principles of the European Social Model. In addition, the unclear definition of the Eurozone as an economic, political and social entity and the inability to establish the notion of a common European identity has serious consequences on the economic governance (Begg, 2010). The harsh policies of 'internal devaluation' lately applied (2010–2014) contribute to the rise of income inequality, worsening unemployment (Figure 9), unprecedented reduction of GDP of some countries (Figure 7) and to soaring public debt (Figure 8). As a result the recession deepens, the countries face deflation and the economic imbalances in the Eurozone are sharpened.

---

[16] In this study, the Diagram shows the Member States of the European North, which are: Germany, France, Netherlands, Belgium, Luxembourg, Austria and Finland, and those of the European South, which are: Greece, Italy, Portugal, Spain, Cyprus and Ireland respectively

Figure 7: Cumulative GDP, (2008–2013) in the Eurozone

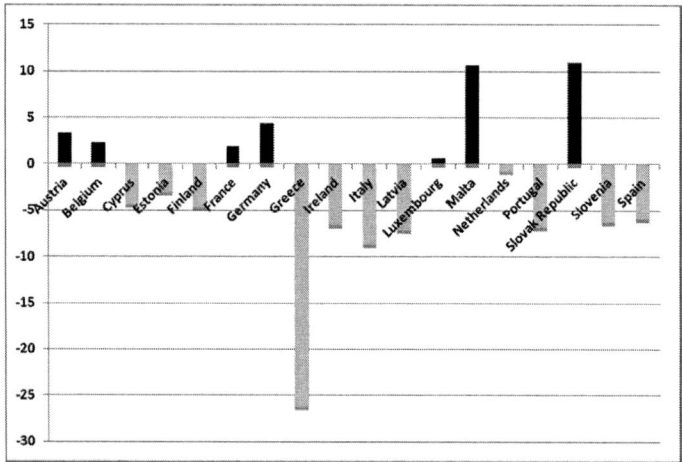

Source: IMF, World Economic Outlook Database, October 2014

Figure 8: General government gross debt (% of GDP), 2008–2013 in selected Eurozone countries

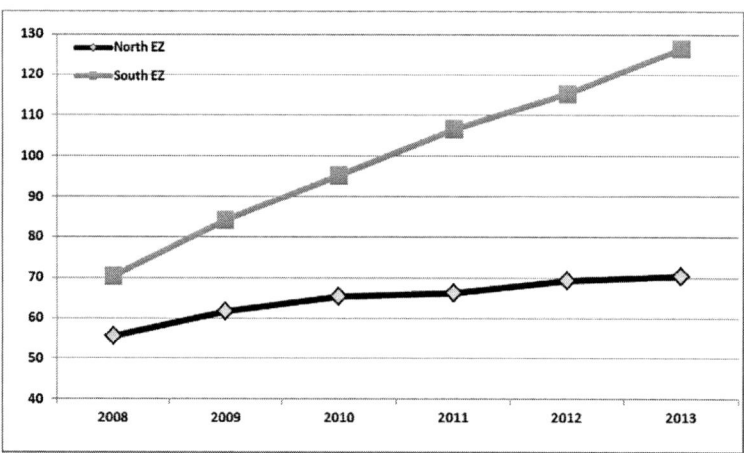

Source: IMF, World Economic Outlook Database, October 2014

Figure 9: Unemployment rate (% of total Labor force), 2008–2013 in selected Eurozone countries

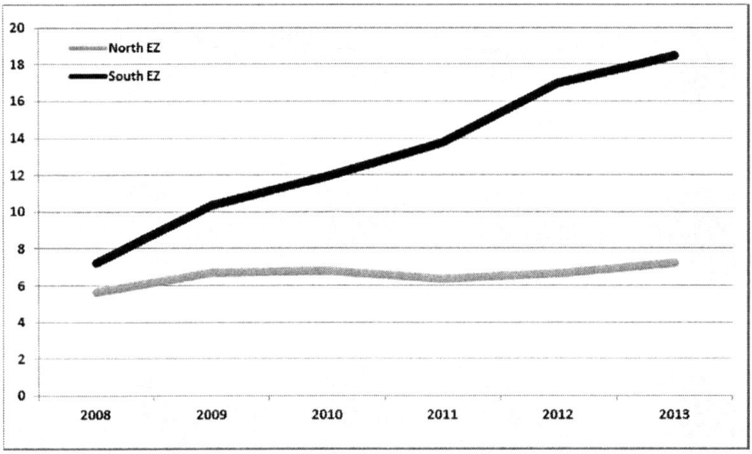

Source: IMF, World Economic Outlook Database, October 2014

When a country aims to achieve social justice whilst going through a period of fiscal consolidation it needs to have a social safety net in order to secure the viability of the program (Blanchard-Cottarelli, 2014).In order for such a program to be successful it needs to:

- Be based on cutting of costs rather than tax increases.
- Have clearly defined targets about spending and be based on fiscal rules.
- Be in accordance with the monetary policy.

The probability of success of such a program of 'fiscal consolidation' is greater as the social benefits are enhanced. The effectiveness of such a program is related to the increase of spending on programs of active labour market policy, vocational training and reduction of tax rates (e.g. reduction of VAT in a basket of goods such as food) (Kaplanoglou - Rapanos and Bardakas, 2014). Therefore, providing support to the more vulnerable social groups during periods of this fiscal consolidation is a factor of vital importance, not only for sustaining the social cohesion but also for the success of the program, the controlled reduction of deficit and the deceleration of public debt as well (Parliament Budget Office, 4th Quarter Report, 2013).

The reminder of De Grauwe (2010), about the 'Fisher Paradox' (1932) is particularly interesting. In this Fisher notes that as governments are forced by credit rating agencies, who downgrade their rating score, to reduce their public debts this then makes the deleveraging of private debt impossible. The reduction of debt in the private sector is only possible if governments are willing to increase the public debt. Thus, the economic policy aiming at reducing both the public and the private sector's debts is self-destructive and impossible and leads the economy to recession and deflation. In addition, according to Robert Barro, in order for countries with high public debt to increase their tax income, they will have to lead the economic policy to reduce their spending and increase the tax rates. As a result the economic growth will drop significantly.

Eurozone's painful experiences during the last few years confirm both, De Grauwe's reminder and Barro's observations. All Member States have increased their taxes and at the same time the economic development has fallen (Wyplosz, 2010). It should be noted that since 2010 in the frame of the economic policies of 'fiscal consolidation', taxation and unemployment are rising whilst wages and pensions are significantly reduced. This fact has aggravated the living standards and has weakened the social fabric especially in the Southern European countries. The recent OECD report (Taxing Wages 2014) (Figure 10–11) confirms these observations as it shows that southern European countries are overtaxed in comparison with other Member States. As a consequence, according to a recent report by the IMF (Ostry - Berg and Tsangarides, 2014), income inequalities are detrimental for growth, for economic and political stability and for social cohesion and investments. Therefore, we can conclude that the existing tax system should be reformed in favor of the income redistribution in order for this to have a significant impact on the growth of the Eurozone.

Figure 10: Tax wedge annual change between 2010 and 2013 as % of labour costs in EZ-15

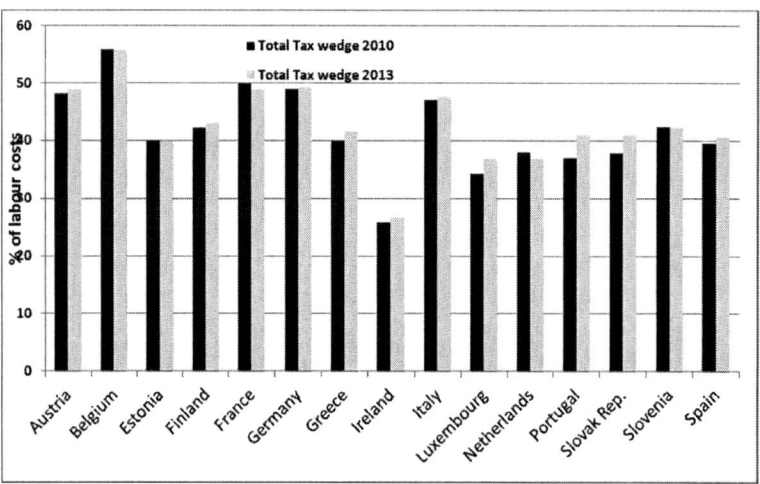

Source: OECD

Figure 11: Comparison of total tax wedge by family type (2013) as % of labor costs in EZ-15

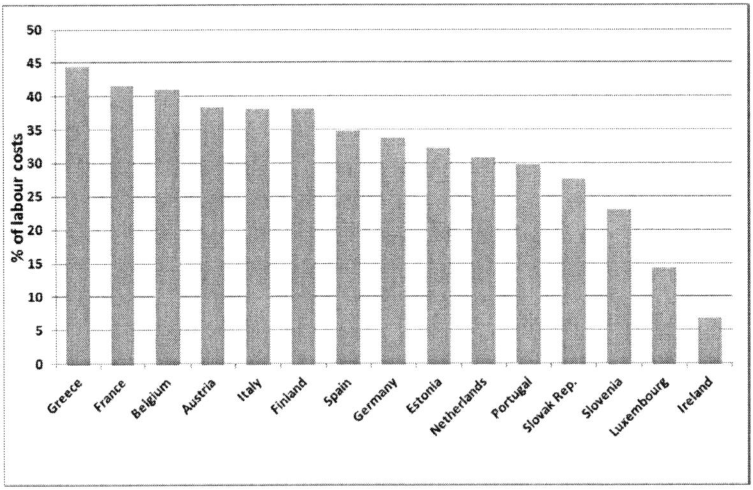

[Bar chart showing % of labour costs by country: Greece ~44, France ~42, Belgium ~41, Austria ~38, Italy ~38, Finland ~38, Spain ~35, Germany ~34, Estonia ~32, Netherlands ~31, Portugal ~30, Slovak Rep. ~27, Slovenia ~23, Luxembourg ~15, Ireland ~7]

Source: OECD

The pressure of global economic competition along with the rapid development of new factors in the international system causes international transformations. According to the convention of the new model of cooperation (EC-IMF-ECB) these transformations necessitate the structural convergence of the Member States of the Eurozone. As a consequence the national differences in the economic management and policy will need to disappear while societies will be forced to adopt similar institutions, models and practices (Gilpin, 2002). In this context, it is evident that the achievement of convergence and harmonization is necessary for the viability of the Eurozone and the elimination of multiformity and diversity.

However, in the frame of cooperation between European and International institutions (EC-IMF-ECB) as part of the process of establishing a new model of economic governance in the E-MU, the trend of the Eurozone gradually transforming to a liberal Anglo-Saxon model is observed. This means that the financial Markets play a central role in the economy and Neo-classical economics determine social activities. Consequently, the occurring transformation and the shrinkage of the welfare state affect the alteration of the whole European social structure. Admittedly, there is a tendency towards the Liberal system, because the framework was not formed as part of social institutions. In fact it reflects the intensification of the imbalances between Member States. This acts as a result both in the economic and in the social field, with enlargement of the disruptive tendency economic effectiveness and social justice.

However, as Adam Smith noted, no society is sustainable and there are no opportunities for growth if the majority of its members are in despair. Thus, according to Polanyi (1944) when a self-regulated market economy system dominates the fundamental social relations there is a danger of erosion of social cohesion. As Economic

History teaches us, when a similar situation arose just before the World War II, social instability favoured the political extremes.

Challenges and Perspectives for the European Social Model

Economic effectiveness and social justice are conflicting elements in the implementation of economic policy and the process of decision making. The achievement of high levels of competitiveness and social justice coupled with internal structural reform is a challenging process (Tsoukalis, 2007). This is because the state mechanism is linked to the mechanism of international capital markets and is vulnerable to intense pressures towards the shrinking of the policies of social cohesion.

The European Social Model is shaped by the notion that Social Justice has to be combined with regulatory rules for the free market economy. Also economies and societies should have the ability to adapt in the economic, social and technological changes; the economic and social interdependence as part of the economic globalization has necessitated the Eurozone to confront multiple challenges on different levels. At the economic level the challenges are the following:

- Rise of Macroeconomic Imbalances between the North and South European countries
- Exacerbation of the competitiveness gap.

As far as the social level is concerned the challenges that the Eurozone faces which threaten the viability of the European social structure are:

- The rise of income inequalities.
- The rise of social exclusion and poverty.
- The increasing trend of exclusion of people, communities and peripheries as a result of social damping, deregulation and lack of democratic processes.

The recent data about the inequalities between Member States in the social field are indicated by the 'Misery Index' (Figure 12) and confirm the aforementioned conclusions.

Figure 12: Misery Index in the Eurozone (2013)

World Misery Index Scores – 2013			
Rank (Worst to Best)	Country	Misery Index Score	Largest Contribuiting Factor
11	Spain	36.9	Unemployment
13	Greece	35.9	Unemployment
21	Cyprus	28.7	Unemployment
33	Portugal	23.8	Unemployment
39	Ireland	22.4	Unemployment
45	Italy	20.4	Unemployment
53	Slovenia	17.8	Unemployment
58	Slovak Republic	17.1	Unemployment
64	Estonia	15.8	Unemployment
71	Finland	14.0	Unemployment
73	France	13.8	Unemployment
76	Belgium	13.4	Unemployment
77	Lithuania	13.4	Unemployment
81	Latvia	12.9	Unemployment
83	Netherlands	11.9	Unemployment
93	Luxembourg	10.8	Unemployment
97	Malta	10.0	Unemployment
98	Germany	9.1	Unemployment
99	Austria	9.0	Unemployment

Source: World Bank, Economic Intelligence unit (EIU), IMF

The lack of Social Justice is also evident from the widening of social division between the South and North European countries as depicted by the European Social Justice Index (Figure 13) and poses a threat to the European economic and political integration (Bertelsmann, 2014a). The European Social Justice Index measures 6 fields[17] according to 35 criteria (Figure 14).

---

[17] The six dimensions in detail: **Poverty Prevention**: Under conditions of poverty, social participation and self- determined life are possible only with great difficulty. Poverty is the strongest determinant of social and economic exclusion of young people. **Equitable Education**: Equal access to good- quality education is an essential factor in providing equitable capabilities and opportunities for advancement (vertical mobility). It is critical to ending hereditary social exclusion, supports integration and includes lifelong learning. **Labor-market access**: Employment both provides an income and facilitates social participation. The degree of inclusiveness is essential since an individual's status is defined in large part by his or her participation in the workforce. Exclusion from the labor market substantially limits individual opportunities for self- realization, contributes to an increase in the risk of poverty, and can even lead to serious health stresses. **Access to Health**: The conditions in which people live and die are shaped by political, social and economic forces. Social and economic policies have a determining impact on whether a child can grow and develop to it's full potential and live a flourishing life, or whether it's life will be blighted. This is why access to healthcare ensures young people can be active in society. **Social cohesion and non-discrimination**: This dimension enables the examination of the extent to which trends towards social polarization, exclusion and the discrimination of specific groups are successfully countered. Developing a community of shared values, shared challenges and

These fields are:

- Poverty Prevention (Figure 15)
- Access to Education.
- Access to Labour Market (Figure 16).
- Access to Health (Figure 17).
- Justice between generations .
- Social Cohesion and Non-Discrimination (Figure 18).

The widening of social gaps and the absence of social security, in combination with the economic imbalances between south and north European countries causes imbalances to societies, socioeconomic divergence and rise of income inequality. These developments have serious consequences to the future prospects of growth of the European economies and challenge the viability of funding of social policies. Economic growth is of vital importance in order to address the effects of the economic crisis and the social and political dangers and propel the economic and social well-being (Pagoulatos, 2014).

Figure 13: EU & EZ Social Justice Index

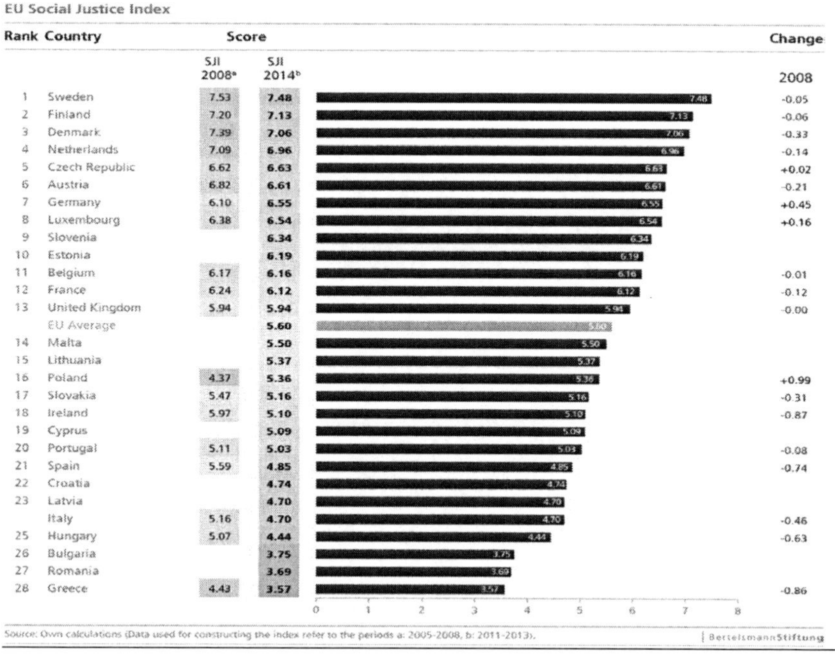

EU Social Justice Index

Rank	Country	SJI 2008[a]	SJI 2014[b]	Change 2008
1	Sweden	7.53	7.48	-0.05
2	Finland	7.20	7.13	-0.06
3	Denmark	7.39	7.06	-0.33
4	Netherlands	7.09	6.96	-0.14
5	Czech Republic	6.62	6.63	+0.02
6	Austria	6.82	6.61	-0.21
7	Germany	6.10	6.55	+0.45
8	Luxembourg	6.38	6.54	+0.16
9	Slovenia		6.34	
10	Estonia		6.19	
11	Belgium	6.17	6.16	-0.01
12	France	6.24	6.12	-0.12
13	United Kingdom	5.94	5.94	0.00
	EU Average		5.60	
14	Malta		5.50	
15	Lithuania		5.37	
16	Poland	4.37	5.36	+0.99
17	Slovakia	5.47	5.16	-0.31
18	Ireland	5.97	5.10	-0.87
19	Cyprus		5.09	
20	Portugal	5.11	5.03	-0.08
21	Spain	5.59	4.85	-0.74
22	Croatia		4.74	
23	Latvia		4.70	
	Italy	5.16	4.70	-0.46
25	Hungary	5.07	4.44	-0.63
26	Bulgaria		3.75	
27	Romania		3.69	
28	Greece	4.43	3.57	-0.86

Source: Own calculations (Data used for constructing the index refer to the periods a: 2005-2008, b: 2011-2013). | BertelsmannStiftung

equal opportunity is the aim. **Intergenerational justice**: The issue at stake here is the need for contemporary generations to lead lives they value without compromising the ability of future generations at the same. Sharing social burdens among young and old, with provision for future generations is the aspiration.

Figure 14: Dimensions & Indicators of the Index

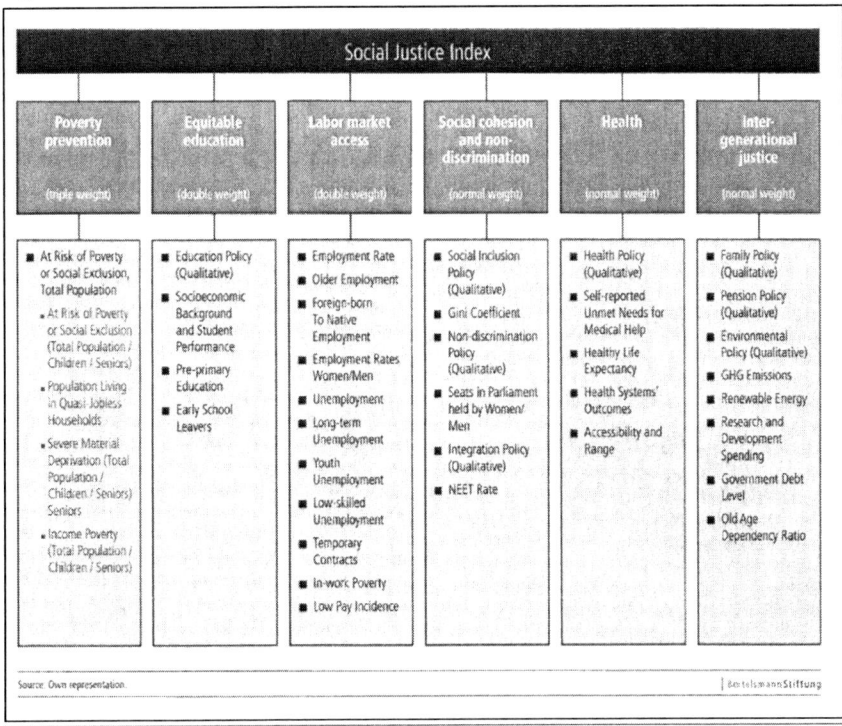

Figure 15: EU & EZ Poverty Prevention
Poverty Prevention

Rank	Country	Score SJI 2008[a]	Score SJI 2014[b]	Change 2008
1	Czech Republic	7.22	7.50	+0.28
2	Netherlands	7.24	7.41	+0.17
3	Sweden	7.67	7.26	-0.40
4	Finland	6.84	7.17	+0.33
5	Luxembourg	7.19	6.60	-0.59
6	Austria	7.00	6.51	-0.50
7	Denmark	6.98	6.46	-0.52
8	France	6.46	6.44	-0.02
9	Germany	6.08	6.32	+0.24
	Slovenia		6.32	
11	Slovakia	5.91	6.27	+0.36
12	Belgium	5.84	5.84	+0.00
13	Malta		5.49	
14	Estonia		5.39	
15	United Kingdom	5.61	5.25	-0.36
	EU Average		5.01	
16	Portugal	5.04	4.97	-0.07
17	Poland	2.81	4.85	+2.04
18	Cyprus		4.54	
19	Spain	5.44	4.49	-0.95
20	Italy	4.80	4.23	-0.57
21	Ireland	5.49	3.85	-1.63
22	Croatia		3.31	
23	Lithuania		3.26	
24	Hungary	4.00	3.02	-0.97
25	Greece	4.26	2.76	-1.49
26	Latvia		2.65	
27	Romania		1.08	
28	Bulgaria		1.00	

Source: Own calculations based on Eurostat Online Database (data refer to a: 2007; b: 2012, 2013). | BertelsmannStiftung

Figure 16: EU & EZ Access to Labor Market
Access to Labor Market

Rank	Country	Score SJI 2008[a]	Score SJI 2014[b]	Change 2008
1	Austria	7.24	7.33	+0.09
2	Denmark	7.89	7.28	-0.62
3	Germany	6.36	7.19	+0.84
4	Finland	7.34	7.10	-0.24
5	Sweden	7.42	7.02	-0.40
6	Netherlands	7.43	6.97	-0.46
7	Estonia		6.78	
8	United Kingdom	7.04	6.67	-0.37
9	Malta		6.29	
10	France	6.47	6.11	-0.36
	Luxembourg	6.33	6.11	-0.22
12	Czech Republic	6.48	6.02	-0.46
13	Belgium	5.98	5.93	-0.04
14	Slovenia		5.79	
	EU Average		5.70	
15	Ireland	7.29	5.65	-1.64
16	Latvia		5.62	
17	Lithuania		5.56	
18	Romania		5.31	
19	Poland	4.55	5.24	+0.69
20	Bulgaria		5.07	
21	Hungary	5.61	4.95	-0.67
22	Portugal	6.14	4.86	-1.28
23	Italy	5.71	4.79	-0.92
24	Cyprus		4.76	
25	Croatia		4.16	
26	Slovakia	4.55	3.98	-0.58
27	Spain	6.06	3.70	-2.37
28	Greece	5.22	3.23	-2.00

Source: Own calculations (Data used for constructing this composite indicator refer to the periods a: 2005-2008, b: 2011-2013). | BertelsmannStiftung

Figure 17: EU & EZ Access to Health
Health

Rank	Country	Score SJI 2008[a]	Score SJI 2014[b]	Change 2008
1	Sweden	7.75	8.15	+0.40
2	Luxembourg	8.24	8.12	-0.12
3	Netherlands	8.18	8.00	-0.18
4	Belgium	7.68	7.92	+0.24
5	Denmark	8.18	7.73	-0.45
6	Austria	7.78	7.48	-0.29
7	Czech Republic	7.01	7.40	+0.39
8	United Kingdom	6.77	7.26	+0.49
9	France	7.34	7.25	-0.09
10	Germany	6.74	7.20	+0.46
11	Malta		7.13	
12	Spain	7.04	7.00	-0.04
13	Ireland	6.74	6.75	+0.02
14	Finland	7.11	6.66	-0.46
15	Slovenia		6.28	
	EU Average		6.27	
16	Lithuania		6.25	
17	Cyprus		6.15	
18	Croatia		6.04	
19	Italy	6.41	5.90	-0.52
20	Portugal	4.23	5.87	+1.64
21	Slovakia	5.42	5.32	-0.10
22	Estonia		5.19	
23	Hungary	5.56	4.97	-0.59
24	Greece	5.68	4.68	-1.00
25	Bulgaria		4.31	
26	Poland	4.47	4.26	-0.21
27	Romania		3.19	
28	Latvia		3.14	

Source: Own calculations (Data used for constructing this composite indicator refer to the periods a: 2005-2008, b: 2011-2013). BertelsmannStiftung

Figure 18: EU & EZ Social Cohesion & Non-Discrimination
Social Cohesion and Non-discrimination

Rank	Country	Score SJI 2008a	SJI 2014b		Change 2008
1	Sweden	7.98	8.06		+0.08
2	Netherlands	8.04	7.96		-0.08
3	Finland	7.88	7.67		-0.21
4	Denmark	7.68	7.45		-0.23
5	Luxembourg	7.12	7.37		+0.25
6	Germany	6.60	7.33		+0.73
7	Belgium	7.16	6.59		-0.56
8	Austria	6.86	6.49		-0.38
9	Slovenia		6.43		
10	United Kingdom	6.29	6.10		-0.19
11	Ireland	6.09	6.07		-0.02
12	France	5.95	5.97		+0.02
	EU Average		5.89		
13	Lithuania		5.88		
	Poland	4.89	5.88		+0.99
15	Czech Republic	6.15	5.84		-0.32
16	Estonia		5.83		
17	Portugal	6.12	5.77		-0.35
18	Spain	6.30	5.45		-0.85
19	Malta		5.22		
20	Latvia		5.16		
21	Slovakia	5.73	5.15		-0.58
22	Cyprus		4.91		
23	Italy	5.13	4.80		-0.33
24	Hungary	5.21	4.61		-0.60
25	Romania		4.46		
26	Bulgaria		4.45		
27	Croatia		4.31		
28	Greece	4.55	3.74		-0.81

Source: Own calculations (Data used for constructing this composite indicator refer to the periods a: 2005-2007, b: 2011-2013). BertelsmannStiftung

In addition, the exacerbation of social imbalance during the economic crisis in the Eurozone is described by the levels of social injustice between generations (Figure 19–20). This is also reflected in the levels of youth unemployment in the age group 15–24 and the soaring numbers of young people who are not in education, employment or training. As a result social tensions and loss of confidence are observed (Unicef, 2014) (Figure 21).

Figure 19: Youth unemployment rate – (%) of active population in the same age group (15–24) in selected Eurozone countries

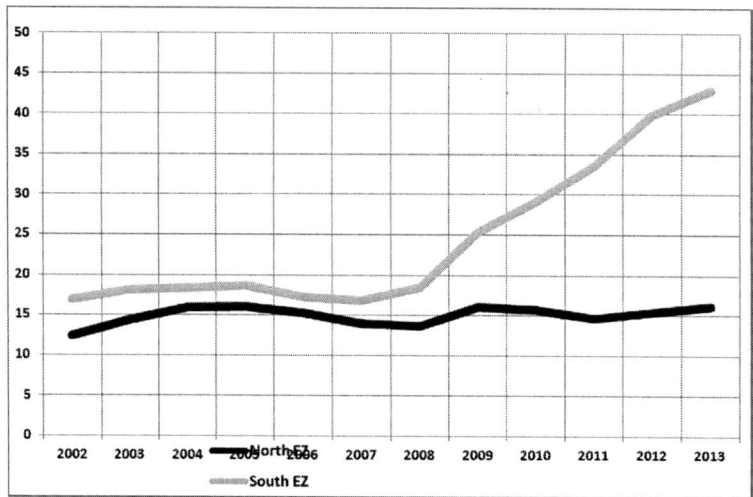

Source: Eurostat

Figure 20: Youth unemployment rate – (%) of active population in the same age group (15–24) in the Eurozone countries, 2008 & 2013

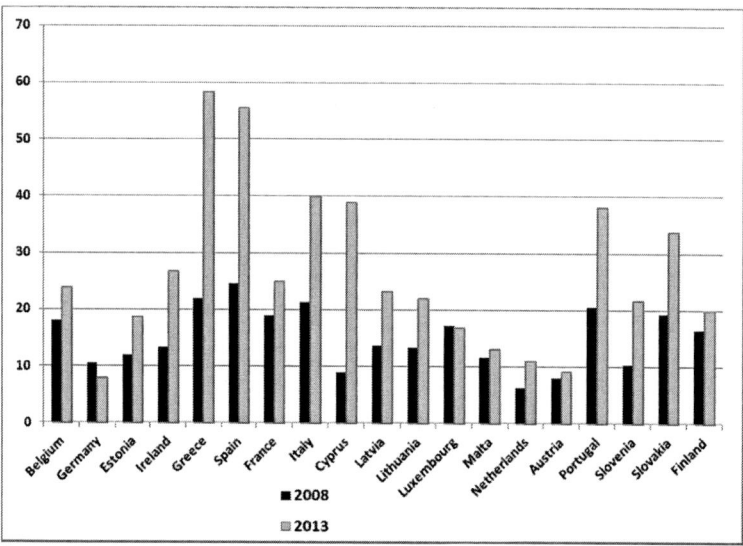

Source: Eurostat

Figure 21: Youth aged 15–24 not in education, employment, training (NEET) (%) 2008 & 2013 in EZ-19

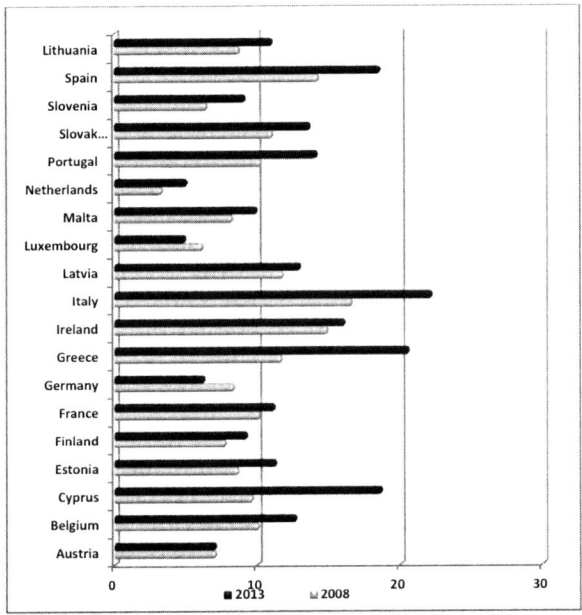

Figure 22

Average annual gain in the real GDP per capita as a result of the growing EU integration in the period from 1992 to 2012 (in euros, rounded).

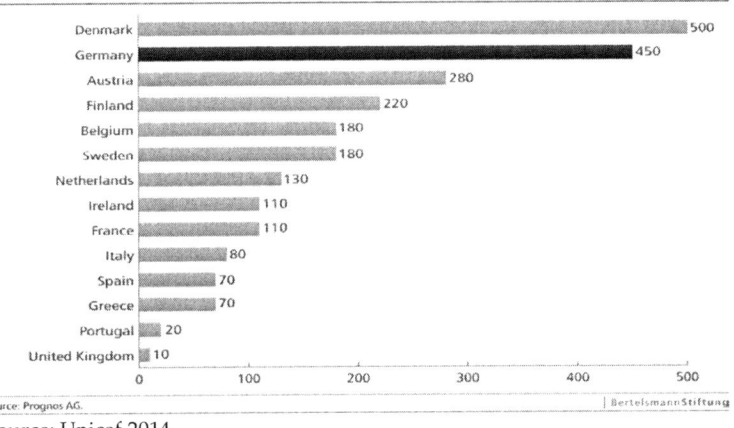

Source: Unicef 2014

Admittedly, social justice should play a key role in the establishment of the future European Social Policy. The development of a complete strategy is necessary, one that will include a coherent policy in order to tackle the social injustice through the promotion of development policies (Bertelsmann, 2014a). The current challenges do not solely concern the establishment of new welfare architecture. The economic and social policy should be reconfigured and regenerated in order to be adapted to the new environment of the post economic crisis Eurozone and tackle the occurring social challenges and economic limitations.

The different level of economic prosperity of Member States in the frame of the Single European Market causes political differences and social divisions between them and these issues need to be addressed. The level of political intervention that is required in order to resolve these differences and address the division between Member States causes political frictions (Nugent, 2010). These observations have been reflected in a recent study by Bertelsmann Foundation (2014b) according to which, the northern European Countries have received greater benefits from their integration to the Single European Market. This is also reflected in the rise of the real GDP per capita (Figure 22). The report notes that the degree of integration of a country to the European Single Market, determines the economic growth of this country. Moreover, the low rise in GDP per capita in southern European Countries (Figure 23–24) is not considered to be the primary result of the European crisis, but has aggravated an adverse situation that already existed. According to the same report the low rhythms of growth of GDP per capita are the result of the insufficient efforts on what concerns the integration of the southern European countries to the Single Europfīean Market since the beginning of the 1990s.

Figure 23: GDP per capita in the Eurozone, (constant prices 2008 & 2013)

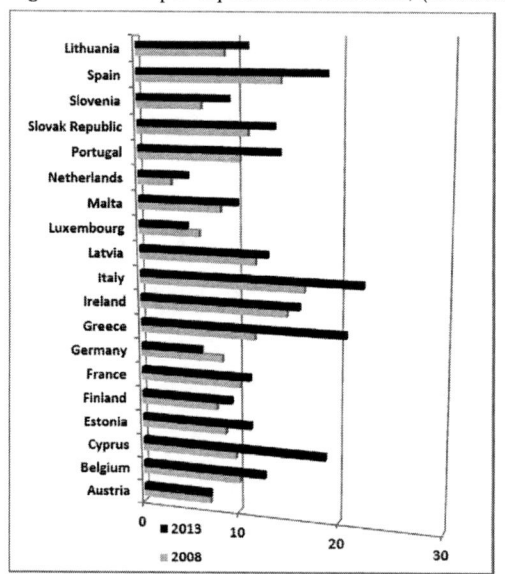

Source: IMF, World Economic Outlook Database, October 2014

Figure 24: GDP per capita in selected countries in the Eurozone, (constant prices 2008 & 2013)

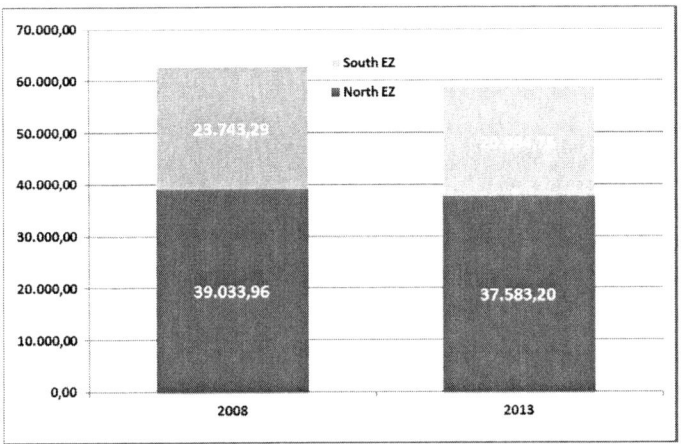

Source: IMF, World Economic Outlook Database, October 2014

These differences of GDP per capita between the Member-States of the Eurozone are determinant factors for the maintenance of social cohesion. According to the report of Bertelsmann Foundation (2014c), the index of social cohesion (Table 1) is a function of three primary social and economic factors. These are: the Gross Domestic Product (GDP), the income inequalities as they are described by Gini and S80 / S20 indices and the level of growth, according to the report, the greater the GDP of a Member-State the higher its social cohesion. The income inequalities are disproportionally related to the social cohesion and the resulting greater social inequality is responsible for the smaller cohesion. In addition, the knowledge index which is a measure of the level of growth of a Member-State correlates with the level of social cohesion. Table 1 depicts the comparison of social cohesion in the Eurozone and Europe-28 in the period 2009–2012. The social division between the north and south European countries is evident.

Table 1: Comparison of social cohesion (2009–2012) in selected countries (EZ, EU-28 & OECD)

Period 2009–2012	Overall index of social cohesion	1. Social relations			2. Connectedness			3. Focus on the common good		
		1.1 Social networks	1.2 Trust in people	1.3 Acceptance of diversity	2.1 Identification	2.2 Trust in institutions	2.3 Perception of fairness	3.1 Solidarity and helpfulness	3.2 Respect for social rules	3.3 Civic participation
Denmark	■	■	■	■	■	■	■	■	■	■
Norway	■	■	■	■	■	■	■	■	■	■
Finland	■	■	■	■	■	■	■	■	■	■
Sweden	■	■	■	■	■	■	■	■	■	■
New Zealand	■	■	□	■	■	■	■	■	■	■
Australia	■	■	□	■	■	■	■	■	■	■
Canada	■	■	■	■	■	■	■	■	■	■
United States	■	■	■	■	■	■	■	■	■	■
Switzerland	■	■	■	■	■	■	■	■	■	■
Luxembourg	■	■	■	■	■	■	■	■	■	■
Netherlands	■	■	■	■	■	■	■	■	■	■
Ireland	■	■	■	■	■	■	■	■	■	■
Austria	■	■	■	■	■	■	■	■	■	■
Germany	■	■	■	■	■	■	■	■	■	■
United Kingdom	■	■	■	■	■	■	■	■	■	■
France	■	■	■	■	■	■	■	■	■	■
Spain	■	■	■	■	■	■	■	■	■	■
Belgium	■	■	■	■	■	■	■	■	■	■
Estonia	■	■	■	■	■	■	■	■	■	■
Malta	■	■	■	■	■	■	■	■	■	■
Poland	■	■	■	■	■	■	■	■	■	■
Slovenia	■	■	■	■	■	■	■	■	■	■
Czech Republic	■	■	■	■	■	■	■	■	■	■
Italy	■	■	■	■	■	■	■	■	■	■
Hungary	■	■	■	■	■	■	■	■	■	■
Portugal	■	■	■	■	■	■	■	■	■	■
Slovakia	■	■	■	■	■	■	■	■	■	■
Israel	■	■	■	■	■	■	■	■	■	■
Cyprus	■	■	■	■	■	■	■	■	■	■
Lithuania	■	■	■	■	■	■	■	■	■	■
Latvia	■	■	■	■	■	■	■	■	■	■
Bulgaria	■	■	■	■	■	■	■	■	■	■
Greece	■	■	■	■	■	■	■	■	■	■
Romania	■	■	■	■	■	■	■	■	■	■

The figure shows mean values for the nine dimensions for the EU and Western OECD countries. The five colors designate the top tier (dark blue = ■), second tier (blue = ■), middle tier (light blue = ■), fourth tier (yellow = ■) and bottom tier (orange = ■). White dots (□) designate dimension values that were estimated based on other time periods.

| BertelsmannStiftung

Undoubtedly, the European Social Model creates interaction among competitiveness, economic effectiveness, innovation, knowledge economy, health, education and social justice. Hence it affects the targets of the economic policy, the social relations and the cultural institutions (Aiginger-Guger, 2007). As Table 2 and Figure 25 show, the rising economic imbalances of the Member States have increased the groups of people that face poverty and social exclusion in several countries and this has had severe consequences to social cohesion.

Table 2: People at risk of poverty or social exclusion by age group in the Eurozone (2012) (%) of total population

Country	Total	Children (0–17)	Adults (18–64)	Elderly (65 years & over)
Spain	28,2	33,8	29,7	16,6
Greece	34,6	35,4	37,7	23,5
Cyprus	27,1	27,5	25,8	33,4
Portugal	25,3	27,8	25,5	22,1
Ireland				
Italy	29,9	33,8	30,4	25,2
Slovenia	19,6	16,4	19,7	22,8
Slovak Republic	20,5	26,6	19,9	16,3
Estonia	23,4	22,4	24,2	21,8
Finland	17,2	14,9	17,3	19,5
France	19,1	23,2	19,8	11,1
Belgium	21,6	23,1	21,6	19,6
Lithuania	32,5	31,9	31,7	35,7
Latvia	36,2	40,0	35,9	33,7
Netherlands	15,0	16,9	16,5	6,2
Luxembourg	18,4	24,6	18,8	6,1
Malta	23,1	31,0	21,1	22,3
Germany	19,6	18,4	21,2	15,8
Austria	18,5	20,9	18,4	16,2

Source: Eurostat

Figure 25: People at risk of poverty or social exclusion in the EZ (2008 & 2013) (%) of total population

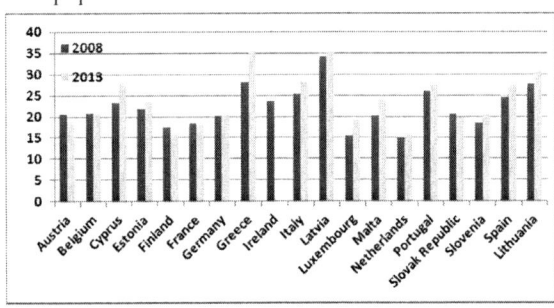

Source: Eurostat

A recent report by Unicef (2014) has drawn the same alarming conclusions about the social division in the Member States and depicts the soaring levels of child poverty

(Figure 26) in a lot of Member States of the Eurozone. This is also an index of the absence of a decisive strategy from the Member States and has adverse long term consequences for the societies.

Figure 26: Change in child poverty (anchored in 2008) (child poverty rate %) 2008 & 2013 in the EZ-19

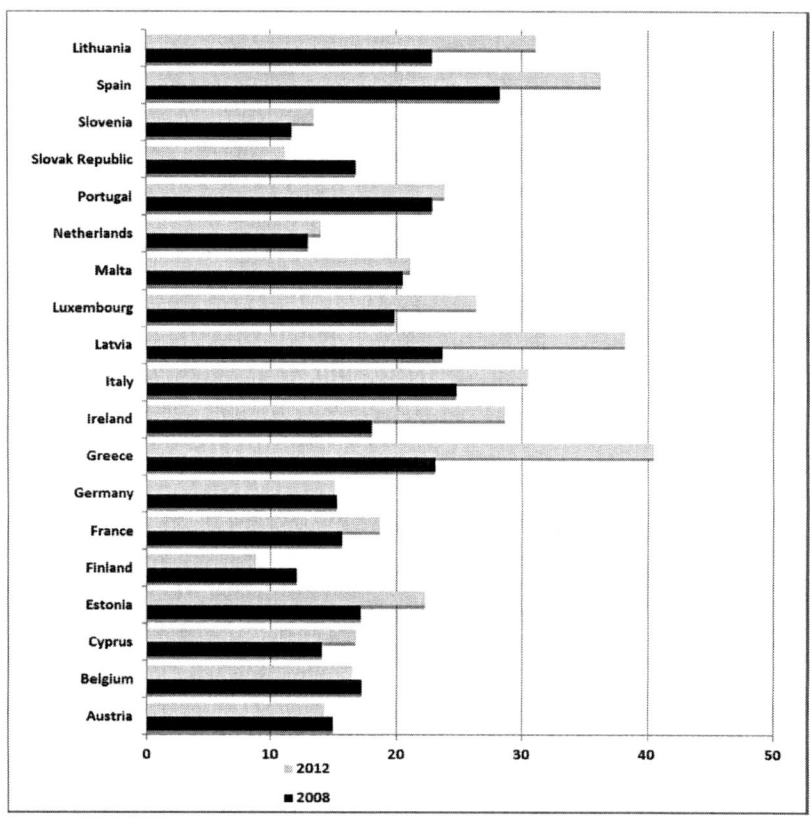

Source: UNICEF 2014

Meanwhile the economic and social imbalances among Member States of the European North-South reflect marked differences in the effectiveness of the Governing level[18] (Figure 27) (European Commission, 2014). It is evident that the assessment of the Governing quality is related directly to the economic and social growth thus, to social cohesion[19]. The above evidence appears in a new index (Map 2) which was created by

---

[18] The World Bank Governance Indicators which cover over 200 countries, consist of six measures: Political stability, Government effectiveness, Regulatory quality, Rule of law, Control of corruption and Voice and accountability.

[19] For relevant analysis see European Commission, (2014), 6th Report on Economic, Social & Territorial cohesion, Brussels, Publications Office of the European Union

the Quality of Government Institute (Gothenburg)[20] as well as in the report of OECD, 'Investing Together' (2013). According to the basic findings of the survey, it is concluded that the low Governing quality constitutes a suspending factor for economic growth. Consequently, it is imperative that this is improved so as to achieve a boost in the developing procedure contributing greatly to the reduction of imbalances.

A correct European Social Model should take into account international competitiveness, austerity, demographic ageing and change in employment life (Hemerijck, 2007). The European Social Model should expand its social dimensions, the social care and solidarity factors whilst also being compatible with the financial markets and competition (Ferrera, 2007). Demographic upheavals (e.g. population ageing (Map 3), the rise of life expectancy of the European peoples (Table 3, Figure 28) which affects pensions and social insurance and the rise of inequalities as a result of economic globalization are inherent weaknesses. These weaknesses dictate a policy planning that would promote social justice. It is true that the European Social Model represents one of the fundamental values of Europe. An equal distribution of social dangers at all social strata of the population, the limitation of inequalities which threaten social cohesion and the provision of a framework for economic and social rights should be provided (Giddens. 2007).

Figure 27: World Bank indicators, 1996 & 2012

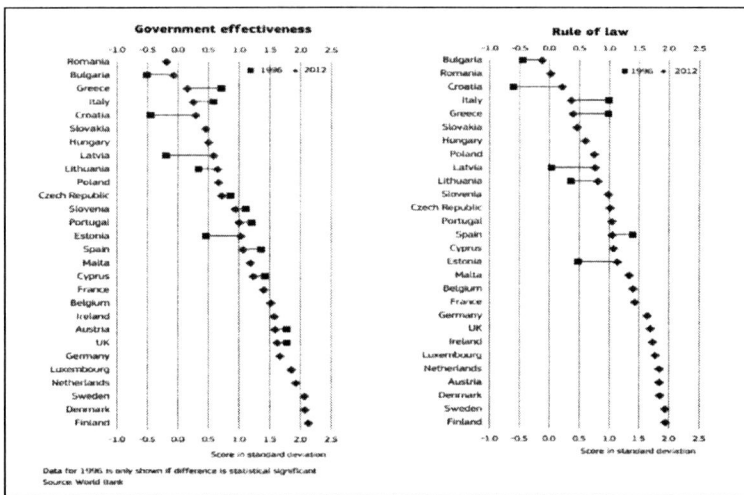

---

[20] This index, commissioned by DG Regional and Urban Policy and first published in 2010, combines World Bank Governance indicators at the national level with a survey that captures regional variations within each country. As a result, the national average of the regional indices equals the World Bank Governance score.

Map 3: World elderly population

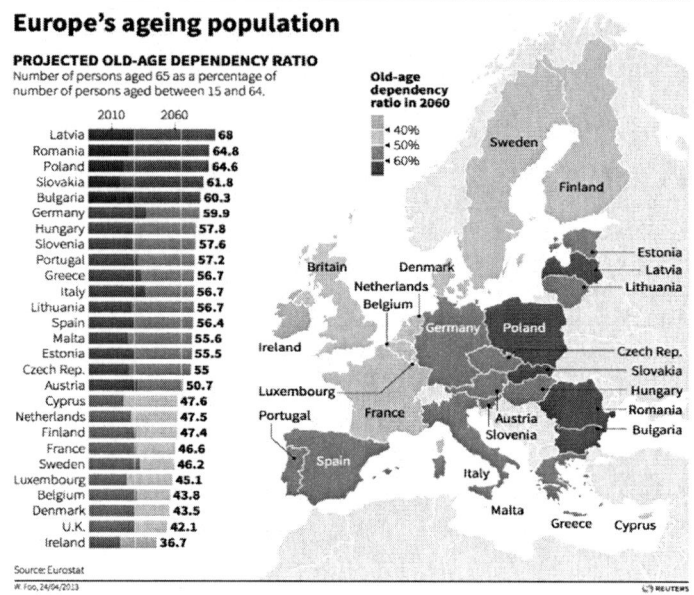

Source: Moody's, 2014

Table 3: Regional averages of life expectancy at birth, 1820s-2000s

	Western Europe (WE)	Eastern Europe (EE)	Western Offshoots (WO)	Latin America and Caribbean (LA)	East Asia (EA)	South and South-East Asia (SSEA)	Middle East and North Africa (MENA)	Sub-Saharan Africa (SSA)	World
1820s	..	..	..	..	..	..	..	..	..
1830s	33.4	..	..	..	..	..	..	..	..
1840s	34.7	..	..	..	..	..	..	..	..
1850s	35.5	..	..	..	..	..	..	..	..
1860s	36.9	..	..	..	..	..	..	..	..
1870s	38.3	..	..	..	..	..	..	..	..
1880s	40.4	..	40.3	..	..	24.6	..	..	27.0
1890s	42.9	34.9	45.6	..	..	24.2	..	..	26.7
1900s	46.3	35.8	50.6	29.4	..	24.5	..	..	30.8
1910s	46.7	..	53.6	31.8	..	25.1	..	..	32.8
1920s	54.7	40.9	56.3	34.7	..	27.8	..	..	36.4
1930s	58.7	44.6	61.3	37.8	35.6	31.9	34.5	..	40.0
1940s	60.1	50.1	65.6	42.8	40.5	34.1	37.0	..	43.5
1950s	68.2	62.5	69.2	53.5	47.4	41.0	43.5	37.9	50.6
1960s	70.7	68.4	70.4	58.5	54.1	48.1	50.3	42.2	56.0
1970s	72.6	68.7	72.4	62.5	66.3	53.6	55.9	46.2	61.6
1980s	75.1	69.2	74.8	66.6	69.2	58.9	61.2	49.4	64.6
1990s	77.2	68.2	76.3	69.9	71.3	62.4	67.4	49.8	66.6
2000s	79.7	69.1	78.1	72.6	74.7	65.9	70.1	52.1	69.1

Source: OECD, 2014

Figure 28: Life expectancy at birth, total (years) in the Eurozone (1960, 2000, 2012)

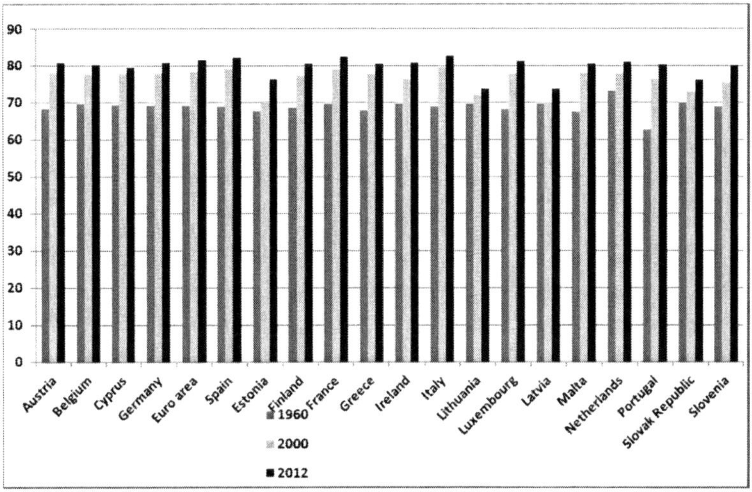

Source: World Bank

Concluding Remarks

According to Esping-Andersen (2002), the Eurozone faces an unfeasible three way issue. It is impossible to foster simultaneously a balanced budget, low level of income inequality and high levels of employment. In order to maintain a certain level of balance in the frame of the consensual new agreement, the supply-side economics (which target the Macroeconomic Consolidation) should be followed by demand stimulation measures (focusing on policies that support employment and economic growth). The sustainability of the single currency necessitates an effective implementation of economic and social policy with more powerful institutional bodies which will be under democratic control thus strengthening the European governance. A specific policy mix is crucial; one which will safeguard the balance between European institutions and all the restricting rules applied to national politics (Tsoukalis, 2014). This will in turn aim at achieving greater economic flexibility and better social security.

The European social model is part of the identity and the common cultural heritage of the European people. At the beginning of a new era, it is imperative that new relationships between the State, the Markets and Society are built. On the basis of a social and democratic approach and in order to achieve economic prosperity and social normality the intense challenges, emerging from the deepening of the economic crisis in the Eurozone, must be overcome. In order to move past the problems that threaten the European architecture it is vital to rely on intergovernmental and supranational cooperation, between the member states, that aims at the deepening of the Eurozone. Through this, the foundations of a new architecture will be laid for the strengthening of the Eurozone and the establishment of new long-term goals that will lead to change.

References

Aiginger, K. and Guger, A. (2007). Stylized facts on the interaction between income distribution and the great recession, Paper prepared for the NERO meeting of OECD in Paris on June 18th

Argeitis, G. (2012). *Greece: Caught fast in the Troika's Austerity trap*, Levy Institute Policy Note 12/2012

Begg, I. (2010). Economic & Social Governance in the Making: EU Governance in flux, *Journal of European Integration*, 32 (1), 1–16

Begg I., Draxler J., Mortensen J. (2008). *Is Social Europe Fit for Globalisation?* Brussels: Centre For European Policy Studies (CEPS),

Bertelsmann Stiftung Foundation, Schraad-Tischler, D. & Kroll, C. (2014a), *Social imbalance in Europe is increasing*, Brussels: Social Inclusion Monitor, Bertelsmann Stiftung

Bertelsmann Stiftung Foundation, Petersen T., Böhmer M & Weisser J. (2014b). *20 years of the European single market: growth effects of EU integration*, Brussels: Bertelsmann Stiftung Foundation, Policy Brief 2014/02

Bertelsmann Stiftung Foundation, Dragolov G., Ignácz Z., Lorenz J., Delhey J. & Boehnke K. (2014c). *Social Cohesion Radar: An International Comparison of Social Cohesion*, Brussels: Bertelsmann Stiftung Foundation

Blanchard, O. and Cottarelli, C. (2014). *Ten Commandments for Fiscal Adjustment in Advanced Economies*, International Monetary Fund's global economy forum

Blanchard O. and Summers, L. (1986). *Hysterersis in Unemployment*, NBER Working paper series No 2035, Cambridge: October

Cerny, G. P. (1997). International Finance & the erosion of Capitalism Diversity. In Crouch C. – Streek W. (eds), *Political Economy of Modern Capitalism: Mapping, Convergence & Diversity*, London: Sage

Chossudovsky, M. (1997). *The Globalization of Poverty*, London: Zed Books

De Grauwe, P. (2012). *The Economics of Monetary Union*, Oxford University Press, 7th ed.

De Grauwe, P. (2010), Crisis in the eurozone and how to deal with it, *Brussels: CEPS Policy Brief, No. 204*, Centre for European Policy Studies,

De Grauwe, P. (1996). *International Money*, Oxford University Press

De la Porte, C. and Pochet, Ph. (2004), The European Employment Strategy: existing research and remaining questions, *Journal of European Social Policy* 14/1, 71–78

Esping-Andersen G. (eds.), (2002). *Why we need a New Welfare State*, Oxford: Oxford University Press

European Commission, (2014). 6th Report on Economic, Social & Territorial cohesion, Brussels, Publications Office of the European Union

European Commission, (2010). *Europe 2020, a strategy for smart, sustainable and inclusive growth*, Brussels, Publications Office of the European Union

European Commission, (1994). *European social policy-a way forward for the Union, a white paper*, Brussels, Publications Office of the European Union

European Council, (2000). *Presidency conclusions*, Lisbon 23–24 March, Europa website

European Parliament, (2010). *The Lisbon Strategy 2000–2010. An analysis and evaluation of the methods used and results achieved*, Brussels: European Parliament's Committee on Employment and Social Affairs

Ferrera, M. (2006). Friends not Foes: European integration & National Welfare states. In Giddens A, Diamond P. & Liddle R., *Global Europe Social Europe*, Cambridge: Polity Press

Fisher, I. (1932), *Booms and Depressions: Some First Principles*, N.Y: Adelphi Company

Gilpin, R. (2002), *Global Political Economy*, Princeton: Princeton University Press

Giddens, A. (2006). A Social Model for Europe?. In Giddens A, Diamond P. & Liddle R., *Global Europe Social Europe*, Cambridge: Polity Press

Hemerijck A. (2006). Social change & Welfare reform. In Giddens A, Diamond P. & Liddle R., *Global Europe Social Europe*, Cambridge: Polity Press

I.L.O. (2014) *World Social Protection Report 2014/15, Building economic recovery, inclusive development and social justice*, Geneva: International Labour Office

Kaplanoglou G., Rapanos T. V. and Bardakas C. I. (2014). *Does fairness matter for the success of fiscal consolidation?*, University of Athens: Economics Discussion Reports

Kenen, P. (1969). The Theory of Optimum Currency Areas: An Eclectic view. In Mundell R.-Swoboda A. (Eds) *Monetary Problems of the International Economy*, Chicago: University of Chicago Press

Krougman P. (1991). *Geography & Trade*, Cambridge, Mass: The MIT Press

Matsaganis, M. (2015). Youth unemployment and the Great Recession in Greece. In Dolado J., (Eds), *No Country for young people, Youth Labour Market problems in Europe*, London: Centre for Economic Policy Research (CEPR)

Matsaganis M. (2013). *The Greek crisis: social impact and policy responses*, Berlin: Friedrich-Ebert-Stiftung.

Matsaganis, M. (2011). Prospects of Social Europe after the crisis, *Hellenic Political Science Review, Athens: Vol. 37*, June (in Greek)

McDonald, I. and Solow, R. (1981). Wage Bargaining & Employment, *American Economic Review 79*: 896–908

McKinnon, R. (1963). Optimum Currency Areas, *American Economic Review*, 53: 717–25

Melitz, J. (1996). The Theory of Optimum Currency Areas, Trade Adjustment & Trade, *Open Economies Review 7*.

Melitz, J. (1995). A Suggested Reformulation of the Theory of Optimal Currency Areas, *Open Economies Review 6*

Mundell, R., (1961). A Theory of Optimal Currency Areas, *American Economic Review*, 51

Nugent, N. (2010). *The Government and Politics of the European Union*, 7th Edition, Palgrave Macmillan

OECD, (2013). *Investing Together report*, OECD publishing

Ostry, J., Berg, A. & Tsangarides, Ch. (2014). *Redistribution, Inequality, and Growth*, International Monetary Fund, Stuff Discussion Note/14/02

Pagoulatos, G. (2014). The growth challenge for Europe and the EMU. In *CHALLENGE EUROPE*, Issue 22, *Challenges and new beginnings: Priorities for the EU's new leadership*, European Policy Centre, September

Pagoulatos, G. (1999). Ideas, Institutions & Interests in Public Policy: The Case of the European Economic Policy, *Greek Political Science Review*, No 13, Athens: Themelio (in Greek)

Parliament Budget Office (2014). *4th Quarter Report, 2013*, Athens Parliament of Greece (in Greek)

Pisany-Ferry, J., Sapir, A., Wolff, G. (Bruegel), (2013). *EU-IMF assistance to euro-area countries: an early assessment*, Brussels: Bruegel Blueprint Series, Volume XIX

Polanyi, K. (1944). *The Great Transformation*, N.Y: Farrar & Rinehart

Prats-Monne, X. (2009). In search of socio-economic reform and innovation: making "Social Europe" stronger. In Liddle, R., *After the Crisis: A New Socio-Economic settlement for the EU*, London: Policy Network

Rodriguez-Pose, A. and Garcilazo, E. (2013). Quality of Government and the Returns of Investment: Examining the Impact of Cohesion Expenditure in European Regions, *OECD Regional Development Working Papers, No. 2013/12*, OECD Publishing.

Sapir, A. (2006). Globalization and the Reform of European Social Models, *JCMS*, 44:2, Blackwell Publishing Ltd

Sutton, J. (2006). Globalization: A European perspective. In Giddens, A., Diamond P. and Liddle R. *Global Europe Social Europe*, Cambridge: Polity Press

Tsoukalis, L, (2014). *The Unhappy state of the Union*, London: Policy network

Tsoukalis, L. (2012). Europe in a dangerous crossroads, *The Athens Review of Books*, No 25, January (in Greek)

Tsoukalis, L. (2006). Economic reform, Further Integration & Enlargement: Can Europe Deliver?. In Giddens, A., Diamond P. and Liddle, R., *Global Europe Social Europe*, Cambridge: Polity Press

Unicef (2014), *Children of the Recession: The impact of the economic crisis on child well-being in rich countries*, UNICEF Office of Research – Innocenti, Innocenti Report Card 12

Vaughan-Whitehead, D. (2013). *Public sector shock: The impact of policy retrenchment in Europe,* Geneva and Cheltenham, ILO and Edward Elgar

Wyplosz, C. (2010). *Germany, current accounts and competitiveness.* In VoxEU, 31 March

(Dis)orienting the Greek Crisis

APOSTOLOS AGNANTOPOULOS

There is a common perception that the Greek sovereign debt crisis has been caused by intrinsic domestic structural weaknesses, which derive from an enduring failure to modernize and adapt to European standards. In this article I use Edward Said's notion of orientalism in order to challenge this perception. I posit that the 'elusive modernization' thesis is problematic, not only because it essentializes and buttresses an intrinsically unequal hierarchy of European nations but also because it paints a fundamentally distorted picture of the problems that Greece face and erroneously restricts the range of possible solutions. In addition to proposing a wider more inclusive discursive space for policy debate the paper addresses the broader issue of the recurrence of stereotypes and in-Europe otherness in the context of the economic crisis, by exposing the various differentiation mechanisms entailed in and reproduced by the dominant discourse.

Dr. Apostolos Agnantopoulos holds a PhD in International Studies from the University of Birmingham and is currently a research associate at the Dublin City University

Keywords: Greece; Debt crisis; Orientalism; Modernization; Metaphorical analysis

Editors' Note

The Greek crisis case, is the one among the so called P.I.G.S. that drew the attention the most and for the longest time on a global level. Decision-makers, academics and journalists spent a lot of written and spoken word in order to approach and explain the Greek crisis. In that procedure, the narrative that prevailed was the one that presents Greece as a non-European country inside the EU, with intrinsic structural problems. Likewise, the Greeks are seen as the typical example of laziness and corruption. This viewpoint bears serious repercussion both Greece and the EU; Greeks were somewhat convinced that there is an intrinsic deviation of their country from the rest of the EU countries, while their EU partners blamed the economic hardships of Greece to an inherent orientalism. As Apostolos Agnantopoulos argues, while Greek structural dysfunctionalities, corruption and tax evasion are part of the problem, the country does not significantly deviate from the EU average in sectors that it was harshly criticized for backwardness. The approach that leads to the conclusion of a primarily "Greek crisis" is reductionist and incomplete. As a result, it narrows the issue, reduces the discursive space for debate and creates a framework for separating the handling of the 'Greek problem' from the broader Euro-zone crisis.

Introduction

The economic malaise that has plagued the Eurozone since 2009 is considered to have exacerbated long-standing tensions and perceived divisions between Europe's north (commonly seen as 'hard-working', 'responsible', 'honest' and 'well-organized') and the south (commonly associated with 'laziness', 'profligacy', 'irresponsibility' and 'corruption' (Ntampoudi 2013). The pejorative acronym PIGS, which has been employed to denote the 'problematic' southern European economies (Portugal, Italy, Greece and Spain) and Ireland attests to this in no ambiguous terms.

In this paper I use the case of Greece—broadly seen as the 'worst performing' of the PIGS—in order to problematize this divide. In particular I take issue with the argument that the ongoing sovereign debt crisis has been caused primarily by intrinsic structural weaknesses, which reflect the country's irreconcilable political, economic, social and cultural misfit with the 'core' of Europe. I contend that the narratives and subject positions that underpin this perception are problematic, not only because they essentialize and buttress an intrinsically unequal hierarchy of European nations but also because they paint a distorted picture of the 'Greek crisis' and erroneously restrict the range of policy options to address it.

I argue that this particular construction of the Greek crisis represents a fragment of Orientalism: a style of thought and a corporate institution that enables Western dominance and authority over the Orient, effectively depriving the latter from its independent existence and recasting it in a simplified manner as the antithesis of the West (Said 1979: 2–3). The notion of Orientalism has been employed by social scientists to explore a variety of issues, including the entrenchment of a deeply discriminatory logic in the non-proliferation regime (Biswas 2001, Gusterson 1999), the securitization of Islamic terrorism (Pavan 2012, Mavelli 2012) and the role of discourses on development and neoliberal economic ideology in perpetuating imperial geographies and patterns of exploitation (Gupta 1998, Doty 1996). This study is embedded in this critical tradition but shifts the focalization from the 'Third World' to Europe's periphery. Although less prominent in the literature, so-called 'Euro-orientalism' (Murawska-Muthesius 2006) has provided a useful framework for analyzing the way in which various constructions of Eastern or Southern Europe have served as a constitutive other for Western or Northern Europe (Kuus 2007, Neumann 1999, Todorova 1997).

Methodologically the paper follows Milliken's (1999) three tier approach and attempts to capture discourse as a system of signification (i.e. the binary oppositions and associated relations of power entailed in the dominant discourse), discourse productivity (i.e. the delineation of authoritative subjects and practices) and the 'play of practices'(i.e. the interaction between the dominant discourse and alternative discourses). To do this, three methodological devices are employed: a juxtapositional analysis, which consists of 'juxtaposing the truth about a situation constructed in a particular discourse with events and issues that this truth fails to address' (Milliken 1999: 243); a metaphorical analysis, which 'focuses on metaphors (conventional ways of conceptualizing one domain in terms of another) as structuring possibilities for human reasoning and action' (Milliken 1999: 235); and a study of subjugated knowledge, which consists in pitting the 'cultural myths' and 'paradigmatic truths' upon which the dominant discourse is based against alternative accounts and marginalized discourses (Milliken 1999: 245). It is important to note that the objective of this discourse analytic approach is not to establish the 'real causes' of the Greek sovereign debt crisis or tell the 'right story'. The aim is to examine how a particular narrative about the crisis became the dominant frame of reference and to reveal its contingent nature, perceptive fallacies and explanatory limits.

The argument proceeds in three steps. In the first part I review five common claims about the Greek crisis and show that, although they all have elements of truth, they also embody several incorrect assumptions, flawed reasoning and significant omissions. The claims are: (1) that the bailout packages effectively reward Greek reckless borrowing and generate moral hazard; (2) that the Greek state is hypertrophic and must be aggressively cut down; (3) that the Greek people are particularly prone to tax avoidance and tax evasion; (4) that extensive structural reform is the key for escaping the current predicament; (5) that the Greek political leadership has been unable to stand up to this task.

In the second part I present three recurrent images that underpin the relationship between Greece and its lenders and show how these legitimize the various disciplinary and control mechanisms imposed. The first image is that of a criminal, who needs to be policed and punished. The second is that of a child, who needs guidance and schooling to make it into adulthood. The third is that of a patient receiving an unpleasant but necessary treatment. Whereas the first establishes Greece as inherently un-European the other two involve less radical differentiation mechanisms and leave open the possibility of redemption. In the third part I critique the discourse on modernization, which has been employed in order to give credence to these binary oppositions. I expose its orientalist underpinnings and explore two alternative readings of the crisis that rely on radically different discursive positions. The concluding section summarizes the argument and raises broader issues that emerge from this study.

The Greek Crisis: Common Arguments and their Discontents.

Reckless Borrowing?

The first common argument about the Greek sovereign debt crisis is that it has been the direct consequence of reckless borrowing by successive Greek governments and therefore any economic assistance would effectively reward the irresponsible behaviour of a nation accustomed to live beyond its means. The fear of moral hazard has been evident in the initial hesitancy to bailout Greece, the punitive interest rates of the first bailout loans and the continuing aversion towards debt relief, despite the fact that most economists agree that it is both inevitable and desirable.

Figure 1: Greece – General government consolidated gross debt (% of GDP)

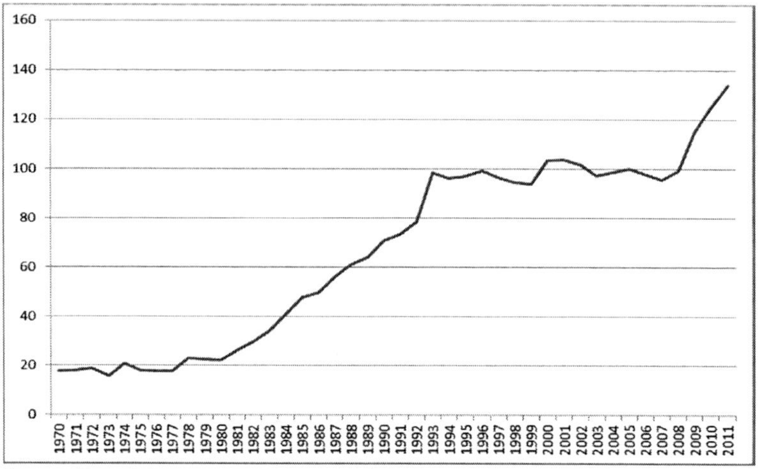

Source: Eurostat

A glance at the evolution of Greek public accounts seems to vindicate these concerns. As can be seen in figure 1, government debt increased exponentially during the 1980s and early 1990s, from just above 20 percent of GDP to around 100 percent and, despite the fiscal consolidation efforts undertaken as part of meeting the Maastricht convergence criteria, it has remained very high ever since. In addition, since entering in the Eurozone, Greece consistently exceeded the 3 percent budget deficit threshold established by the Stability and Growth Pact (SGP) and also ran large primary deficits (i.e. before interest payments), which in 2009 reached an astonishing €24 billion or 10 percent of GDP (ELSTAT 2014: 18). Unsurprisingly, when the crisis broke out Greece was considered to have the worst fiscal position in the Eurozone, recording both the highest public debt / GDP and public deficit / GDP ratios (Oxford Economics 2010: 3).

Figure 2: Total indebtedness (public & private) in selected Eurozone states, 2009 (% GDP)

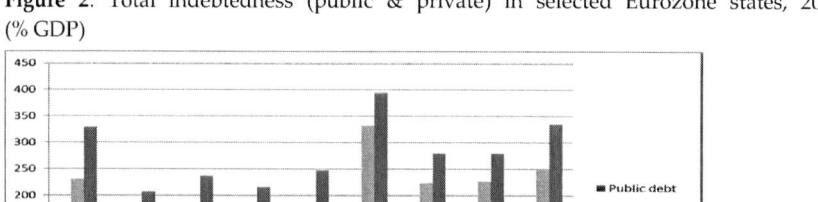

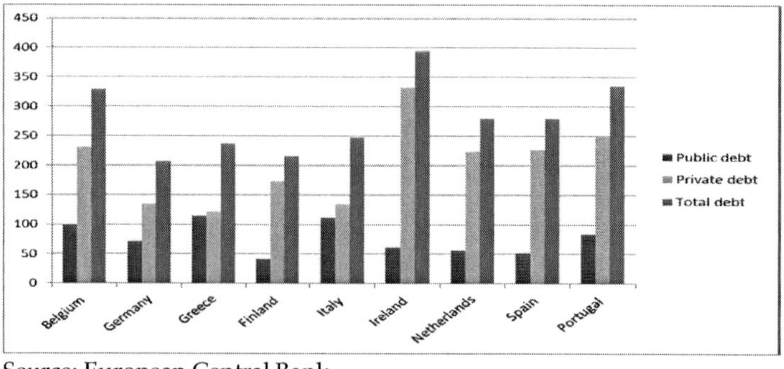

Source: European Central Bank

However, on closer inspection it becomes apparent that 'reckless borrowing' and 'profligacy' were not Greek prerogatives. More precisely, since 1999 there has been a tremendous increase in private indebtedness throughout the Eurozone, with household debt rising from 52 percent to 70 percent of GDP and the debt of non-financial corporations rising from 60 percent to 80 percent of GDP (ECB 2012: 88). Although Greek households and business also increased their indebtedness, they did so at a lesser extent than their counterparts in other Eurozone countries. Consequently, despite having a relatively high public debt, Greece's overall indebtedness level, when the crisis broke out, was lower than many Eurozone countries, including presumably thrifty Netherlands (see figure 2). This suggests that the distinction between 'profligate crickets' and 'prudent ants' is in many respects artificial. No country was immune from the lending frenzy unleashed by the spread of financialization. The peculiarity of the Greek case was that over-borrowing was mainly assumed by the government and subsequently trickled down to the economy.

A "Hypertrophic State"?

Related to the above discussion is the castigation of Greece's hypertrophic state, together with proposals about the need to drastically reduce the number of public employees and curtail overgenerous state benefits.

Figure 3: General government expenditure (% of GDP)

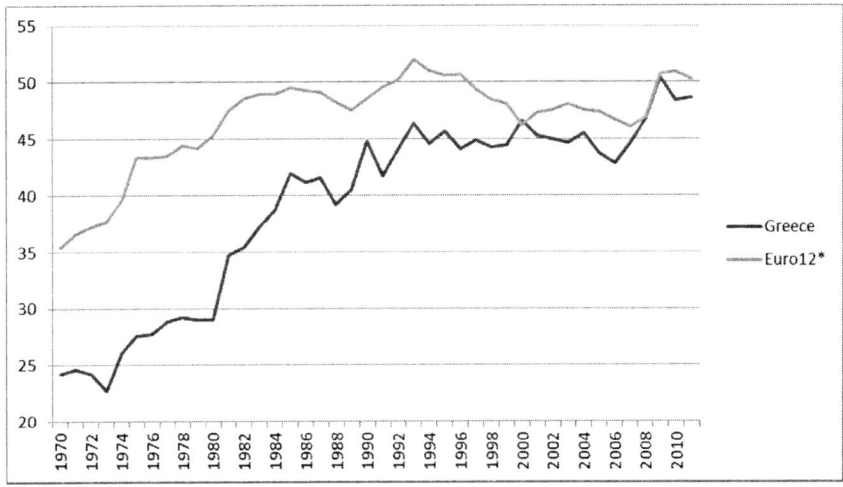

Source: Eurostat
* Until 1994 it excludes Luxemburg

Such arguments, which are often backed by striking statistical data and anecdotal evidence suggesting unspeakable waste, overstress the size of Greek public sector. For instance the frequently mentioned fact that 'Greek public expenditure surpassed 50 percent of GDP in 2009' ignores that the said year was in many respects atypical due to the repercussions of the sub-prime mortgage financial crisis and that the mean general government expenditure as a percentage of GDP between 2000 and 2009 stood at 45.57 percent, slightly below the Eurozone average (see figure 3). More generally, whereas public expenditure to GDP ratio has almost doubled since the 1970s, it is important to note that this was not a 'Greek phenomenon'. The average government expenditure within the Eurozone, for instance, rose from 35 percent of GDP in 1970 to 51 percent in 1994 and remained close to the 50 percent threshold thereafter. Moreover, between 2000 and 2009 Greek government expenditure per capita stood at around $12000, roughly comparable to OECD averages (OECD 2011a: 65). If anything therefore, the trajectory of Greek public spending reveals a gradual convergence to Eurozone and global standards rather than an idiosyncratic path to profligacy.

Figure 4: Public sector employment in selected EU countries in 2008 (% of labor force)*

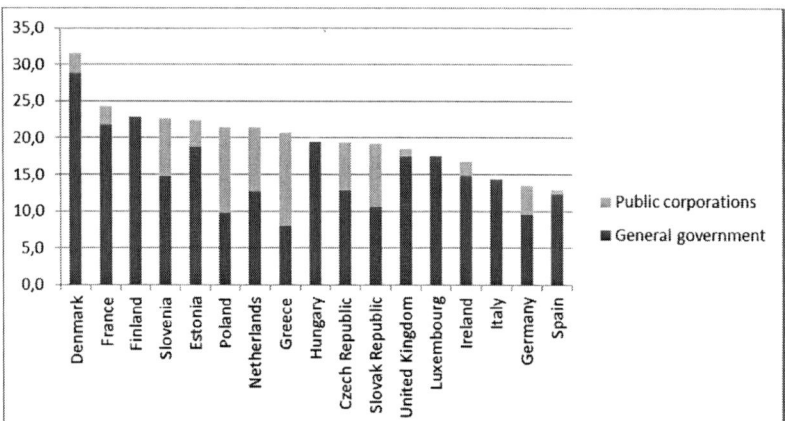

Source: OECD

A similar conclusion can be reached if one examines the available data on public employment. Whereas the number of public employees almost doubled over 30 years, one has to take into account that this increase has taken place from a relatively low base point (510,000 in 1980) (Iordanoglou 2013: 33). It is characteristic in that respect, that the total public employment to labor force ratio in 2008 stood at just above 20 percent— hardly an excessive weight when set against other EU countries (see figure 4).

Figure 5: Public social expenditure (% of GDP)

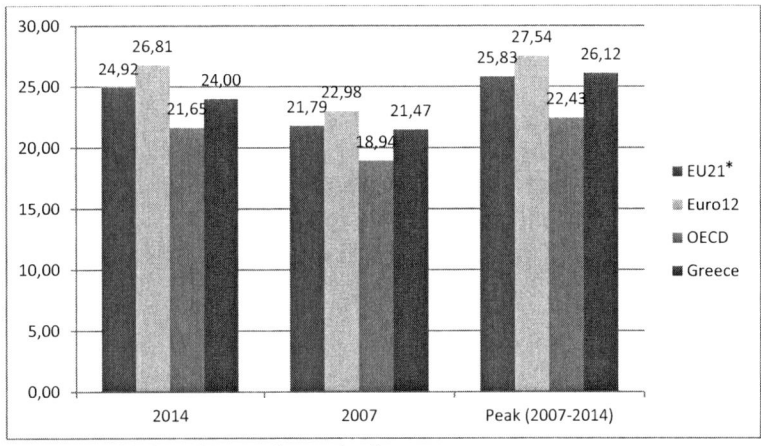

Source: OECD Social Expenditure database.
* EU21 (excludes Bulgaria, Croatia, Cyprus, Latvia, Lithuania, Malta, Romania).
** "Peak level after 2007" refers to the highest level over the period 2007–2014, ie. to 2009 except for Slovenia (2011), Greece (2012), France, Belgium, Denmark, Italy, Spain, Portugal, Poland, Slovak Republic (2013), Finland, Netherlands, Czech Republic (2014).

The view of the Greek state as a distributor of generous benefits also stands on shaky grounds. According to OECD data, social public expenditure in Greece stood at 21.47 percent of GDP, higher than the OECD average of 18.94 percent but lower than average public social spending in the Eurozone and the EU (22.98 and 21.79 respectively). What is more, if one excludes pensions and health, social welfare benefits amounted to merely 4.25 percent of GDP in 2009, which is the lowest in the EU and below the OECD average (OECD 2013: 28). This suggests that part of the (allegedly) generous pensions effectively substitutes for the lack of social assistance (ibid.).

To sum up the size of the Greek state has increased over the last 40 years but is broadly in line with other EU and OECD countries. This is not to say that public sector reform is not required. However, the assertion that Greece's troubles are due to the existence of an over-bloated public sector that has to be ruthlessly cut down is erroneous. The real question is whether Greece had adequate resources to sustain it.

A Culture of Tax Evasion / Avoidance?

Another common feature of the dominant narrative is the portrayal of the Greek people as rampant tax evaders who have starved the government coffers by concealing their real revenues and refusing to pay their dues.

Figure 6: General government revenue (% of GDP)

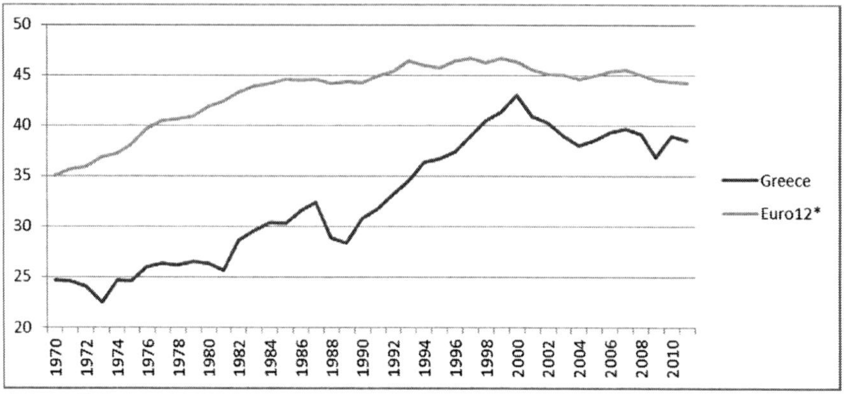

Source: Eurostat
*Until 1995 it excludes Luxemburg.

The argument that Greece faces an enduring tax collection problem is based on solid grounds. As can be seen in figure 6, general government revenue to GDP ratio increased gradually for most of the 1980s and 1990s, peaked at 43 percent in 2000 and followed a downward path thereafter, remaining constantly below 40 percent and falling to 36.9 percent in 2009. When set against the evolution of public expenditure in figure 2 it is obvious that public revenues failed to keep up, trailing by around 6 percentage points. What is more they have remained constantly well below the Eurozone average for most of that period. In addition, despite the fact that statutory tax rates have fluctuated around EU averages, the ratio of direct taxes to GDP has been relatively low (8 percent as opposed to 12.2 percent for the EU-27) while the proceeds from personal income tax have been almost half of the EU average (4.7 percent as opposed to 8.1 percent) (Eurostat 2010: 201). Indirect taxation has not fared better partly due to the widespread application of reduced VAT rates (Eurostat 2010: 99) and partly due to non-compliance and non-collection, which has resulted in significant VAT gap—more than double the EU average (Matsaganis et al. 2012: 26).

Arguably this shortage in government revenues is linked to the enormous size of the 'informal' sector in Greek economy which is estimated to stand at between 25 and 30 percent of GDP—double the OECD average (Schneider 2007). A much quoted recent study by Artavanis et al. (2012), for instance, estimated that total tax evasion from self-employed stood at €28 billion in 2009, close to 30 percent of the total tax base, with the lost revenues representing 31 percent of the budget deficit shortfall for that year. In a similar vein an OECD report reckoned that 'if Greece collected its VAT, social security contributions and corporate income tax with the average efficiency of OECD countries, tax revenues could rise by nearly 5 percent of GDP' (OECD 2011b: 35).

This suggests that there is indeed a strong case for reforming the tax collection system. However, the often heard corollary claim that Greeks display a culturally nurtured, inherent propensity to 'dodge the taxman' needs certain qualifiers.

To start with, tax avoidance and tax evasion are global problems. Multinational companies have for a long time tried to play the system by shifting profits to affiliates based on low-tax countries. According to some estimates, more than half of world trade, a third of foreign direct investment and the majority of international financial transactions is channelled, in one way or another, through offshore centres (Shaxson 2011: 1–2). Thus, there is nothing intrinsically Greek in the desire to reduce the tax bill. What seems unique in the Greek case is the fact that the option of doing so has been widely available, not only to big companies, with access to offshore financial centres and sophisticated accounting, but to myriad of self-employed and owners of small business.

This leads to a second qualifier. As pointed out by Aristos Doxiadis, although the average hidden income by self-employed in Greece does not deviate from international standards, the fact that their weight in the workforce is more than double the OECD average (35 percent as opposed to 15.8 percent) would by itself suffice to explain up to a 3 percent shortage in direct tax revenues (Doxiadis 2013: 162). If one also takes into account that the shipping sector, which represents 3–6 percent of GDP or 1–2 percent of tax revenues, is legally exempted from paying taxes, for reasons that go beyond the immediate control of the Greek government,[1] then a persuasive argument can be made that the observed shortage in government revenues relative to EU averages does not emerge from cultural flaws but is in fact the result of the structure of the Greek economy (ibid.).

A Rigid, Closed and Unproductive Economy?

A fourth recurrent argument about the Greek crisis focuses on the long-standing 'structural weaknesses' of the Greek economy and the need to undertake overarching reforms in order to improve its international competitiveness. Consistent with this representation, the bailout packages were accompanied by ambitious structural adjustment programmes based on the trinity of market liberalization, deregulation and privatization.

On the face of it, the case for 'structural reform' seems irrefutable. To start with, Greece has had a relatively large non-tradable sector, representing 65 percent of Gross Added Value in 2008, which is 3–4 points higher than European averages (McKinsey & Company 2011: 12–13). The combination of high wages and low productivity in this sector is considered to have generated a crowding out effect for the tradable sector and to have decreased its international competitiveness, thus making the existence of current account imbalances inevitable (Kyrkilis and Hazakis 2014, Malliaropoulos and Anastasatos 2011).

The Greek product and labor markets have also been characterized as excessively rigid and protectionist. It is characteristic in this respect that in 2008 Greece occupied the

---

[1] As in the rest of the world, shipping is subject to a modest tonnage tax but individual and corporate ship owners are exempted from income tax liabilities on the profits derived from operating Greek and foreign flagged registered vessels. Although this special regime has often been criticized as being unfair, the fear that its reversal could lead to the depletion of the industry (through reflagging and relocation to other shipping centers) has deterred successive governments from adopting a heavy handed approach.

second highest place in OECD's Product Market Regulation Index with a score of 2.21 as opposed to 1.6 OECD average (OECD 2011b: 39). Moreover, the existence of more than 150 'closed professions' has constituted a major source of large rents and inefficiencies with negative spill-over effects (in the form of rising input costs) for the entire economy (OECD 2011b: 140). In a similar vein a recent OECD study on food processing, retail trade, building materials and tourism has identified 555 regulatory restrictions that were assessed as being 'potentially harmful to competition' and 40 provisions that constitute administrative burden on businesses, with a total estimated cost of more than €5 billion (OECD 2014).

More generally, Greece is widely perceived as not conferring a business-friendly environment. It consistently performed poorly in the World Bank's Ease of Doing Business Index, occupying places close or above the top 100 and, although its ranking has improved significantly over the last four year (65th in 2014, 61st in 2015) (see World Bank 2015), it continues to have third lowest place in the EU, just above Cyprus (64th) and Croatia (65th).[2] In a similar vein the 2010 Transparency International's Corruption Perceptions Index put Greece in 78th place—the most corrupt EU country (Transparency International 2012: 25), with only slight improvement recorded over the next three years.[3]

---

[2] See http://www.doingbusiness.org/rankings. I thank one anonymous reviewer for highlighting this.
[3] In 2013 and 2014 Greece was marked equally with Bulgaria, Romania and Italy. I thank one anonymous reviewer for highlighting this.

Figure 7: Competitiveness gap in the Eurozone

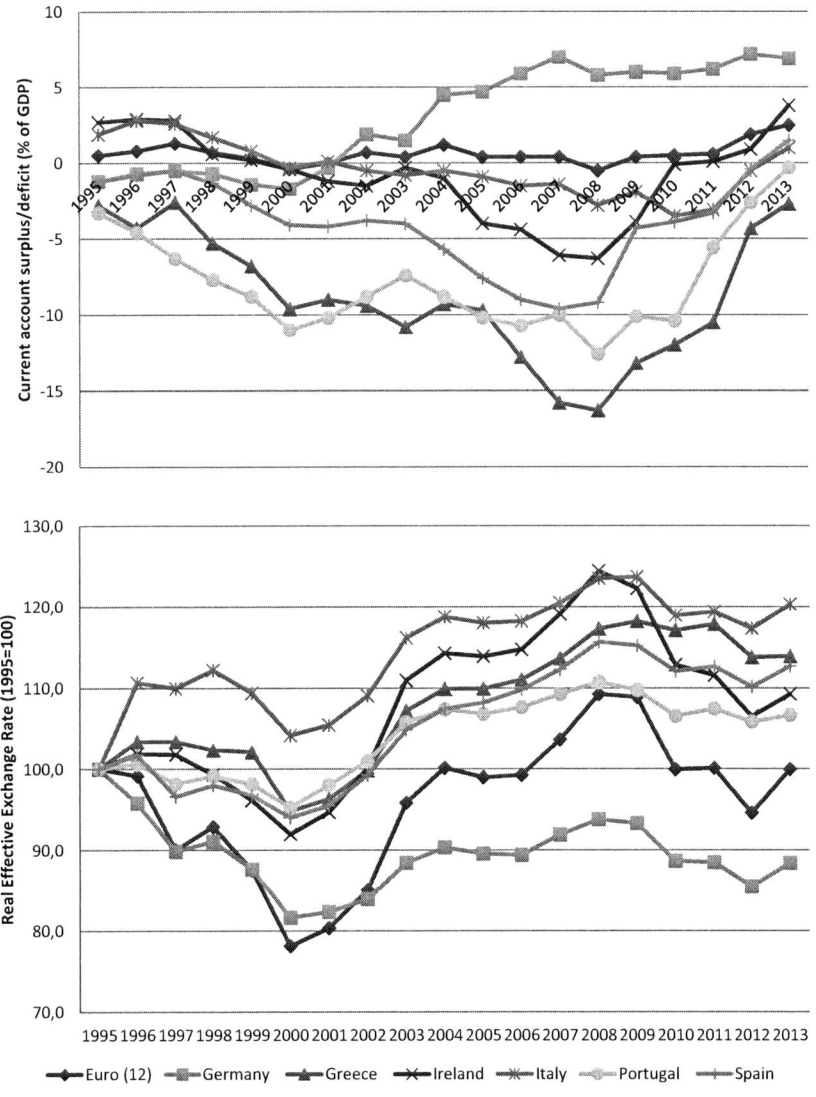

Source: Eurostat, Bruegel

Impressive as these figures may be, they only tell half of the story. Whereas Greece has had a long history of 'low competitiveness' and trade deficits, EMU membership unleashed a sharp deterioration in all relevant indicators. As can be seen in figure 7, between 1995 and 2008 Greece's current account deficit as a percentage of GDP increased from 2.8 to 16.3, with the bulk of the increase emerging after the finalization of EMU accession. During that time its Real Effective Exchange Rate was also appreciated by about 18 percent. What is more, a similar decline in international competitiveness occurred in other periphery countries, while Germany, recorded hefty current account surpluses (close to 4 percent of GDP on average) and a decrease in its real exchange rate of more than 10 percent.

The widening trade imbalances within the Eurozone have led some analysts to turn the competitiveness debate on its head by pointing to Germany as the main beneficiary of the EMU and culprit for the crisis (Wolf 2010a). Their main argument is that Germany's export–led strategy based on wage moderation and labor market reforms effectively turned into a 'beggar-thy-neighbor policy' that eroded the competitive advantage of peripheral countries and established a two speed Europe (see De Grawe 2009, Lapavitsas et al. 2010 and for a critical review see Young and Semmler 2011). From this perspective, the attempt to transpose the German economic growth model in Greece is futile, because within a monetary union surpluses in some countries are conditioned upon the existence of deficits in others and vice-versa. Thus, instead of insisting on austerity and internal devaluation, Germany, together with other net exporters, should take measures to foster domestic demand and reduce their enormous trade surpluses (Stockhammer2011, Wolf 2010b).

Lack of Political Will?

The last common argument about the Greek crisis concerns the perceived failure of domestic political elites to take 'ownership' of the adjustment programmes and the inability of the Greek dysfunctional political system to enact and implement reforms.

An examination of Greece's reform record shows that this perception is misleading. It is widely recognized, for instance, that Greece broadly succeeded to meet the (admittedly ambitious) deficit reduction targets, thus achieving the biggest and fastest fiscal consolidation in the OECD over the last thirty years (OECD 2011: 12) and the strongest cyclically-adjusted fiscal position within the euro area (IMF 2014: 22).[4] Moreover, Greece has achieved the highest responsiveness to OECD Going for Growth recommendations (OECD 2013: 19) and, since 2012, has ranked first in the Adjustment Progress Indicator calculated by the Lisbon Council for the 17 Euro area countries (IMF 2014: 2).

To be sure, such assessments usually measure the formal adoption of reforms and therefore tend to underestimate the severe problems underpinning their implementation. It is also true that the reform process has been fragmented, with some sectors being able to maintain their privileges more than others. Nevertheless, the representation of Greece as being impenetrable to reform is erroneous. If anything, it helps obscuring the severe drawbacks in the design of the adjustment programmes. It has been argued, for instance, that the delays in establishing a rescue package and undertaking a private debt restructuring—despite IMF's recommendations—worsened

---

[4] The cyclically adjusted budget balance takes into account cyclical effects and temporary measures. It corresponds to the budget balance prevailing if the economy was running at potential.

the debt problem and increased the costs for both Greece and its lenders (Jones 2010: 22; Xafa 2014). In a similar vein, it has been widely recognized that the initial bailout programme put excessive emphasis on austerity without taking into account the negative repercussions that this would have on economic output and, by corollary, debt sustainability. Crucially, an examination of decision-making in other Eurozone countries reveals that their governments were not immune to domestic political pressures and short term electoral considerations.[5]

In short, there may indeed have been a lack of political will, but this characterized all Eurozone governments, not merely Greek ones.

Elucidating the Greek 'Other'

The common denominator in the above arguments is a construction of Greece as being an exceptional case; an allusion to deviation from European normalcy; localization of Greece as being *in* but not *of* Europe. This process of othering was activated through the mobilization of images and metaphors depicting Greece as criminal, child and patient. These metaphorical representations are particularly powerful because, as Gusterson (1999: 131) notes, in his insightful analysis of nuclear orientalism, they have the ability to 'assimilate domestic hierarchies [and] use their symbolic force to buttress and construct the global hierarchy of nations'.

Greece as a Criminal

The construction of Greece as a criminal was very prominent during the early phase of the crisis. Greece stood accused not only of violating the Maastricht deficit rules but also of attempting to conceal its fiscal delinquency through misreporting and creative statistics. The fact that this fraud could not have occurred without the complicity of private investors, rating agencies and EU institutions who had turned a blind eye to obvious signals not hidden by Greek statistics (such as the enormous current account deficit) and had silently endorsed, if not assisted, Greece's fiscal engineering was omitted from this image.

Arguably the most prominent portrayal of Greeks as criminals was a notorious cover by the German magazine Focus in February 2010, which displayed an image of the Aphrodite of Milo armless statue, showing her middle finger next to the heading 'Swindlers in the European family'.[6] There are two noteworthy representational practices in this cover: Firstly, the 'fact' of having being caught to lie and cheat is constituted as rendering modern Greeks unworthy of the Ancient Greek heritage, which comes back, in the form of a famous statue, to haunt them. The second is the depiction of the EU / Eurozone as a family, making claim to common values and a common ancestry of which Ancient Greece is presumed to be part. The subtext is that, just like Greece's

---

[5] It has been pointed out for instance that beyond genuine fear about the economic implications of bailing-out Greece, Angela Merkel's procrastination in approving the first bailout programme was motivated by the desire not to irritate the skeptical German public ahead of a crucial election in North-Rhine Westphalia, which was due to take place on 9 May (Featherstone 2011: 201, Schmidt 2014: 199).

[6] The cover can be found in http://www.spiegel.de/international/europe/bird-trouble-angry-greeks-to-sue-german-magazine-for-defamation-a-758326.html

membership in the Eurozone was fabricated on a false claim of having sound public finances, so its 'Europeaness', has been predicated on a false claim to a glorious past. In this way the cover casts doubt not only on Greek membership in the Eurozone but also on the foundational myth upon which Modern Greek identity has been built.

The representation of Greece as a fraudster that deserves to be penalized also featured in the official discourse. In his highly acclaimed book *Stress Test: Reflections on Financial Crises* for instance, former US Treasury Secretary Timothy Geithner recalls that during a G7 meeting, shortly after the revelation that Greek public accounts were flawed, the Europeans were calling for 'Old Testament justice' against Greece. An interview transcript, leaked to the Financial Times, left no doubt as to what this entailed:

> "We're going to teach the Greeks a lesson. They are really terrible. They lied to us. They suck and they were profligate and took advantage of the whole basic thing and we're going to crush them," was their basic attitude, all of them […] They just wanted to take a bat to them.
>
> (Spiegel 2011)

The language of criminality was also employed in calls for tighter oversight on national budgets and penalties for those who violated the EU budgetary rules. In the wake of the crisis for instance, the Commission, announced that it would begin *legal proceedings* against Greece for *breaching* EU Treaty rules (quoted in Papadimitriou and Zartaloudis 2014) and the EU Economy Commissioner Olli Rehn proposed the withholding of cohesion funds aid for repeated budget *offenders* (Euractiv 2010). Along similar lines, the German Chancellor Angela Merkel said that countries 'that repeatedly *flout* euro-zone stability rules need to live with the possibility of *interventions* in their national budget authority' (Radowitz2011), while the Dutch government proposed to set up a Commissioner for budgetary discipline with the authority to veto national budgets that violate the EU rules and impose *sanctions* including the withholding of voting rights and forcing countries to leave the Euro (Euractiv 2011).

It is easy to spot the hierarchical subject positioning entailed in these statements: the criminal (Greece) is set apart from other law-abiding countries, while EU institutions are assigned the role of law-enforcer charged with preserving fiscal order through preventive and punitive measures. The threat of exclusion from the Eurozone is particularly significant in that respect because it is predicated on the presumption that a 'serial', 'unrepentant' violator of budgetary rules ceases to be a worthy member of the Euro-in group and must be isolated, in the same way that a prisoner is 'kept away' from society as a measure of discipline and prevention.

Greeks as (Spoilt) Children

The depiction of Third World states as children has been a common orientalist trope, particularly in discourses on development that portray Western capitalist economies as a more advanced model to emulate (Gupta 1998). In the context of the Greek sovereign debt crisis, the child metaphor was often combined with the unflattering epithet 'spoilt' in order to chastise those who opposed the austerity programmes. In a highly critical piece in the UK daily *Independent*, O'Grady compared the rioting which took place throughout 2011 in Athens to 'a tantrum by a spoilt child' (O'Grady 2011). In a similar vein, Daniel Howden (2012) asserted that the skyrocketing of anti-bailout vote at the May 2012 elections was 'the last tantrum of a spoilt child [who] punished moderates who refused to lie to the people about the dilemma they faced and rewarded extremists on the right and left who wilfully ignored reality and responsibility'(Howden 2012)—an unwarranted conclusion given that the elections were also marked by impressive performance from openly pro-reform political parties (e.g. *Dimiourgia Ksana, Drasi*) and that the vote was almost evenly split between parties that accepted, one way or another, the necessity of conditional bailout, and those who clearly advocated a break up with the 'troika'.

Casting those who oppose the bailout programme as 'children' is a very significant discursive strategy because a childish behaviour denotes 'immaturity', 'irrationality', 'irresponsibility', 'lack of discipline' and 'impulsiveness'. Therefore this representation writes off the possibility that their objections may emerge from logical and sound reasoning. By contrast the parent / adult is presumed to be 'mature', 'rational', 'responsible' and, when necessary, oblivious to childish 'capricious' demands.

The child / adult binary also featured prominently, albeit in a less pejorative manner, in the assertion that before getting an agreement Greece must 'first do its homework', which was enunciated on several occasions by, among others, the German Foreign minister Guido Westerwelle (The Guardian 2010), the French President Nicola Sharkozy (The Independent 2012) and the German Chancellor Angel Merkel (BBC 2012). In this formulation being a child is not associated with 'undisciplined' behaviour but with the status of a minor who is in need of protection and guidance from an enlightened paternal figure as she makes her way into adulthood.

Interestingly the image of the undisciplined child has also found advocates within Greece. In an interview with German magazine Spiegel, Greek crime writer Petros Markaris stressed that the Greeks 'urgently need reprimands' in order to do the 'correct thing' (Spiegel online 2010). Along similar lines, Kostas Euthimiou, vice-president of the Panhellenic Psychologists Union, criticized, in an interview with German newspaper Die Welt, the Greek's 'seriously warped sense of reality' which he saw as reminiscent of that of 'little children':

> They're living in a fairy-tale world ... When problems come up, they think a fairy or a mayor will come along and make everything better. They haven't learnt to solve problems for themselves and expect that someone from the outside world will come and solve it for them'.
>
> (Die Welt 2010)

The infantilized image evokes a relationship of difference with the EU and Europe, albeit less radicalized than the image of a criminal. That is, whereas criminality is couched in the language of 'surveillance', 'punishment' and even 'exclusion', the child-adult relationship denotes 'advice', 'guidance' and 'positive inducement'. Moreover, the child imaginary evokes a sense of 'purity' and 'innocence' that warrants 'empathy', 'generosity' and 'patience'.

Greece as a patient

The representation of Greece as a patient undertaking a necessary, if unpleasant, treatment has been recurrent in quality press and elite discourse. An article featuring in the *Guardian* illustrates this imagery very eloquently and therefore deserves to be reproduced in length.

> Greece was *diagnosed* as critically insolvent a year ago. It was *placed* in the Eurozone's *intensive care ward*, treated with an *infusion* of €110bn and put on a *crash diet* to thin its bloated state sector. But 12 months on, the patient is *getting sicker* […] If this is the *cure*, the Greeks are telling their Eurozone peers, we prefer to take our chances with the *disease*. The *doctors* in Berlin take a dim view of that. They might *sugar the pill* with another €30bn or so to tide Greece through next year and *spare it the pain* of the bond markets. They might also agree to a "soft restructuring" by swapping debt for longer-term, lower-interest loans. But they will agree to this only if the *medicine is stronger* and the Greeks promise to *take it all*.
>
> (Traynor 2011 – my emphasis)

The patient-doctor dichotomy in this representation assigns Greece with a passive role of following the guidelines of those who are in a position to 'know' what the right treatment is, its input being confined to supplications for 'easing the pain'. The possibility of substantive input on the type and length of the therapy is instead ruled out, because those who suffer usually lack 'sound judgement'. The alleged response of a high ranking EU official to the news that Greece intended to 'end the memorandum' eloquently exemplifies this. The announcement, he claimed, was reminiscent of 'a patient who has survived intensive care but wants to leave the hospital early […] a relapse is certain and the subsequent care will be much more involved than if the patient had stayed in the hospital long enough for full recovery' (Pauly et al.2014).

The patient metaphor also featured prominently in countless analyses that evoked the fear of 'contagion', to other Eurozone countries. In this context it is possible to identify two variants. The first, which was prominent in early 2012, when exit from the Eurozone looked imminent, constructed Greece as an infected, gangrenous limb and considered 'amputation' as a painful but perhaps necessary option in order to preserve the health of the EU-body (McCarthy 2010). The second, which was more benign, made allusions to the need to 'quarantine' Greece by placing other peripheral economies under a protective firewall (Schneider 2011).

In terms of degree of otherness, the representation of Greece as a patient stands somewhere between the previous two. On the one hand it implies Greek responsibility for its current condition and warrants isolation in order protect the other members of the in-group. On the other hand, it conjures Greek suffering with feelings of compassion and sympathy which is absent in the criminal imagery.

The Underlying Discourse

The Elusive Modernization

The perception of Greek exceptionalism has been very influential because it resonates with a reading of Modern Greek history as an elusive process of transition to modernity, characterized by a struggle between reformist and anti-reformist forces. The elusive modernization thesis has been formulated by Nikoforos Diamandouros in the early 1990s. Its basic tenet is that Greece's modernization has been hampered by the fact that western liberal political institutions had to be grafted onto pre-capitalist structures deriving from Byzantine and Ottoman heritages (Diamandouros 1994). This incongruence was manifested, according to Diamandouros, in the creation of a pervasive cleavage between two cultural traditions: A reformist culture, which gets inspiration from the French revolution and Enlightenment, is extrovert and secular, embraces competition and market mechanisms and aspires to a quick adaptation to western European norms; and an 'underdog' culture, which displays parochial and primordial attachments, shows preference for statist and paternalistic economic structures and has an inward looking international orientation, often bordering a siege mentality (ibid).

The elusive modernization thesis has been very influential in Greek academic discourse, with the resilience of the underdog culture being targeted as the cause of all presumed 'Greek pathogeneses': The weak administrative capacity of the Greek state, the excessive polarization of the Greek political system, the prevalence of corporatist and clientelistic relations, the drive towards rent seeking, the endemic corruption, the tendency towards 'free riding', the appeal of populist and conspiratorial frames, the weak and dependent nature of civil society and so on so forth (see Featherstone 2005, Mouzelis 1996, Pagoulatos 2004, Tsoukalas 1995). The dualistic culture scheme has also been embraced by the Europeanization literature in order to analyze the impact of EU membership on Greek economy, society and politics. The consensus view is that, despite the existence of external adaptational pressures and the sustained effort of domestic reformers to co-opt the EU in their political agenda, the reform process has been thwarted by domestic structural constraints and therefore instead of the anticipated deep transformation, the observed change has been patchy and superfluous (Featherstone 2005, Gemenis and Lefkofridi 2013, Kazakos 2004).

From this perspective the crisis is the logical outcome of Greece's failure to meet the challenge of modernization and Europeanization (Featherstone 2011). Had Greek politicians and people exploited the opportunities conferred by EU membership, the argument goes, the country would have been spared from its current predicament.

Challenging 'Greek Exceptionalism'

The orientalist essence of the elusive modernization thesis cannot go unnoticed. Couched into American political science, the discourse on modernization presupposes an evolutionary and linear conceptualization of history embodying a Western notion of rationality and progress. It also involves an unquestioned acceptance of Western positional superiority and equates modernization with Westernization (or

Europeanization). In this context, Greek society is defined by 'what it is not', through a binary juxtaposition to a 'Western ideal type' (Liakos2004: 358).

A number of authors have challenged this dichotomous logic, arguing that it is underpinned by essentialist tendencies (Tsoukalas 1995) and conceals the way in which tradition and modernity can coexist in a symbiotic relationship (Babiniotis 1995, Kokosalakis and Psimenos 2002). In this context, it has also been argued that the clear delineation of competing camps ignores the complexity of subjectivities and political reality (Stavrakakis 2002: 46) and the inter-constituted and interrelated relationship between tradition and modernization (Demertzis 1997: 118). Taking these arguments further, Gropas and Triandafyllidou (2009: 11) have employed Eisenstadt's multiple modernities theory and argued that the western pattern of modernity entailed in Diamandouros' work is not the only authentic modernity and therefore instead of classifying Greece as pre-modern or anti-modern it may be more appropriate to cast it as proposing an alternative Eastern path to modernity, which follows a different set of norms.

But the problem with this orientalist reading of the Greek crisis is not only meta-theoretical or normative. As mentioned above the dominant narrative provides a fundamentally distorted image of the crisis. Against this reductionist notion of Greek exceptionalism it is possible to identify two alternative discursive positions that focus primarily on the systemic causes of the crisis.

The first, which is rooted in Marxist and neo-Marxist political economy, locates the Greek crisis within a broader crisis of capitalism and especially the neo-liberal ideology that has come to dominate international institutions, including the EU. From this perspective the main culprits are the prevalence of 'neo-liberal production prototypes and social inequalities' (Laskos and Tsakalotos 2013), the 'overacccumulation of capital' in the developed capitalist economies (Overbeek 2012) and the 'financialization' of mature economies (Lapavitsas *et al.* 2010, Fouskas and Dimoulas 2013). Moreover, the weakness of the Greek political system is not understood in terms of maladjustment to western European norms, but in terms of perpetual dependence and coalescence of political elites with a parasitic capitalist class (Katrougalos 2013). Finally, rather than offering a way out of the crisis, the adjustment programs are considered to be part of a premeditated neoliberal onslaught against the European social model (Petmetzidou 2013, Papadopoulos and Roumpakis).

The second discursive position assembles a heterogeneous group of economists, political scientists and journalists who point to the significant institutional deficiencies of the Eurozone and the fallacy of the expectation that the precipitation of monetary integration would act as a catalyst for economic convergence. Even before the establishment of the EMU, several economists had warned that the countries that aspired to become members did not form an Optimum Currency Area and therefore the prospective Eurozone would be vulnerable to asymmetric shocks particularly as the EU lacked automatic fiscal transfers to smooth their negative effects (Krugman 1991). In this context it was also pointed out that there was no precedent of successful monetary union in the absence of fiscal and political union (McNamara 2005). Others have criticized the narrow scope of the SGP rules, which failed to take into consideration important factors such as private debt and current accounts deficits (Kutlay 2011).

In presenting these alternative perspectives, I do not claim that they provide necessarily a better or more accurate account of the Greek crisis. After all, they tend to follow their own (reductionist) grand theories and metanarratives. However, by writing them off and opting for a one-sided explanation that focuses exclusively on Greece's internal weaknesses and failures, the elusive modernization thesis has provided a poor frame for analysis and policy-making.

Conclusion

In this chapter I have argued that the dominant narrative about the Greek sovereign debt crisis provides a reductionist and incomplete account of its causes and implications. I have established that reckless borrowing and consumption-led growth were not confined to Greece; that the size of the Greek state, in terms of public spending and number of public employees has not diverged significantly from the EU average; that the observed shortage in public revenues may result from the structure of the Greek economy rather than an idiosyncratic tax evasion culture; that structural reforms are a necessary but not sufficient condition to overcome the crisis; that the Greek reform record is better than often assumed and, conversely, that other Eurozone governments have not been immune to populist and short-term considerations.

Although there is no shortage of work trying to add nuance to the dominant narrative by pointing to the systemic flaws of the EMU (see Panagiotarea 2013, Tsoukalis, 2012 Featherstone 2011, Monastiriotis 2013), the fundamental logic remains unchallenged: This is primarily a 'Greek crisis', reflecting a lingering maladjustment to European standards. I have tried to push these critiques one step further, by problematizing the underlying discursive structures that produce such unbalanced blame rhetoric. More precisely, I have argued that the notion of 'Greek exceptionalism' derives from an orientalist reading of Greek history as an elusive process of transition to modernity underpinned by a constant struggle between a reformist and an underdog culture. By challenging the modernization discourse I do not deny that Greeks bare a great deal of responsibility for their economic predicament. Nor do I refute the need for political and economic reforms. However, I contend that debates on the content of these reforms, should go beyond the dominant 'adaptation' frame and incorporate alternative discursive positions that do not embed orientalist hierarchies and assumptions. My aim, in other words, is not to prescribe a 'better' policy but to propose a wider and more inclusive discursive space for debating policy.

The paper also contributes to the broader debate on the crisis related 'recurrence of stereotypes and in-Europe otherness', by exposing the various differentiation mechanisms entailed in and reproduced by the dominant discourse. In particular, I have argued that the images of children and patient involve a non-radical differentiation which leaves open the possibility of redemption. This construction bears similarities with the way other southern European countries have been perceived. On the contrary the image of criminal constructs Greece as inherently un-European, a radical other, and therefore paves the way for separating the handling of the 'Greek problem' from the broader Euro-zone crisis.

References

Artavanis, N., Morse, A., and Tsoutsoura, M. (2012). Tax Evasion Across Industries: Soft Credit Evidence from Greece. *Chicago Booth Research Paper, No. 12–25*. Available at: http://papers.ssrn.com/sol3/papers.cfm?abstract_id=2109500

Babiniotis, G. (1995). The Blending of Tradition and Innovation in Modern Greek Culture. In Constas, Dimitri and Stavrou, Theophanis (eds.) *Greece Prepares for the Twenty-first Century*. Washington: Woodrow Wilson Center Press.

BBC (2012). *Merkel: Eurozone Must Avoid Greek Exit*. 26 March. Available at: http://www.bbc.com/news/world-europe-17497656

Biswas, S. (2001). "Nuclear Apartheid" as Political Position: Race as a Postcolonial Resource? *Alternatives, Vol. 26*, No 4, 485–522.

De Grauwe, P. (2009). Some Thoughts on Monetary and Political Union. In Simona L. Talani (ed.) *The Future of EMU*. New York: Palgrave Macmillan, 9–28.

Demertzis, N. (1997). "Greece". In Eatwell Robert (ed.) *European Political Cultures: Conflict or Convergence?* London: Routledge, 107–122.

Diamandouros, N. (1994). Cultural Dualism and Political Change in Post-Authoritarian Greece, *Working Paper 50*, Madrid: Instituto Juan March de Estudios e Investigaciones.

Die Welt (2010). *Die Griechen Sind WieVerzogene Kinder'*, 29 April. Available at: http://www.welt.de/welt_print/debatte/article7387461/Die-Griechen-sind-wie-verzogene-Kinder.html

Doty, R. L. (1996). *Imperial Encounters: The Politics of Representation in North–South Relations*. Minneapolis: University of Minnesota Press.

Doxiadis, A. (2013). *The Invisible Rift*, Athens, Polis. (in Greek)

European Central Bank, 2012. Corporate Indebtedness in the Euro Area, *ECB Monthly Bulleting, No. 352*, 87–103.

ELSTAT, (2014). The Greek Economy. Available at: http://www.statistics.gr/portal/page/portal/ESYE/BUCKET/General/greek_economy_24_12_2014.pdf

Euractiv, (2010). "EU Threatens Regional Aid Cuts for Budget Offenders". Available at: http://www.euractiv.com/regional-policy/eu-threatens-regional-aid-cuts-for-budget-offenders-news-445970

Euractiv, (2011). "Commission Rebuffs Dutch Calls for Euro 'Exit Plan'. Available at: http://www.euractiv.com/euro-finance/commission-rebuffs-euro-exit-debt-offenders-news-507495

Eurostat, (2010). *Taxation Trends in the EU: Data for the EU Member States, Iceland and Norway*. Eurostat Statistical Book.

Featherstone, K. (2005). Introduction: "Modernisation" and the Structural Constraints of Greek Politics, *West European Politics, Vol. 28*, No. 2, 223–241.

Featherstone, K. (2011). The JCMS Annual Lecture: The Greek Sovereign Debt Crisis and EMU: A Failing State in a Skewed Regime, *Journal of Common Market Studies, Vol. 49* (2), 193–217.

Fouskas, V. and Dimoulas, C. (2013). *Greece, Financialization and the EU: The Political Economy of Debt and Destruction*. Basinkstoke: Palgrave Macmillan.

Gemenis, K. and Lefkofridi Z. (2013). The Europeanization of Greece: A Critical Assessment. In Mike Mannin and Charlotte Bretherton (eds.) *The Europeanization of European Politics*. Basingstoke: Palgrave Macmillan.

Gropas, R. and Triandafyllidou, A. (2009). The State of the Art: Various Paths to Modernity. *Identities and Modernities in Europe Greek Case Report*. Available at: http://www.eliamep.gr/wp-content/uploads/2010/06/WP4-Greece.pdf

Gupta, A. (1998). *Postcolonial Developments*, Durham, NC: Duke University Press

Gusterson, H. (1999). Nuclear Weapons and the Other in the Western Imagination, *Cultural Anthropology, Vol. 14* (1), 111–143.

Howden, D. (2012). *Greek Elections Were the Last Tantrum of a Spoilt Child*. The Independent, 12 May.

IMF (2014). *Greece: Fifth Review under the Extended Arrangement under the Extended Fund Facility*.

Iordanoglou, C. (2013). *State and Interest Groups*, Athens, Polis. (in Greek).

Jones, E. (2010). Merkel's Folly. *Survival, Vol. 52* (3), 21–38.

Katrougalos, G. (2013). "Memoranda": Greek Exceptionalism or the Mirror of Europe's Future". In Triantafyllidou, A., Gropas, R. and Kouki, H. (eds). *The Greek Crisis and European Modernity*. London: Palgrave.

Kazakos, P. (2004). Europeanisation, Public Goals and Group Interests: Convergence Policy in Greece, 1990–2003, *West European Politics, Vol. 27* (5), 901–918.

Kokosalakis, N. and Psimmenos, I. (2002). *Modern Greece: A Profile of Identity and Nationalism*, EURONAT Report.

Krugman, P. (1991). *Geography and Trade*. Cambridge: MIT Press.

Kutlay, M. (2011). Stopping "Blame Game": Revealing the Euro Zone's Design Faults 'Complex Interdependence Within the Nation-State Framework, *Uluslararası Hukukve Politika, Vol. 7* (27), 87–111.

Kuus, M. (2007). Something Old, Something New: Eastness in European Union Enlargement, *Journal of International Relations and Development, Vol. 10* (2), 150–167.

Kyrkilis, D. and Hazakis, K. (2014). *The Impact of Economic Adjustment Programmes on Greek Competitiveness.* Paper presented at the conference 'The Greek economy from crisis to development', 4–5 April, Volos, Greece.

Lapavitsas, C., Kaltenbrunner A., Lindo D., Michell, J., Painceira, J. P., Pires E., Powell, J., Stenfors A. and Teles, N. (2010). Eurozone Crisis: Beggar Thyself and Thy Neighbour, *Journal of Balkan and Near Eastern Studies, vol. 12* (4), 321–373.

Laskos, C. and Tsakalotos, E. (2013). *Crucible of Resistance: Greece, the Eurozone and the World Economic Crisis.* London: Pluto Press.

Liakos, A. (2004). Modern Greek Historiography (1974–2000). The Era of Tradition from Dictatorship to Democracy. In Brunbauer, U. (ed.) *(Re)Writing History. Historiography in Southeast Europe after Socialism.* Münster: LIT Verlag, pp. 351–378.

Matsaganis, M., Leventi, C., and Flevotomou, M. (2012). The Crisis and Tax Evasion in Greece: What are the Distributional Implications?. *CESifo Forum No. 2*, pp. 26–32.

Mavelli, L. (2012). Between Normalisation and Exception: The Securitisation of Islam and the Construction of the Secular Subject. *Millennium - Journal of International Studies, Vol. 41* (2), 159–181.

McCarthy G. (2010). Eurozone Contagion: Here's What's at Stake. Available at: http://blogs.wsj.com/marketbeat/2010/04/27/eurozone-contagion-heres-whats-at-sta ke/

McNamara (1998). *The Currency of Ideas: Monetary Politics in Europe.* Ithaca: Cornel University Press.

Michaels, A. (2010). *Germany Wants to Punish the Euro Offenders*, The Telegraph 12 March.

Milliken, J. (1999). The Study of Discourse in International Relations: A Critique of Research and Methods, *European Journal of International Relations, Vol. 5* (2), 225–254.

Monastiriotis, V. (2013). A Very Greek Crisis, *Intereconomics, Vol. 48* (1), 4–32.

Mouzelis, N. (1996). The Concept of Modernization. Its Relevance for Greece, *Journal of Modern Greek Studies, Vol.14*, 215–227.

Murawska-Muthesius, K. (2014). Small Children: Nations Eastern Punch and Bullied Draws Europe, *The Slavonic and East European Review, Vol. 84*, (2), 279–305.

Neumann, I. B. (1999). *The Uses of the Other: 'The East' in European Identity Formation,* Minneapolis, MN: University of Minnesota Press.

Ntampoudi, I. (2013). *The Good Guys, The Bad Guys and The Ugly Debt: The Eurozone Crisis and the Politics of Blaming.* Paper presented at the UACES conference Evolving Europe: Voices of the Future Loughborough, 8–9 July.

O'Grady, S. (2011). *Greek Rage Will Remind Many of a Spoilt Child's Tantrums*, The Independent, 22 June.

OECD (2011a). *Government at a Glance.* OECD Publishing. Available at: http://www.o ecd.org/gov/governmentataglance2011.htm

OECD (2011b). *OECD Economic Survey: Greece.* OECD Publishing. Available at http://www.oecd.org/greece/economicsurveyofgreece2011.htm

OECD (2013). *OECD Economic Survey: Greece.* OECD Publishing. Available at: http://www.oecd.org/eco/surveys/economic-survey-greece.htm

OECD (2014). *OECD Competition Assessment Reviews: Greece.* OECD Publishing. Available at: http://www.oecd.org/competition/greece-competition-review-2013.htm

Overbeek, H. (2012). Sovereign Debt Crisis in Euroland: Root Causes and Implications for European Integration, *The International Spectator, Vol. 47* (1), 30–48.

Oxford Economics (2010). *Is Greece Heading for Default?* Available at: http://www.google.gr/url?sa=t&rct=j&q=&esrc=s&source=web&cd=1&ved=0CCEQFjAA&url=http%3A%2F%2Fwww.oxfordeconomics.com%2Fpublication%2Fdownload%2F214082&ei=InDDVN6DFovmaNCPgNAP&usg=AFQjCNHBoJuWnYGMhGn0EGNqyRF3nVLYcA&bvm=bv.84349003,d.d2s

Pagoulatos, G. (2004). Believing in National Exceptionalism: Ideas and Economic Divergence in Southern Europe, *West European Politics, Vol. 27* (1), 43–68.

Panagiotarea, E. (2013). *Greece in the Euro: Economic Delinquency or System Failure?* Colchester, ECPR Press.

Papadimitriou, D. and Zartaloudis, S. (2014). *European Discourses on Managing the Greek Crisis: Denial, Distancing and Blaming,* Paper prepared for the Annual PSA Conference Manchester, 14–16 April.

Papadopoulos, T. and Roumpakis, A. (2013). From Anti-Social Policy to Generalised Insecurity: The Greek Crisis Meets the Decline of the European Social Model, *Social Policy, No. 1.*

Pauly, C., Reiermann, C. and Schult, C. (2014). *The Greek Patient: Europe Debates Third Bailout Package for Athens.* Spiegel online. 1 December. Available at: http://www.spiegel.de/international/europe/euro-zone-debate-third-bailout-package-for-greece-a-1005977.html

Pavan Kumar, M. (2012). Introduction: Orientalism(s) after 9/11. *Journal of Postcolonial Writing, Vol. 48* (3), 233–240.

Petmetzidou, M. (2013). Is the Crisis a Watershed Moment for the Greek Welfare State? The Chances for Modernization amidst an Ambivalent EU Record on "Social Europe". In Triantafyllidou, A., Gropas R. and Kouki, H. (eds). T*he Greek Crisis and European Modernity*, London: Palgrave.

Radowitz, B. (2011). *Merkel: Euro Stability Offenders May Face Budget Intervention,* http://www.efxnews.com/story/5580/merkel-euro-stability-offenders-may-face-budget-intervention

Said, E. W. (1979). *Orientalism,* New York: Vintage Books.

Saxson, N. (2011). *Treasure Islands.* Bodley Head.

Schmidt, V. (2014). Speaking to the Markets or to the People? A Discursive Institutionalist Analysis of the EU's Sovereign Debt Crisis, *The British Journal of Politics and International Relations*, Vol. 16 (1), 188–209.

Schneider, F. (2012). *The Shadow Economy and Work in the Shadow : What Do We (Not) Know?* IZA Discussion Paper No. 6423.

Schneider, H. (2011). *Euro zone: Greek Contagion Quarantined*, The Washington Post. Available at: http://www.washingtonpost.com/business/economy/eurozone-greek-contagion-quarantined/2011/07/22/gIQA1Q9XTI_story.html

Spiegel online (2010). *The Greeks Must Suffer*, Available at: http://www.spiegel.de/international/europe/interview-with-greek-crime-writer-petros-markaris-the-greeks-must-suffer-a-681705.html

Spiegel, P. (2011). *Draghi's ECB Management: the Leaked Geithner Files*. Available at: http://blogs.ft.com/brusselsblog/2014/11/11/draghis-ecb-management-the-leaked-geithner-files/

Stavrakakis, Y. (2002). Religious Populism and Political Culture: The Greek Case. *South European Society and Politics*, Vol. 7 (3), 29–52.

Stockhammer, E. (2011). Peripheral Europe's Debt and German Wages : the Role of Wage policy in the Euro Area, *International Journal of Public Policy*, Vol. 7 (January), 83–96.

The Guardian (2010). *German Opposition to Greek Debt Bailout Gathers Pace*, 26 April. Available at: http://www.theguardian.com/business/2010/apr/26/germany-condemns-greece-debt-bailout

The Independent (2012). *Greece is Being Screwed Down so Sarkozy can Meet his Deadline*. 8 February. Available at: http://www.independent.co.uk/voices/commentators/hamish-mcrae/hamish-mcrae-greece-is-being-screwed-down-so-sarkozy-can-meet-his-deadline-6655136.html

The Independent (2013). *Angela Merkel Says Greece Should Never Have Joined*. 28 August

Todorova, M. (1997). *Imagining the Balkans*, New York: Oxford University Press.

Transparency International (2012). *National Integrity System Assessment: Greece*. http://www.transparency.org/whatwedo/publication/nis_greece_2012

Traynor, I. (2011). *The Greek Patient is Getting Sicker and Dr Merkel's Reputation is at Stake*, The Guardian, 9 May.

Triantafylidou, A., Gropa, R. and Kouki, H. (2013). *The Greek Crisis and European Modernity*, London: Palgrave.

Tsoukalas, C. (1995). Free riders in Wonderland: or of Greeks, in Greece. In Constas, D. and Stavrou, T. (eds), *Greece Prepares for the Twenty-First Century*, Washington: Woodrow Wilson Center Press, pp. 191–222.

Tsoukalis, L. (2012). Greece in the Euro Area: Odd Man Out, Or Pre-cursor of Things to Come?. In William Cline and Guntram Wolff (eds.), *Resolving the European Debt Crisis Washington*, DC: Peterson Institute for International Economics, pp. 19–35.

Wolf, M. (2010a). *Germans are Wrong: the Eurozone is Good for Them*, Financial Times, 8 September.

Wolf, M. (2010b.). *The Eurozone Needs More than Discipline from Germany*, Financial Times, 22 December.

World Bank (2015). *Doing Business: Economy Profile 2015: Greece*. http://www.doingbusiness.org/data/exploreeconomies/~/media/giawb/doing%20business/documents/profiles/country/GRC.pdf?ver=2

Xafa, M. (2014). *Sovereign Debt Crisis Management: Lessons from the 2012 Greek Debt Restructuring*. CIGI Papers, No 33.

Young, B. and Semmler, W. (2011). The European Sovereign Debt Crisis: Is Germany to Blame?. *German Politics and Society*, Vol. 29 (1), 1–24.

Tsoukalis, L. (2012). Greece in the Euro Area: Odd Man Out, Or Pre-cursor of Things to Come?. In William Cline and Guntram Wolff (eds.), *Resolving the European Debt Crisis* Washington, DC: Peterson Institute for International Economics, pp. 19–35.

Wolf, M. (2010a). *Germans are Wrong: the Eurozone is Good for Them*, Financial Times, 8 September.

Wolf, M. (2010b.). *The Eurozone Needs More than Discipline from Germany*, Financial Times, 22 December.

World Bank (2015). *Doing Business: Economy Profile 2015: Greece*. http://www.doingbusiness.org/data/exploreeconomies/~/media/giawb/doing%20business/documents/profiles/country/GRC.pdf?ver=2

Xafa, M. (2014). *Sovereign Debt Crisis Management: Lessons from the 2012 Greek Debt Restructuring*. CIGI Papers, No 33.

Young, B. and Semmler, W. (2011). The European Sovereign Debt Crisis: Is Germany to Blame?. *German Politics and Society*, Vol. 29 (1), 1–24.

Conflict of Identity or Conflict of Interest: The two Facets of the EU North-South Divide

NIKOS PASAMITROS

The EU North-South divide is an issue that re-emerged with the proliferation of the EU crisis. This scheme is influenced by the Dependency Theory of the uneven distribution of resources between a centre of wealthy states and a periphery of poor ones. However, this approach attempts to examine only one facet of the divide, based on the distribution of material resources. The other aspect of the issue is the negative images that emerge between peoples of the EU states that were heavily stricken by the crisis and the ones that remain relatively unharmed. This paper attempts to examine two levels of the alleged divide caused by the EU crisis; (1) the level of resources and (2) the social psychological level. The first part is based on the Realistic Conflict Theory and uses hard data (Income per Capita, employment and unemployment data, annual earnings and minimum wage). The second part starts from the Social Identity Theory and uses data that monitor perceived well-being (life satisfaction, happiness, positive and negative affect, net affect and Quality of Support Network). In order to develop the argument, two sets of states are utilized; a "north group" consisting of Austria, Finland, Germany and Sweden and a "south group" represented by Cyprus, Greece, Portugal and Spain. The aim is to examine the explanatory power of the two theories and draw useful conclusions from both.

Nikos Pasamitros is a PhD candidate at Panteion University and co-founder of the Inter Alia think tank

Keywords: EU North-South Divide; Social Identity Theory; Realistic Conflict Theory; Stereotypical Images

Editor's Note

The European Union has diachronically been a field of difficult concessions, that have largely defined the integration process. However, the current crisis has consolidated political disagreements and negative images of member states and has re-contextualized them in an old-new debate about the north-south divide. The way in which this discourse unravels and the terms in which it is perceived is not politically neutral. On the contrary, it indicates a related understanding of the Union and a different vision for its future. Contextualization of the north-south divide in fiscal or economic terms brings along a different, top-down toolbox for solutions in comparison to an identitarian one, that necessitates a long-term involvement and a bottom-up approach. While different in nature and effect, both readings of the north-south divide constitute oversimplifications. Pasamitros claims, that a common, sustainable European future depends on the capacity of the EU leadership, be it national or supranational, to invest in forming a common identity that, will irreversibly deprive essence and applicability from the north-south divide.

Introduction

Discussions on multi-speed Europe, EU North-South and West-East divide are always present in the European Union as asymmetry and divergence are key characteristics that originate from the birth and evolution of the EU itself. Since the appearance of the global crisis in the European space, the notion of the EU North-South divide dynamically re-emerged in the political rhetoric and the media. The proliferation of the EU crisis sparked a protracted period of critique to the dominant political forces of Europe. Much of the criticism that emerged utilized the narrative of the widening economic divide between the wealthy states of the European North and those of the poor European South. This explanatory model is systematically met in the rhetoric of the European Left, the Europe-wide indignados movements, the newfound apolitical populist movements and the Eurosceptic and anti-EU parties. On the one hand, the left and leftist parties use the euro-dependency approach in order to stress the need for a *"Europe for the people"*. On the other, the apolitical and extreme right parties evoke it in order to accentuate the failure of the EU, and the parasitic dependency of the European South to the North, or the other way around, the authoritarian behavior of the North to the South. From time to time, the dominant EU political forces invoke themselves the north-south gap when convenient but in general they refrain from using dividing terms.

The paper attempts to explore the EU alleged north-south divide on two levels; (1) the level of material resources and (2) the social-psychological level. For the former, the explanatory framework is the *Realistic Conflict Theory* and for the latter, the *Social Identity Theory*. For that purpose, I use hard data to explore the resources level, and perception and self-report data to examine the social-psychological one. The aim is to examine the explanatory power of the two theoretical approaches and draw results on the implications of an EU divide on both levels. In the *Theoretical Framework*, I offer a brief overview of the two theoretical approaches, the *Realistic Conflict Theory* and the *Social Identity Theory*. *Data and Data Analysis*, which is the main body of the research is divided in two parts; *Realistic Conflict Theory Approach* and *Social Identity Theory*. In the *Realistic Conflict Theory Approach* Chapter, I appose and examine the data on economics, income and employment that support the Realistic approach. A brief analysis of the explanatory capability of the *Realistic Conflict Theory* on the EU North-South case follows. In the *Social Identity Theory* Chapter, I supplement the gap left by the *Realistic Conflict Theory* analysis, based on the *Social Identity Theory*. Then, I present and analyse the data on life satisfaction, happiness and affect. In the *Conclusions* Chapter I present some final thoughts on the EU North-South divide and its implications on the crisis and post-crisis Europe.

Theoretical Framework

Theoretical Aid #1: Realistic Conflict Theory

The *Realistic Conflict Theory* accentuates the central role of competition for the rise of conflict among groups. According to the *Realistic Conflict* approach, real conflict of interests produces competition and hostility towards the out-group and favoritism and solidarity for the in-group. However, when the groups need to accomplish a superordinate goal, hostility decreases and intergroup friendship and harmony are promoted (Valentim, 2010, p. 587). Social psychologist John Duckitt in his work *The Social Psychology of Prejudice* furthers the realistic theory to unequal status groups by alleging that if a higher status group dominates a subordinate group, the subordinate group may either respond by accepting the higher status group behavior to avoid conflict or by judging the behavior of the dominant group as oppressive and unacceptable. In the latter case, the dominant group may judge the contestation as justified or unjustified. If it is judged as unjustified, the top dog will respond in a hostile manner. If the underdog's uprising is viewed as justified the claim for change is accepted (Whitley & Kite, 2010, pp. 327–329). Hugh Donald Forbes points out (1997, p. 31), that when it comes to prejudice or discrimination within a society where the structure is not clearly built for competition as in the interstate level, the explanatory power of *Realistic Conflict Theory* is significantly reduced.

Theoretical Aid #2: Social Identity Theory and Self-categorisation Theory

The *Social Identity Theory* can be seen as contesting and, controversially enough, at the same time complementary to the *Realistic Conflict Theory*. That is, *Social Identity Theory* does not accept conflict of interests as an essential prerequisite for intergroup antagonism to rise (Forbes, 1997, pp. 32, 33). In many cases though, *Social Identity Theory* functions as a supplement to the *Realistic Conflict Theory* by attempting to enrich it with "*an appropriate analysis of the social psychology of social conflict.*" (Tajfel & Turner, 1986, p. 8) In practice the *Realistic* approach is not rejected at all. As Tajfel and Turner put it (1986, p. 23):

> "It is nearly impossible in most natural social situations to distinguish between discriminatory intergroup behavior based on real or perceived conflict of objective interests between the groups and discrimination based on attempts to establish a positively-valued distinctiveness for one's own group."

Social Identity Theory is based on the fundamental hypothesis that social categorization of people into distinct groups can produce favoritism to the in-group over the out-group. Based on observational and experimental research, this theory asserts that the awareness of belonging to a group is, under certain conditions, sufficient to foster discrimination and competition. As people perceive social identification as part of their existence, they demonstrate the need to achieve a positive self-evaluation of the in-group through comparison (Turner, 1999, p. 8). In the specific cases of low status or disadvantaged groups, *Social Identity Theory* bears that the disadvantaged position of the low status group brings to the surface a group identity problem. The reaction of the group members will either be social mobility, if the society permits it or social change where the group attempts to change its status through collective effort. (Tajfel & Turner, 1986, pp. 9–10)

Social behavior varies along a continuum from interpersonal where interaction is determined by personal relations and individual characteristics, to intergroup where behavior is determined by membership in social groups. The aforementioned continuum is shaped by the interaction between social and psychological factors (Turner, 1999, pp. 9–10). In the case of mobility of disadvantaged groups, a group closer to the interpersonal end of the continuum would choose individual mobility, while a group closer to the intergroup end of the continuum would pursue social change.

Self-categorisation Theory which is often mentioned together with *Social Identity Theory* maintains that where self-perception is based on a social category, people tend to exaggerate intragroup similarities and intergroup differences. Therefore, people stereotype themselves as kin to the in-group and distinct from the out-group (Turner, 1999, pp. 10–11).[1] Depending on different situations, the relative salience of the different self-categorisation levels determines behavior as based on the personal (personalisation) or on the social (depersonalisation) identity. As Tajfel et al show in their manipulative matrices experiments (1971, pp. 172–174), contrary to the claims of the *Realistic Conflict Theory*, norms not based on utilitarian or rational norms drive individuals to intragroup favoritism.

Self-categorisation Theory attempts to avoid theoretical oversimplifications by approaching stereotypes as dynamic aspects of social reality. Turner (1999, p. 26) underlines that stereotypes are neither rigid, nor irrational. On the contrary, they are perceptions through the prism of group membership. Their psychological validity is related to perception and interaction and as such they are fluid, variable and context-dependent.

Data and Data Analysis

The selection of the states that constitute the "north" and "south" groups is based on several factors such as antiquity in the European family, rough population criteria and qualitative standards. Concerning antiquity, the intention was not to include establishing members in order to avoid deep divisions from the outset. Secondly, I wanted to include, more or less, states that would represent arithmetically small nations (Cyprus and Finland), small-medium (Austria, Greece, Portugal and Sweden) and big

---

[1] German Sociologist Berndt Simon in his book "Identity in Modern Society" (2004, p. 37) clearly illustrates the core of the *Self-categorisation Theory* : "*The [...] approach is based on the distinction between personal identity and social identity. Personal identity means self-definition as a unique individual in terms of interpersonal or intragroup differentiations, whereas social identity means self-definition as a group member in terms of ingroup-outgroup differentiations.*"

ones (Germany and Spain). Specific selections and exceptions were applied for the improvement of the argument and the corresponding conclusions. For example, Germany, even though it does not exactly match the antiquity criteria (establishing member of the European Coal and Steel Community and 1990 reunification), could not be left out since it was constantly on the spotlight since the emergence of the crisis. Spain was included instead of Italy for several reasons (not a founding member, hit earlier than its neighbor by the crisis, strong popular reaction to austerity). Sweden despite the fact that it is not a member of the European Monetary Union could not be left out since it is often referred to as, the ideal European state, economy, social care and healthcare example to follow, and is usually considered as a "typical North country" in the North-South divide logic.

The data selected for the analysis follow the specific perceptions that result from the explanatory models of the two theories applied in the article. The *Realistic Conflict Theory* that focuses on conflict over resources is supported by indicators that show the capability of the countries under consideration to produce and maintain wealth (GDP per capita, Government Surplus / deficit, minimum wage, average gross annual earnings, GDP per person employed and employment / unemployment rates). Accordingly, the *Social Identity Theory* that focuses on conflict due to in-group / out-group dichotomies is supported by data that attempt to depict psychological features like positive distinctiveness and psychological security (average life satisfaction, average happiness, positive / negative / net affect and quality of support network).

Realistic Conflict Theory Approach

According to the *Realistic Conflict Theory*, hostility among groups arises from antagonistic goals and struggle over limited resources. In our case the competing groups are the national groups (Austria, Cyprus, Finland, Greece, Germany, Portugal, Spain and Sweden). In the wider Centre-Periphery line of thought, we can see two sets of national groups; the wealthy north (Austria, Finland, Germany and Sweden) and the poor south (Cyprus, Greece, Spain and Portugal). We will follow the north-south divide concept in order to properly explore the possible antagonisms arising from real conflict of interests.

Economics

Gross Domestic Product offers an overview for an approach based on resources. It depicts a wide image of economic activity based on production. Diagram 1 shows that the "south group" faces a reduction of the GDP per capita from the crisis eruption in 2009 up to now. Portugal demonstrates an upward trend for 2013, Spain is stabilized, while Cyprus and Greece continue to shrink. As for the north, Austria, Finland and Germany show a slightly downward trend while Sweden is ascending. Notably, the "north group" is diachronically above the EU average while from the "south group" Greece and Portugal have never surpassed the EU average in the period under consideration (2002–2013).

Diagram 1
GDP per capita in PPS
Index (EU28 = 100)

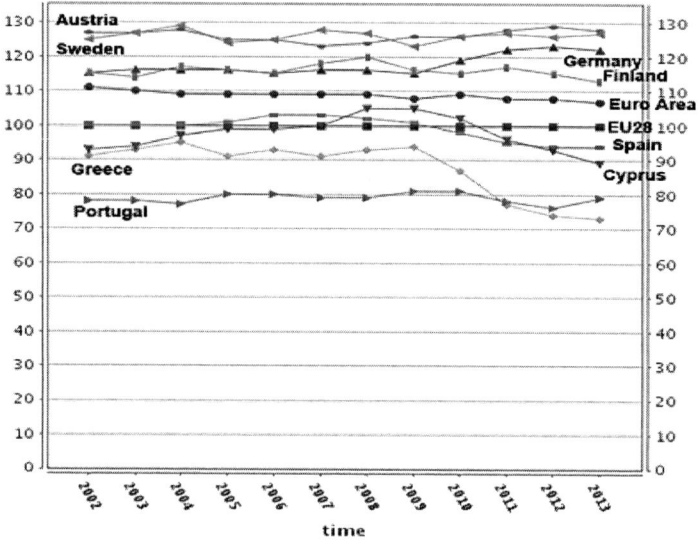

Source of Data Eurostat

Gross domestic product (GDP) is a measure for the economic activity. It is defined as the value of all goods and services produced less the value of any goods or services used in their creation. The volume index of GDP per capita in Purchasing Power Standards (PPS) is expressed in relation to the European Union (EU28) average set to equal 100. If the index of a country is higher than 100, this country's level of GDP per head is higher than the EU average and vice versa. Basic figures are expressed in PPS, i.e. a common currency that eliminates the differences in price levels between countries allowing meaningful volume comparisons of GDP between countries. Please note that the index, calculated from PPS figures and expressed with respect to EU28 = 100, is intended for cross-country comparisons rather than for temporal comparisons."

Concerning central government sector (Diagram 2), only Germany demonstrates surplus for 2013. Sweden and Finland show a small increase of their deficit and Austria is steadily reducing its deficit since 2009. Cyprus, Portugal and Spain seem to be reducing their deficit after the bleak 2009 while Greece, which seemed to move the same way, demonstrates a new downturn in 2013. For an advocate of the *Realistic Conflict Theory*, the deficit / surplus diagram clearly depicts the clash for resources. As the GDP above may be read as "the dominant set of states are above and the subordinate, below EU average", the deficit / surplus could be interpreted likewise

Diagram 2

General government deficit/surplus
% of GDP
Percentage of GDP

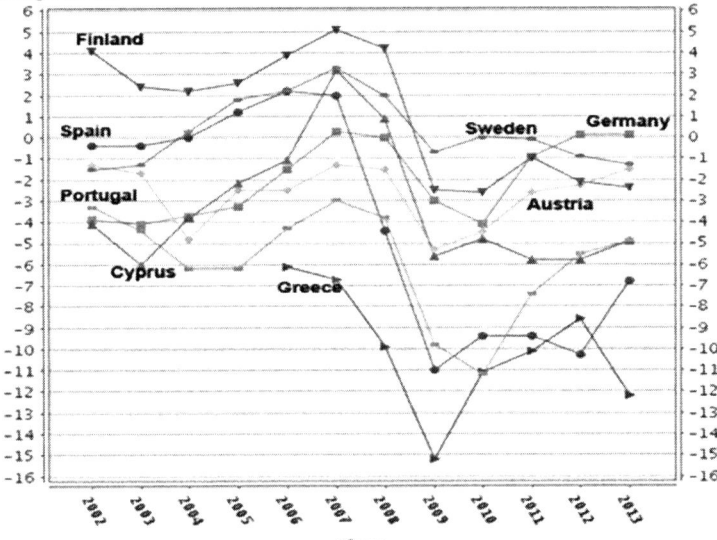

■ Germany ■ Greece ■ Spain ■ Cyprus ■ Austria ■ Portugal ■ Finland ■ Sweden
• Unavailable data is ignored

Source of Data Eurostat

Short Description: Public deficit/surplus is defined in the Maastricht Treaty as general government net borrowing/lending according to the European System of Accounts. The general government sector comprises central government, state government, local government, and social security funds. The relevant definitions are provided in Council Regulation 479/2009, as amended.

Income Data

The minimum wage graph (Diagram 3) shows a constant increase for Greece, Portugal and Sweden until 2010. Thereafter, there is a stabilisation for Portugal and Sweden and a great leap for Greece from 2012 to 2013. Obviously the lack of data in this indicator does not lead to safe conclusions. In some countries the minimum wage does not exist. In addition, this indicator, if the data was sufficient, could only reflect an established level of resources guaranteed for the peoples.

Diagram 3

Minimum wages
EUR/month

Source of Data: Eurostat

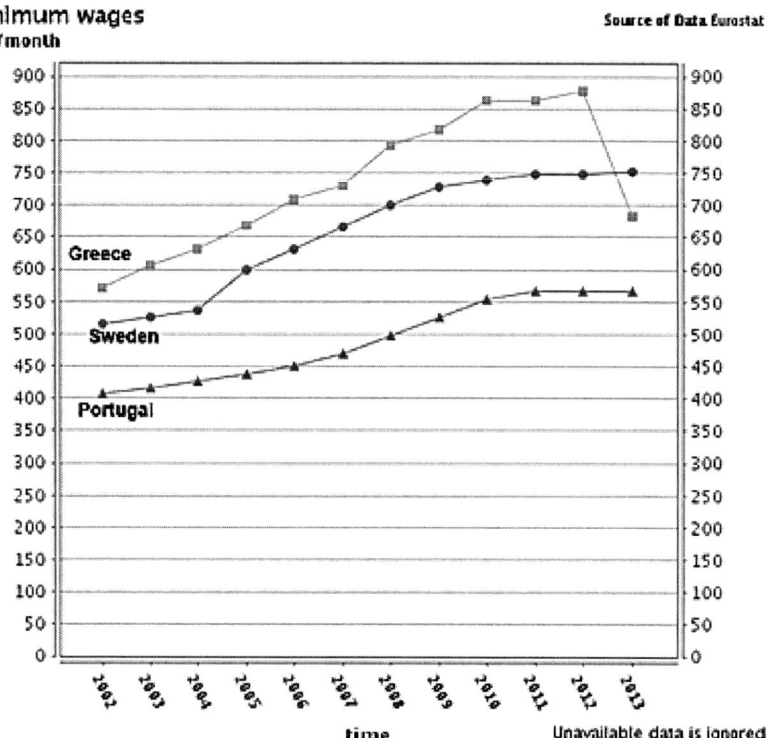

time — Unavailable data is ignored

The data on annual earnings of employees in industry and service (Diagram 4) is more informative than the previous one. Finland, Germany and Sweden demonstrate a steady rise since 2009 while Spain and Portugal hold a steady pace. Here, we see increased capability of the "north group" to produce and maintain wealth contrary to the "south group" that holds a steadily low capability.

Diagram 4

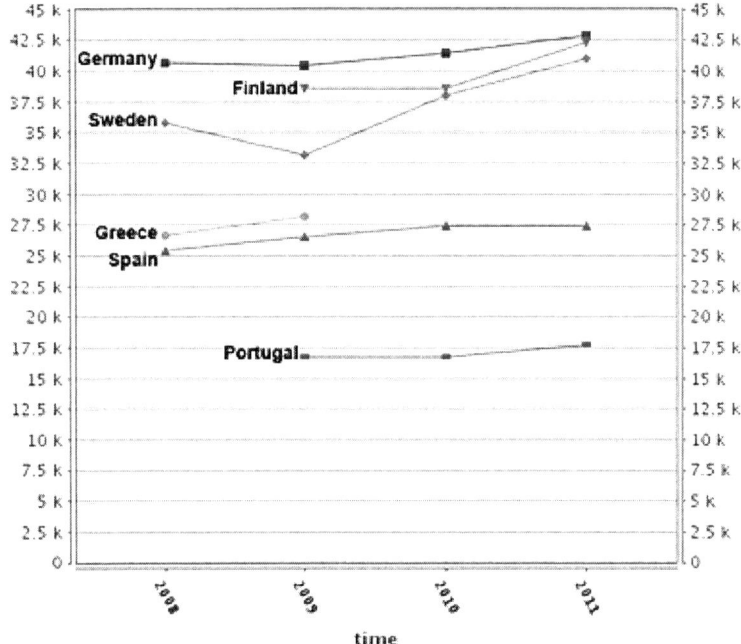

Likewise, the GDP per person employed (Diagram 5) shows that Austria, Finland, Germany and Sweden along with Spain have an upward trend contrary to Cyprus and Greece that show a slight decrease. Portugal is stabilized. The GDP per person employed diagram could not support the Realistic Conflict Approach argument, at least not in an absolute sense.

Diagram 5

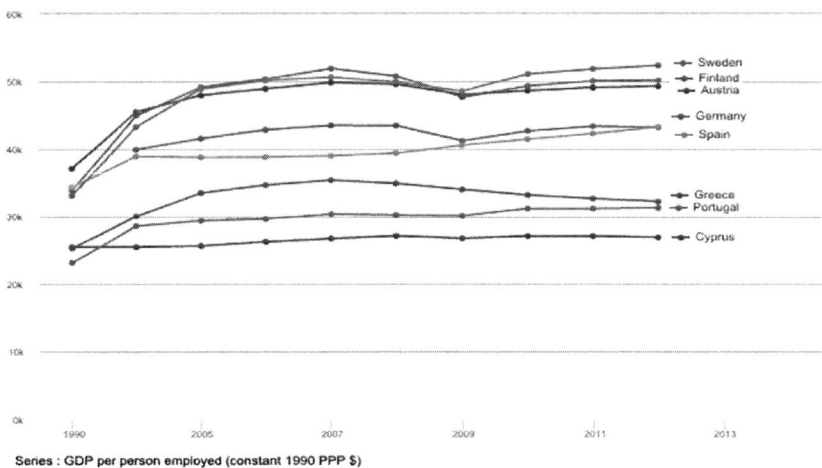

Source: http://data.worldbank.org

Employment / Unemployment

The employment data reflect a steep fall in employment for the "south group" (Diagram 6). On the contrary, the "north group" has an increasing employment rate except from Finland that demonstrates a slight drop in 2013. In this diagram, Duckitt's expansion of the *Realistic Conflict Theory* seems to be right. The dominant "north" has a robust performance while the "subordinate" south cannot perform accordingly.

Diagram 6
Employment rate
%
Total

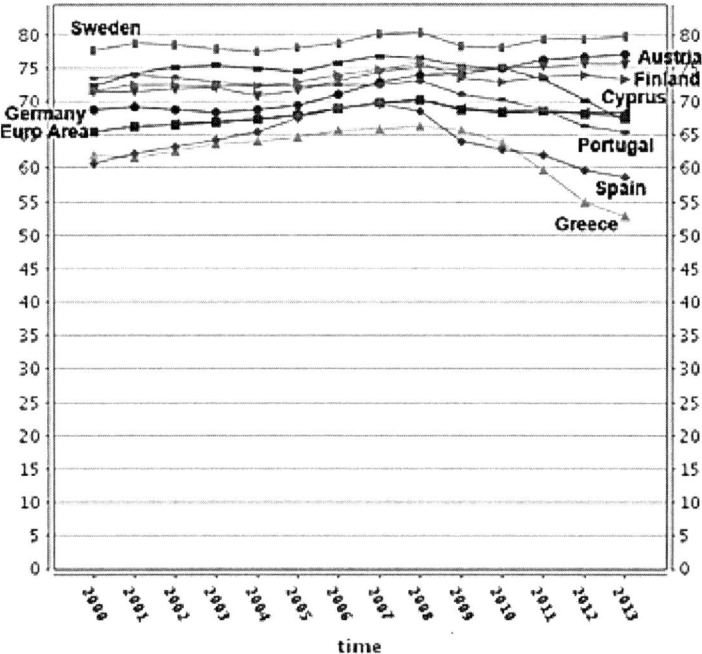

Correspondingly, the unemployment rates for Greece and Spain are strikingly high and continue to follow an upward tendency. Portugal and Cyprus follow similar rising trends. On the other hand, Finland, Sweden and Austria have stable rates while Germany reduces its rates (Diagram 7). Unemployment statistics for the under 25 year old population (Diagram 8) are dark for Greece and Spain and depressing for Cyprus and Portugal. For Sweden and Finland youth unemployment is at the 25–74 age group levels (see Diagram 9) with a slightly upwards trend. For Austria and Germany stats are comparatively low.

Diagram 7

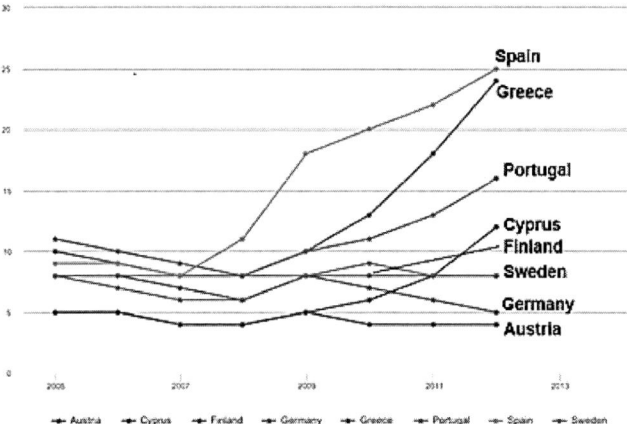

Series: Unemployment, total (% of total labor force) (national estimate)
Created from: World Development Indicators
Created on: 12/18/2014

Diagram 8

Unemployment rate by age group
%
Less than 25 years

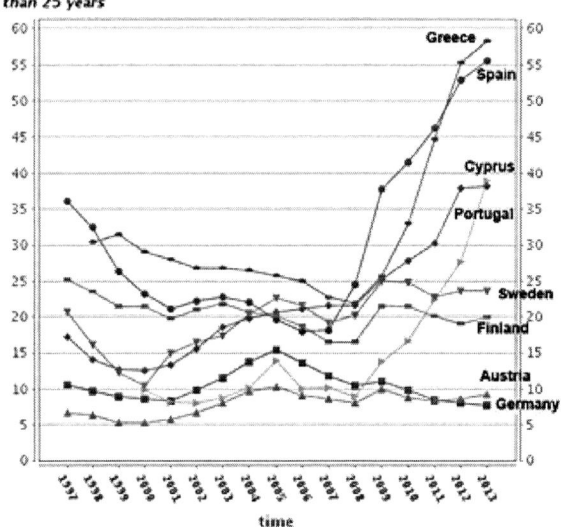

• Unavailable data is ignored Source of Data Eurostat

Short Description: Unemployment rates represent unemployed persons as a percentage of the labour force. The labour force is the total number of people employed and unemployed. Unemployed persons comprise persons aged 15 to 74 who were: a. without work during the reference week, b. currently available for work, i.e. were available for paid employment or self-employment before the end of the two weeks following the reference week, c. actively seeking work, i.e. had taken specific steps in the four weeks period ending with the reference week to seek paid employment or self-employment or who found a job to start later, i.e. within a period of, at most, three months.

Diagram 9
Unemployment rate by age group
%
From 25 to 74 years

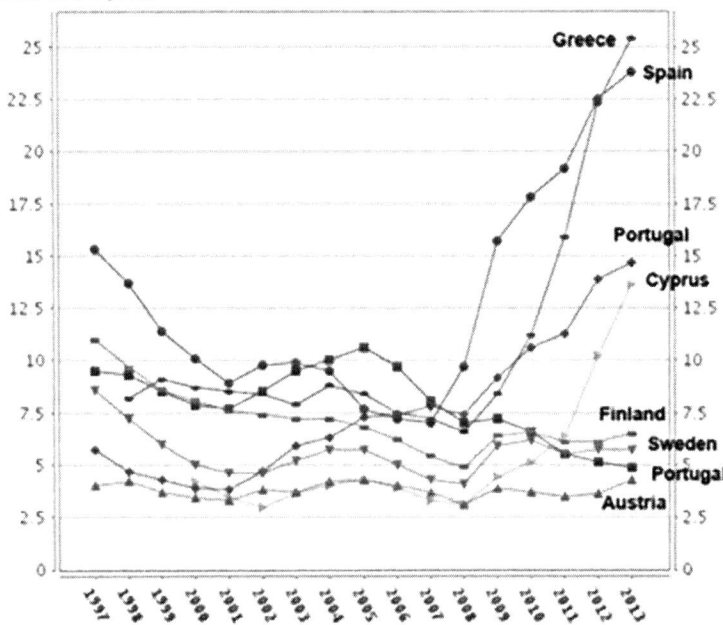

■ Germany ■ Greece ■ Spain ■ Cyprus ■ Austria ■ Portugal ■ Finland ■ Sweden

• Unavailable data is ignored

Source of Data Eurostat

Short Description: Unemployment rates represent unemployed persons as a percentage of the labour force. The labour force is the total number of people employed and unemployed. Unemployed persons comprise persons aged 15 to 74 who were: a. without work during the reference week, b. currently available for work, i.e. were available for paid employment or self-employment before the end of the two weeks following the reference week, c. actively seeking work, i.e. had taken specific steps in the four weeks period ending with the reference week to seek paid employment or self-employment or who found a job to start later, i.e. within a period of, at most, three months.

The indices above are just a sample of the data that could be used on the topic. In any case, whatever data a researcher chooses to use for the subject, the indicators would, more or less, demonstrate a specific pattern; the "south group" is a set of countries with weak and indebted economies, bad record on labor and comparatively poor performance in almost every meaningful economic indicator. Far from it, the "north group" is a block of solvent states with clean and tidy economics that ensure prosperity for their citizens. In that sense, there exists a generic divide between our "north group" and our "south group".

The source of conflict in our case is the fact that these sets of countries attempt to coexist under the EU structure of common rules and try to jointly shape their fate. Following the *Realistic Conflict* approach, conflict arises as the groups compete over finite resources or over resources perceived as such. In the above analysis we emphasized the ability to produce and maintain wealth. Thus, conflict arises from the attempt of the groups to ensure wealth for themselves and the fact (or the perception) that obtaining wealth is a zero-sum game even inside the European space. We should mention that the cause of friction can never be one-dimensional. Other sources such as EU political predominance and social and political status on the European level are not to be overlooked. Given these, there are three possible explanations related to the *Realistic* explanatory framework; 1) the *Realistic Conflict Theory* is incapable of analyzing the EU North-South divide issue because as Forbes stressed its explanatory power is significantly reduced on the interstate level, 2) the *Realistic Conflict Theory* is inadequate for unequal status groups cases or 3) The "north group" the "south group" and the European Union have, so far, failed to bring out the superordinate goal(s) above in-group interests. Thus, regardless if one argues that the EU crisis factor unmasked or aggravated the inability of some EU states to produce and maintain wealth, the EU superordinate goal(s) did not prevail so far.

As presented in the theoretical aids part, John Duckitt's extension of the *Realistic Conflict Theory* seeks to study competition of unequal status groups, a venture the original theory did not attempt. In the present study, the "north" and "south" are the unequal status groups with the former being the dominant and the latter the subordinate one. In the compliance scenario, the underdog accepts the dominance of behavior and values of the top-dog. In the case where the underdog does not accept its subordination, the top-dog either tries to repress it or, if its claims are judged to be justified, is allowed to pursue change. In our case, the subordinate "south group" has not, so far, questioned the value system of the dominant "north group", in a uniform and organized manner. Therefore, the non-compliance version is out of the question.

The EU North-South divide has another serious implication on the EU structure. It is not only competition per se that bitters intra-EU relations but also negative stereotypes and discrimination that are fostered by competition. The dominant group, in order to maintain its superiority constructs legitimising myths that affirm it. Legitimizing myths are *"attitudes, values, beliefs, stereotypes, and ideologies that provide moral and intellectual justification for the social practices that distribute social value within the social system."* (Sidanius & Pratto, 1999, p. 45)

Social Identity Theory Approach

Stereotypes, discrimination and prejudice interpretation though, is the key weakness of the *Realistic Conflict Theory*. The Realistic approach holds that prejudice and discrimination are the result of competition over resources. Consequently, if there is no intergroup competition there should be no prejudice and discrimination (Whitley & Kite, 2010, p. 329). It is then quite problematic to explain the diachronic existence of stereotypes between the European north and south. The *Realistic Conflict Approach* fails to answer the question, why in times of no competition or in times where the superordinate goal(s) prevail, stereotypes persist. Research conducted by Optem S.A.R.L. for the European Commission in 2001—a time of European euphoria—suggested that the North–South divide had deepened during the last 15 years, the feeling of "Europeanness" had been diluted in the northern countries and, in the countries of southern Europe the attraction for the northern values of modernity and organisation had faded. Moreover, while the report sees a widespread feeling of empathy among Europeans based on common roots, people in Finland, Germany and Ireland do not feel strongly about these cultural ties. One step further, discussants from Denmark, the Netherlands, Sweden and the UK, show high in-group favoritism as they hold the belief that their societal models are superior and that their countries have developed with their own values. Based on that, there is a weak propensity to share with others, who tend to be seen as a threat. In these countries empathy for other Europeans is weak. Particularly those from the South are seen as having a very different mentality and are even quite overtly despised for not being responsible, hard-working, orderly, etc. (Debomy, 2001, pp. 5, 6)

The weakness of the *Realistic Conflict Theory* is one of the strong points for the *Social Identity Theory*. According to the latter approach, the sense of belonging to an in-group creates more positive perceptions towards it and less positive ones towards the out-group (Whitley & Kite , 2010, p. 330). Based on this, the *Social Identity Theory* bears that awareness of belonging to and social identification with a group is, under certain conditions, enough to foster discrimination and consequently lead to competition. Thus, *Social Identity Theory* would suggest that existing stereotypes and prejudice are strengthened and brought to the surface by the circumstances of competition or friction. Dichotomisation through positive in-group perceptions and negative out-group stereotypes feed and are fed by inter-group antagonism. A mutually accepted distribution of resources and a possible amelioration of intergroup relations would not mean immediate retreat of prejudice and stereotypes. Negative perceptions can remain latent until another stimulus resurfaces them.

Perceived Prosperity Data

Apart from the hard data, there exist sociological indices that picture the aspects of satisfaction, happiness and perceived prosperity of the peoples. These indices based on individual self-reports may not be objective in a strictly positivist sense but they can offer a view of the human sentiment and perceived well-being. As, more than often, behavior is determined by the perception of reality rather than reality itself[2], these indicators are very important for understanding socio-political behavior. After all, everyday experience often shows that prosperity does not always cover the psychological needs necessary for happiness. Contrarily, in many instances it is either supplementary or not closely attached to perceived happiness.[3] The *OECD index on Life Satisfaction* is based on the evaluation of general satisfaction with life on a scale from 0 to

---

[2] Kenneth Ewart Boulding, in his work *National Images and International Systems* (1959, p. 120) suggests that, "*it is always the image not the truth that immediately determines behaviour. We act according to the way the world appears to us, not necessarily according to the way it "is"*".

[3] Measuring or assessing happiness in social science is a vast topic. An alternative to the traditional tools is the *Gross National Happiness (GNP)* concept and philosophy that shifts attention away from the economic perspective towards spiritual values. (For more information see: http://www.grossnationalhappiness.com)

10 while the Quality of Support Network on data evaluating the quality of social network support. The *World Happiness Report* is based on data of the Gallup World Poll, the World Values Survey / European Values Survey and the European Social Survey. The *World Happiness Report* indicators attempt to take into account both momentary assessment and remembered affect so that both experiencing and remembering are considered.[4] Finally, the *World Database of Happiness* data on "Happiness by Country" are based on the question; "Taking all together, how satisfied or dissatisfied are you with your life-as-a-whole these days?" (Veenhoven, 201?).

Diagram 10, which is based on the OECD Better Life Index, shows that the people of the "north group" show a high level of overall life satisfaction[5] on the 0 to 10 scale unlike the "south group" that scores low with Greece and Portugal below 6.

Diagram 10

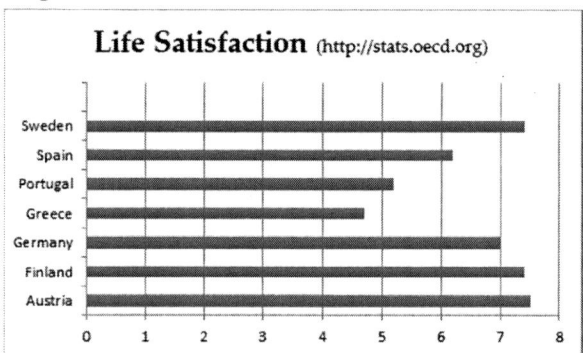

Diagram 11 drawn from the World Happiness Report (Helliwell, Layard, & Sachs, 2012, pp. 36, 37) shows a similar pattern on Average Life Satisfaction[6] with only Spain from the "South group" surpassing Germany of the "North group".

---

[4] For a detailed analysis of the data used see the *World Happiness Report* p.11–22
[5] Life satisfaction measures how people evaluate their life as a whole rather than their current feelings. It captures a reflective assessment of which life circumstances and conditions are important for subjective well-being.
[6] The life satisfaction question in the European Social Survey and the World Values Survey asks "All things considered, how satisfied are you with your life as a whole nowadays?" (on a 0 to 10 scale).

Diagram 11

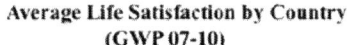
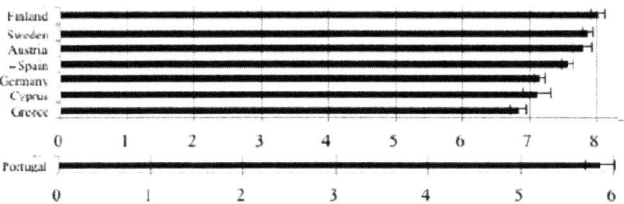

Source: World Happiness Report pp. 36–37

In the same report the European Social Survey data on Average Life Satisfaction show a rather mixed image that does not demonstrate any clear distinction between the countries of the two groups (Diagram 12). The same stands for, Average Happiness with life as a whole[7] (Diagram 13) (Helliwell, Layard, & Sachs, 2012, pp. 40, 41).

Diagram 12

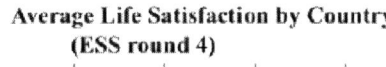
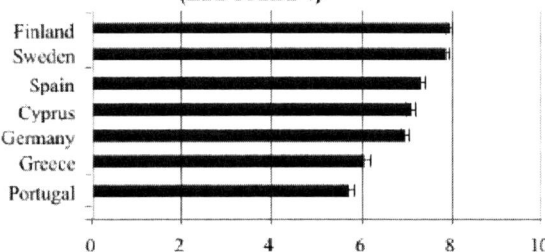

Source: World Happiness Report pp. 40

Diagram 13

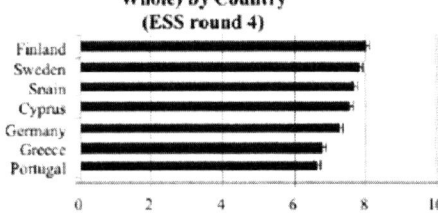

Source: World Happiness Report pp. 41

---

[7] For the Happiness measures, data from several years are combined, so that the sample size is several thousand for most countries. The large sample size, coupled with the fact that the year-to-year changes in happiness averages are small relative to the inter-country differences, means that it is possible to establish many significant inter-country differences.

The Gallup World Poll Average Happiness (yesterday) shows a gap between the two groups with only Spain and Sweden breaking the pattern (Diagram 14).

Diagram 14

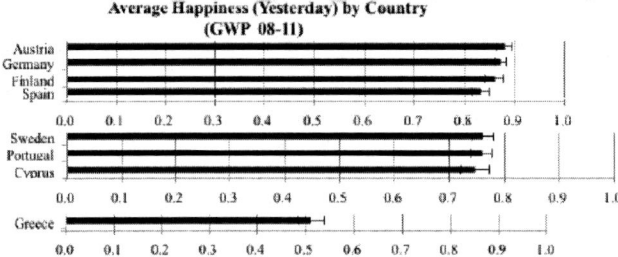

Source: World Happiness Report pp.44–46

The north-south contrast is obvious in the World Database of Happiness data (Diagrams 15 and 16). Not only the north group historically holds a higher average happiness but also the effect of the EU crisis is obvious in the south countries. Data indicate that 2009–2010 is a mark that signals a downward trend for the "south group" countries. On the contrary, the "north group" countries remain unaffected by the EU crisis.

Diagram 15

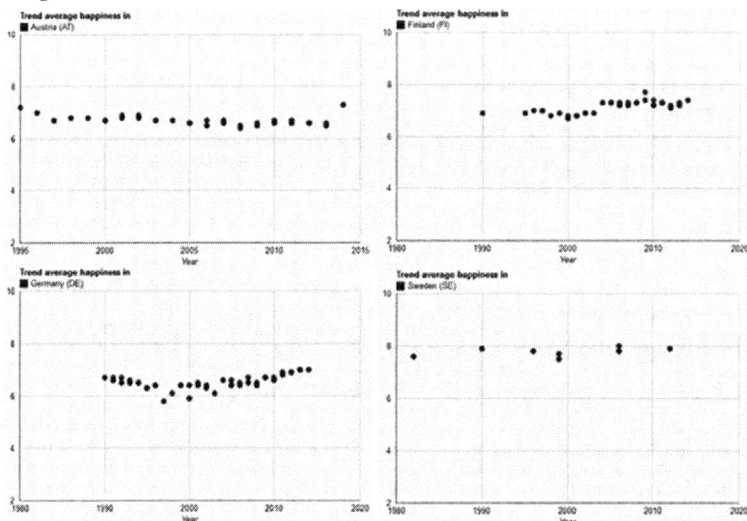

Source: World Database of Happiness http://worlddatabaseofhappiness.eur.nl/

Diagram 16

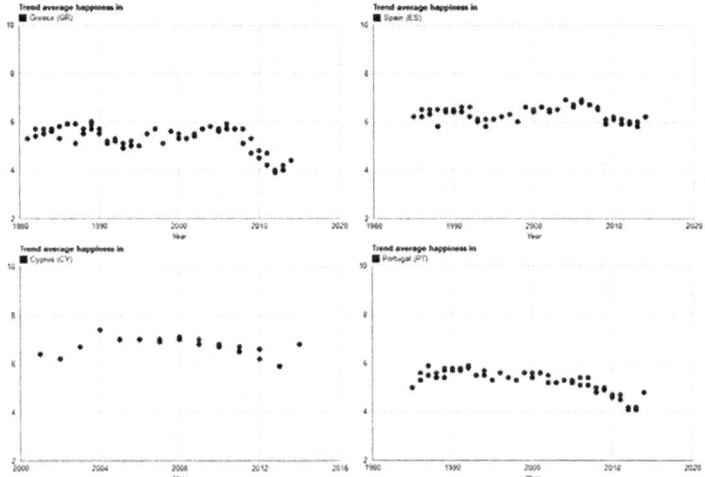

Source: World Database of Happiness http://worlddatabaseofhappiness.eur.nl/

The Average Positive Affect also shows mixed results for the group members (Diagram 17). Significant here, is the increasing gaps as we move from countries with higher to ones with lower positive affect.

Diagram 17

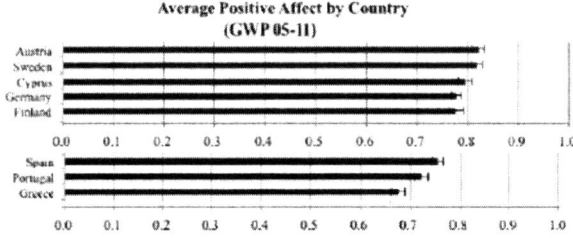

Source: World Happiness Report pp. 47, 48

The Average Negative Affect table though (Diagrams 18) demonstrates a clear distinction between the "north" and the "south group". Not only the "north group" countries have a higher average but also the "south group" is strikingly low apart from Greece.

Diagram 18

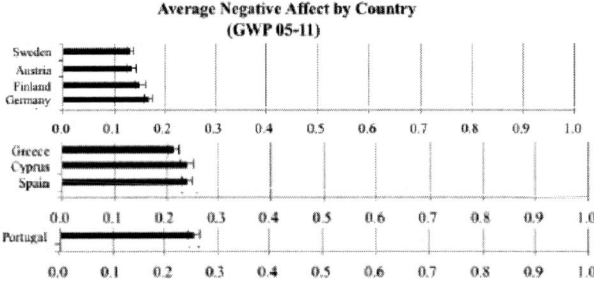

Source: World Happiness Report pp. 50–52

The same goes for the Average Net Affect where the "north" countries have higher and the "south" lower average (Diagram 19).

Diagram 19

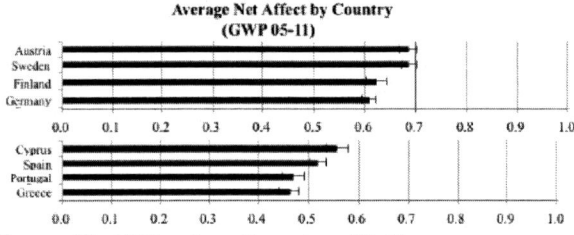

Source: World Happiness Report pp. 53–55

Finally, the Quality of Support Network data[8] (Diagram 20) do not support the divide hypothesis. Only Greece scores significantly lower than the other countries (68)

Diagram 20

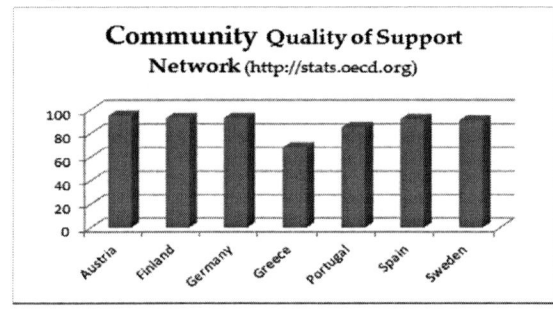

---

[8] The Quality of Support Network / Community / Social Network data are important determinants of well-being since they attempt to illustrate the frequency of contact with others, the quality of personal relationships and the degree of social isolation. Social association is associated with a higher average level of positive feelings and a lower average level of negative feelings.

Social Identity Theory, Positive Distinctiveness and the North-South Divide

As seen in the theoretical aid part, *Social Identity Theory* bears that in the case of low status groups, there are two types of reactions for the disadvantaged group members in their search for positive distinctiveness; social mobility, if the society permits it or social change where the group attempts to change its status through group effort. In our case, members of the "south group" have chosen the individual mobility path by migrating either to EU or to non-EU countries in order to achieve their objective (prosperity and wealth) or their subjective (life satisfaction and personal / family happiness) goals. Individual mobility offers people the opportunity to move to another group that better suits their needs when the societal context is flexible or permeable. In the social change category, two group reactions are possible; social creativity and social competition. The social creativity path offers the group members the opportunity to increase their positive distinctiveness without changing the resources of the groups involved in the strife. This may be achieved by adjusting group comparison; the disadvantaged in-group members may choose some new attribute for inter-group comparison (i.e. no northerner could endure the austerity imposed on southerners) or may choose a whole different out-group to compare with (our countries may perform badly compared to EU states but on a global level things are not bad at all). Finally, social competition is the strategy chosen when conditions are inflexible and consists of direct competition with the out-group and in-group favoritism. Since the eruption of the EU crisis, the individual mobility strategy has been largely applied by members of the "south group" (Diagram 21). On the contrary group, social change efforts have not been applied by the "south group" countries, at least not in an organized, noteworthy manner.

Diagram 21

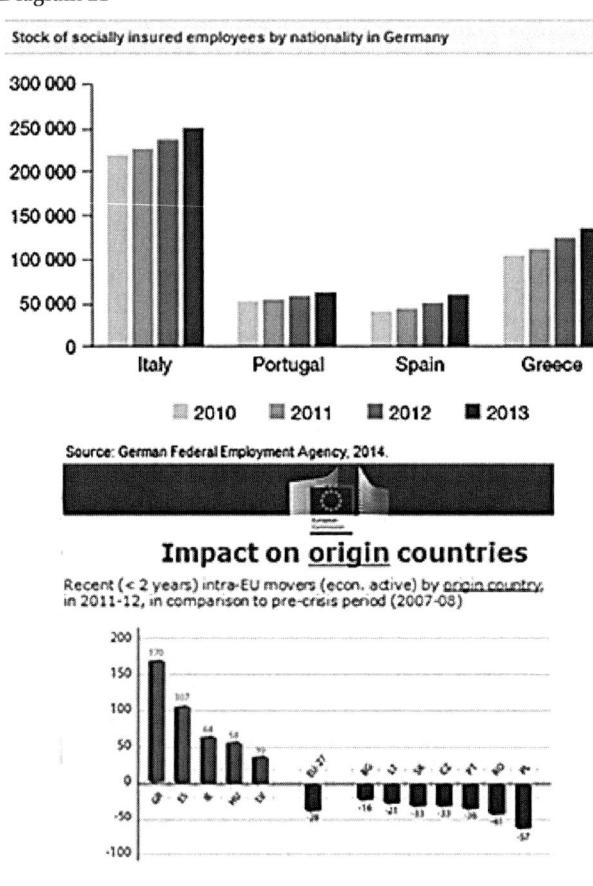

Source: (Barslund & Busse, 2014)

Conclusions

Realistic Conflict and Social Identity; EU lessons
The *Realistic Conflict* approach shows that there is a manifest pattern of a north-south divide concerning the ability to produce and maintain wealth. This is, more or less, what a *dependency* theorist would call unequal distribution of wealth. This unequal distribution, if widened by intended and unintended political acts would lead from a multi-speed Union to an economically fractured Europe. On the prejudice dimension, according to the *Realistic Conflict Theory*, the legitimizing myths created by the dominant group for the preservation of the status quo, as well as the ones constructed by the

subordinate group for the legitimization of the unfavorable reaction to the dominant group, could irreversibly harm the EU if preserved and solidified.

Social Identity Theory stresses the need to break intra-EU stereotypes and negative perceptions. Competition brings to the surface latent stereotypes and strengthens negative perceptions between "scrupulous" and "negligent" nations. On the economic aspect, the EU could attempt to bridge the north-south wealth gap through financial assistance or through development policies. On the social one, educational, training and other immaterial European policies should be continued and strengthened for fighting existing and halting new intra-EU stereotypes from growing. In any case, facing such Europe-wide issues is essential for both the material and psychological needs of the peoples of Europe to be met in a sustainable manner. The individual mobility strategy in the flexible European system is a problematic solution since it has negative implications on the sending groups / countries and also fails to deal with the needs of the EU peoples that are holders of multilevel identities.

One can argue forever on the explanatory power of the *Realistic Conflict Theory* on the wealth division during the EU crisis. What is highly problematic and calls for a solution is the hard feelings caused by the (real or perceived) wealth gap. Peoples of the "south" should not be left with feelings of harsh punishment and the ones of the "north" with a sentiment that they are paying for the lazy. This is where national governments are responsible for systematically building legitimizing myths (distorted images) in order to maintain political approval for their decisions. Regarding the decision-makers, one may argue that in the democratic regimes, the elites cannot diverge too much from the image held by the people because such a move is costly in support and power (Boulding, 1959, pp. 121, 122). However, decision-makers have also the ability to manipulate the images. This strategy is often supported by canalized information that is intentionally or unintentionally reproduced by the mass media. One step further, the media, having their own agenda, promote images that are stereotypical, caricatured, unreal and even overtly hostile towards the "other". In this case, where the decision-makers walk a tightrope by trying to balance two fronts, the domestic and the EU one, national media complicate things by evoking introvert, nationalistic, in-group favoritism.[9]

Leaderships of EU states have persistently applied their demonising rhetoric to justify unpopular political decisions. The media all across Europe, ignoring the magnitude of the European crisis, promote the "us" versus "them" viewpoint in its bluntest and cheapest form, just to serve their own aspirations. Thereby, we have politicians and media that foster the narratives that the iron-hearted northerners have imposed suffering upon the poor southerners and, on the other hand, that the lazy southerners misspend the money of the law-abiding northerners while laughing at them.

By throwing the *Social Identity Theory* into the equation, we see stereotypes originating from the lack of positive distinctiveness and stereotypes coming to the

---

[9] A fine example of the contribution of the national media to the building of negative stereotypes and bleak political atmosphere is the German-Greek case throughout the European crisis and in specific times of crucial political instances. For more information on the specific issue see specific chapters in the current volume

surface because of the wealth divide. Despite the differentiation from the *Realistic Conflict Theory* on the origin of stereotypes, a *Social Identity* application would suggest the bridging of both the material and psychological needs gap, as mentioned above.

All in all, EU peoples should not be left with the impression of a zero-sum game between "north" and "south" rivals over limited resources. Not because people should love each other at any cost, but because such a viewpoint is in contrast to the fundamental values of the EU. The EU was not meant to be, and is not, up to now, a zero-sum game. It is a group of states struggling for a win-win community. Even if the superordinate goal(s) of the *Realistic Conflict Theory* seem pale, the main game in the EU, more than any other supranational union, remains dialogue, consensus and common solutions.

Ideological Divide?

A class struggle hypothesis could also derive from the dependency theory approach. The 2014 European Parliament Elections that could be considered an indicator of the crisis-stricken EU political reality does not show a clear cleavage between northern and southern citizens, at least not in the Lipset-Rokkan[10] sense of the division of voters. The majorities of the two of the four northern countries voted for the European People's Party (EPP) candidates (Austria and Germany) while the others voted for the Alliance of Liberals and Democrats for Europe (ALDE) and the Progressive Alliance of Socialists and Democrats (S&D) parties (Finland[11] and Sweden respectively). As for the south, Cyprus and Spain chose the EPP while Greece voted for European United Left / Nordic Green Left (GUE / NGL) and Portugal for the S&D (European Parliament).

Towards a Sustainable European Reality; the Need for Prosperity and Identity

The European Union holds outstanding achievements for its members-states and its citizens. Under a common European vision and a set of tangible superordinate goals, the EU member-states can benefit significantly from their joint course. However, given the impact of the crisis, a sustainable future for the EU should include the addressing of two burning issues in dynamic manner; the issue of the living standards and wealth gap and the matter of group identity and group positive distinctiveness. The first one creates disparities between peoples and promotes actual economic imbalance and feelings of inequality. These facts undermine the EU superordinate goals and bring competition to the surface. The second boosts negative intergroup perceptions, stereotypes and prejudice and turns group members to in-group favoritism, introversion and radical

---

[10] According to Seymour Martin Lipset and Stein Rokkan, there are some main cleavages (Center-Periphery, Owner-Worker, State-Church and Land-Industry) that emerged after the Industrial Revolution and determine all post-1920s European parties.

[11] In Finland the majority party in the 2014 EP Elections was the *Kansallinen Kokoomus* that belongs to the EPP. Yet, the European the political group that earned the most seats (4) was ALDE. In addition, the sum of the two parties that belong to the ALDE group - the *Suomen Keskusta* and the *Svenska folkpartiet (Ruotsalainen kansanpuolue)* - earned the 26.5% of the votes combined, while the *Kansallinen Kokoomus* the 22.6%. The article does not intend to misquote the victory of the *Kansallinen Kokoomus*. It rather attempts to illustrate the political and ideological preferences of the majority of the voters in the particular election.

political choices. It is in the hands of the EU and its members to stress the importance of the superordinate goals, regional otherness and European commonality in order to overcome these hurdles towards a deeper and wider Europe.

References

Barslund, M., and Busse, M. (2014, May / June). Too Much or Too Little Labour Mobility? State of Play and Policy Issues. *Intereconomics: Review of European Economic Policy, 49*(3). Retrieved from http://www.intereconomics.eu/archive/year/2014/3/labour-mobility-in-the-eu-dynamics-patterns-and-policies/

Blanchet, A., and Trognon, A. (1997). *Ψυχολογία Ομάδων - La Psychologie des Groupes.* Αθήνα: Εκδοσεις Σαββάλα.

Boulding, E. K. (1959, June). National Images and International Systems. *The Journal of Conflict Resolution, 3*(2).

Debomy, D. (2001). *Perceptions of the European Union A Qualitative Study of the Public's Attitudes to and Expectations of the EU in the 15 Member States and in 9 Candidate Countries.* Gambais: OPTEM S.A.R.L.

European Parliament. (n.d.). Retrieved December 2014, from http://www.europarl.europa.eu: http://www.europarl.europa.eu/elections2014-results/en/country-introduction-2014.html

Forbes, H. D. (1997). *Ethnic Conflict: Commerce, Culture and the Contact Hypothesis.* New Haven: Yale University Press.

Helliwell, J., Layard, R., and Sachs, J. (2012). *World Happiness Report.* The Earth Institute Columbia University.

Sidanius, J., and Pratto, F. (1999). *Social dominance: An intergroup theory of social hierarchy and oppression.* New York: Cambridge University Press.

Simon, B. (2004). *Identity in Modern Society: A Social Psychological Perspective.* Malden, Oxford, Victoria: Blackwell Publishing Limited.

Tajfel, H. and Turner, C. J. (1986). The Social Identity Theory of Intergroup Behavior. In S. W. (eds.), *Psychology of Intergroup Relations.* Chigago: Nelson-Hall.

Tajfel, H., Billig, M. G., Bundy, R. P. and Flamant, C. (1971). Social Categorization and Intergroup Behaviour. *European Journal of Social Psychology, 1*(2), 149–178.

Turner, J. C. (1999). Some Current Issues in Research on Social Identity and Self-categorization Theories. In N. Ellemers, R. Spears, & B. Doosje, *Social Identity* (pp. 6–34). Oxford, Massachusetts: Blackwell Publishers Ltd.

Valentim, J. P. (2010). Sherif's Theoretical Concepts and Intergroup Relations Studies: Notes for a Positive Interdependence. *Psychologica, 2*(52), 585–598.

Veenhoven, R. (201?). *Happiness in Nations*. Erasmus University Rotterdam. Rotterdam, The Netherlands: World Database of Happiness,. Retrieved from http://worlddatabaseofhappiness.eur.nl/index.html

Whitley, B. E., & Kite, M. E. (2010). *The Psychology of Prejudice and Discrimination (2nd Edition)*. Belmont, CA: Wadsworth Cengage Learning.

EU's Discourse 'Invisibility' on Social Europe and the European Social Model. Exploring New Legitimacy and Validity from a New Public Discourse Perspective in the Post-Economic Crisis Period

VASSILIKI DELLI

Promoting 'Social Europe' through the European Social Model (ESM) as an essential counterweight to the economic orientation of the European Union project constitutes an important objective for the EU, one that is re-emerging nowadays, following the crisis and its severe repercussions. Yet, there has always been a polysemy and ambiguity on what composes the concepts of Social Europe and the ESM which has often resulted in their 'invisibility' or poor understanding by the European citizens. In this article, I attempt to distinguish the different meanings that Social Europe and the ESM have acquired in the scientific and political discourse in Europe and argue that their polysemy can be explained both at a political and discourse level. Using the principles of post-structuralist discourse analysis (Foucault, Laclau and Mouffe) this article will extend the literature on the European social agenda and explore the resulting social discourse in 'early Europe' and during the Lisbon Strategy Process. I conclude by arguing that in order to increase 'visibility' especially in the post-crisis era, Social Europe must reinforce political legitimacy and encourage democratic participation of European people.

Vassiliki Delli is a PhD candidate in the department of Philosophy, Pedagogy & Psychology of the University of Athens

Keywords: Social Europe; European Social Model; Invisibility; Political legitimacy; Discourse theory

Editors' Note

For many thinkers and practitioners, the *European Social Model* is one of the adhesive elements of the European Union and could constitute one of the main visions that would boost European integration of states and peoples. Since there is no pan-European social model and because of the broad and general sense of the common social model characteristics shared by EU states, social policies related to it differ from state to state. Hence, the lack of a tight social vision and the state differences result in a vague, ambiguous concept of what the European Social Model is. The *European Social Model*, along with the kindred *Social Europe* concept, has re-emerged in the political and academic agenda due to the developments caused by the EU crisis on the societal level. In this chapter, Vassiliki Delli attempts a post-positivist analysis of this European-wide nebulous issue. According to Delli, ambiguity and polysemy of the concepts have to be approached from both a political and a discourse level. Delli suggests that Social Model and Social Europe should be transformed into a more coherent whole by increasing political legitimacy through bottom-up approaches and by encouraging and enhancing democratic participation.

Introduction

Mapping the Impact of the Crisis on Political and Social Europe: 'Fragmented' Concepts or 'Invisible' Discourse?

Half a century after the EU was formed, the very nature of its constitution and the values that govern its development trigger unceasing political debates and doubt[1]. Lacking a unanimous conclusion about what the European Union is, the anguished yet still constructive impetus to the 'end' of the European project was intercepted by an undisputable reality; Europe was faced with an almost 'epidemic' type of crisis: economic, social, political and, for many scholars, deeply existential. The European Union has entered a grave, ongoing, crisis whose impact became evident early enough but whose definition and roots still grasp analysts' attention and remain a matter of contention, thus, rendering the early post-crisis discourse even more intense.

Along with the skepticism that the crisis brought about and its long-discussed economic implications, it directly or indirectly shifts the focus to the organic concerns about the EU's political and social constitution, both at an institutional and discourse level. Unfortunately, the crisis seemed to reinforce the idea that the EU remains "a political conundrum both as to what it is about and what it should do", especially in times of hurdles (Williams 2010: 2). In line with many observers, rather than creating another potentially exclusionary identity, what Europe calls for in the post-crisis era is "a community of responsibility" (Esposito 2009) with a firm political model and corresponding political institutions that will enhance integration altogether. Therefore, the quest for the political identity and 'telos' (end goal) of the EU has given rise to the issue of democratic legitimacy and the legitimization of the European governance anew.

New 'politicization' of the European project emerges as a primary impulse in the post-crisis period. However, along with a new political orientation, the need for a new 'socialization' of Europe follows, once more at both an institutional and discourse level. While the economic and financial crisis has created serious concerns about the EU's political route, one of its positive effects has been to increase awareness of the important role that social policy in general and social protection systems in particular can play as economic stabilizers. This in turn has underlined the need to address the tensions between economic, employment and social objectives towards a more sustainable approach in the future. For many, the so-called 'trickle down' ideology that assumed that economic growth through increased competition would automatically benefit all, clearly has not worked (Frazer et al. 2010). But the truth is that levels of poverty,

---

[1] I use the term 'EU' or 'European Union' throughout this article to signify the entity that has been in existence since 1957 (the EEC Treaty signed in Rome). I mention the term 'European Community' where that particular term relates to a specific time and event.

inequality and social exclusion in the EU stood at high levels even prior to the crisis. The challenges of the ageing population of Europe and the effects of increased mobility and diversity were seen to have serious social consequences already putting economic progress at risk and undermining social cohesion (Frazer et al. 2010). Indeed, the crisis aggravated the concerns held by many EU citizens that the EU's 'primarily economic' project has not been beneficial to them and that it may be endangering the social standards they were aspiring to (Frazer et al. 2010). In a different context, Social Europe was characterized as inadequate due to its fragmentary and, for many, 'invisible' social provisions or its non-transparent and complex agenda. Once more, what was called into question was the political support for the Union and, therefore, its democratic legitimacy.

As an essential component of 'Social Europe', the European Social Model (ESM) constitutes 'a social and political construct' promoted by the EU institutions to deal with the diverse socioeconomic challenges of the European route (Demertzis 2010; Jepsen, Pascual 2006). Social actors' awareness of the need to reinforce the supranational dimension of social cohesion has gradually turned the ESM into a 'conceptual tool' or a 'catch-all' concept in the various debates on social responses to globalization (Jepsen, Pascual 2006). As a result, its content, references and uses vary greatly in the socioeconomic history of the Union. Equally then, the ESM appears to have a polysemous nature while a clear definition of what constitutes its essence remains ambiguous. Furthermore, insofar as definitions are to be found in the relevant literature, the ones provided do not necessarily converge despite the fact that EU continues to reiterate its commitment to the ESM even today (Jepsen, Pascual 2006; Yfantopoulos 2007; Moreau 2011).

Is the polysemy surrounding 'Social Europe' then, (i.e. the social policies, their coordination and implementation and the ESM) a reflection of the lack of scientific precision or continuity in EU's social plan and social discourse? Is there a 'patchwork' in the European social agenda with its incoherence to blame for the probable 'fragmentary' and impenetrable effect of social Europe on its people? What is being done in the early post-crisis era in order to render social Europe more 'visible' to contemporary Europeans?

In what follows, I will explore the ambiguous and contested concept of 'Social Europe' in a political and rhetorical framework, venturing to show that its construction is indeed the outcome of a blend of several meanings the concept has acquired in European, scientific and public discourse. Furthermore, this paper attempts to demonstrate that 'Social Europe' is the result of a *social practice* (Foucault 1985) where the rules of formation are modified following *social antagonisms* (Mouffe 1993 / 2005) in line with the main principles of post-structuralist discourse theory. By tracing the EU's social agenda in the past two decades and in the current, early post-crisis period, my aim is to address its assumed 'invisibility' and put forward the imperative of political legitimacy as probably the most important means to give 'Social Europe' new impetus and validity.

Methodological Framework: Discourse Analysis and Post-Structuralist Theory

Underlying the word 'discourse' is the general idea that language is structured according to the different patterns that people's utterances follow when they take part in different domains of social life, typical examples being 'medical discourse' and 'political discourse'. 'Discourse' is defined as a "particular way of talking about and understanding the world (or an aspect of the world)" (Jørgensen, Phillips 2002: 1). Hence, 'discourse analysis' emerges as the analysis of these patterns (Jørgensen, Phillips 2002). In particular, social constructionist discourse analysis shares the starting point that our ways of talking do not neutrally reflect our world, identities and social relations but rather play an active role in creating and changing them. The key premises of social constructionism are found in French post-structuralist theory and its rejection of totalizing and universalizing theories such as Marxism and psychoanalysis. Thus, social constructionism is understood as a broader category of which post structuralism is a subcategory (Jørgensen, Phillips 2002: 6). In this article, I put forward Laclau and Mouffe's discourse theory as one of the three approaches to social constructionist discourse analysis, along with critical discourse analysis (CDA) and discursive psychology. Discourse theory aims at an understanding of the *social* as a 'discursive construction' whereby, in principle, all social phenomena can be analyzed using discourse analytical tools. The overall idea of discourse theory is that social phenomena are never finished or total. Meaning can never be ultimately fixed and this admittance opens up the way for constant social struggles about definitions of society and identity, with resulting social constructions and social effects (Jørgensen, Phillips 2002: 24).

My discourse analysis approach is also built on Foucault's postulations that adhere to the general social constructionist premise that knowledge is not just a reflection of reality (Jørgensen, Phillips 2002). According to Foucault, truth is a discursive construction and different regimes of knowledge determine what is true and false. Foucault's perspective focuses on the investigation of the structure of different regimes of knowledge—that is the rules for what can and cannot be said and the rules for what is considered to be true and false. Contemporary discourse theories follow Foucault's conception of discourse as "relatively rule-bound sets of statements which impose limits on what gives meaning" (Jørgensen, Phillips 2002:13). They also build on his ideas about truth being something which is, at least to a large extent, created discursively. For Foucault, in common with discourse, power does not belong to particular agents or individuals; rather is spread across different 'social practices'. Thus, power is responsible for creating our social world and for the particular ways in which the world is formed and can be talked about, ruling out alternative ways of being and talking (Jørgensen, Phillips 2002: 13–14). Accordingly, power becomes both a productive and a constraining force. Foucault's conception of power is adhered to by Laclau and Mouffe's discourse theory. However, their theory diverges from Foucault's tendency to identify only one knowledge regime in each historical period. In their approach, a more "conflictual picture" is operating in which "different discourses exist side by side or struggle for the right to define truth" (Jørgensen, Phillips 2002: 13–14). Laclau and Mouffe further develop and radicalize Gramsci's theory of hegemony by abolishing the objectivism and essentialism found in him. For the two theorists, "there are no objective laws that divide society into particular groups; the groups that exist are always created in political, discursive processes" (Jørgensen, Phillips 2002:33).Their theory is based on "an idealist social ontology which emphasizes that all social and natural phenomena acquire meaning through discourse" (Montessori 2011:172).

Exploring the Polysemous Nature of Social Europe and the ESM
The use of 'Social Europe' and ESM in academic and political debate is characterized by two main and interconnected features; on one hand, the assumption, usually taken-for-granted, of the reality status of the concept; on the other hand, its highly diverse nature. 'Social Europe' is therefore articulated by differing meanings with rather ambiguous definitions (Jepsen, Pascual 2006). On embarking to explore this polysemy, at least two distinct meanings that are meant to provide a definition for 'Social Europe' and illuminate its composite discourse can be discerned.

First, Social Europe designates an area of EU policies. The main issues in this area are related to social cohesion, social inclusion and poverty, combating unemployment and ensuring quality of work, health and gender equality. These policies are mainly the responsibility of the European Commission's Directorate General for Employment, Social Affairs and Equal Opportunities but they are directly linked with many other areas of European action, including education, training and lifelong learning (Rasmussen et al. 2004).

Secondly and in a broader sense, the ESM and 'Social Europe' are used to designate qualities of social life and welfare that the EU has always strived to guarantee in direct contrast to other parts of the world and particularly the United States. These qualities are often promoted by the EU discourse itself as an alternative to pure-market form of capitalism. However, as the relative literature demonstrates, their character is neither clear nor consistent since the national systems and traditions of the welfare in the member states differ widely and vary in the course of time (Rasmussen et al. 2004). What is more, the constructed dichotomy between US and European welfare has created "two rhetorical contrasting poles which trap the research within a fixed analytical framework" (Abélès 2002; Alber 2010). It is often assumed that the US social model is the negative reference pole versus the hypothetically superior EU social model, a discrimination that sets the boundaries within which differences are constructed and thus may inhibit impartial and truthful thinking on the subject (Alber 2010; Jepsen, Pascual 2006).

Imprecision and ambiguity can be said to exist in the core of 'Social Europe', namely the ESM, despite long years of discussion in academic and political circles. For many scholars, the ESM represents the EU's venture to promote economic growth and social cohesion simultaneously. The basic idea that underlies its content is that economic and social progress must go hand in hand if the European project is to be sustainable at present and in the future (Jepsen, Pascual 2006). Towards illustrating this concept, the definitions that have been provided by scholars can be summarized into three, though not mutually exclusive, categories (Jepsen, Pascual 2006).

In the first group of definitions, the ESM is considered "the model that incorporates certain common features, i.e. institutions and values that are inherent in the status quo of the EU member states and are perceived as enabling a distinctive mode of regulation as well as a distinctive competition regime" (Jepsen, Pascual 2006: 26–27). In this context, the ESM is described as a specific common European aim, an entity, geared to the achievement of full employment, adequate social protection and equality, suggesting a normative approach within the EU construction.

A second conceptual approach establishes the ESM as "being enshrined in a variety of different national models, some of which are put forward as good examples" (Jepsen, Pascual 2006: 28). More specifically, in search of the ideal European social model, the United Kingdom, Sweden and Germany pose socially ideal organizational and administrative patterns, hence, the 'Anglo-Saxon model', the 'Scandinavian model' and the 'Continental model' respectively. These constitute paradigm cases along with certain countries (e.g. Denmark, Austria and the Netherlands) whose social security policy becomes a role-model towards combining economic efficiency with social justice. Esping – Andersen (1990) is an advocate of this approach. Other scholars illustrate the key features of the ideal model by proposing extensive social security for all citizens, a high degree of interest organization along with coordinated bargaining and a more equal wage and income distribution compared to other parts of the world (Ferrera et al. 2001). Far from acquiring any single best institutional model, Ebbinghaus (1999) calls for a 'European social landscape' by identifying four groups of welfare state; the 'Nordic model', the 'Anglo-Saxon model', 'Europe's Centre model' and the 'Southern model'. For him, 'unity' in combination with 'diversity' will result in an ideal social model.

The third way of identifying the ESM is by perceiving it as a 'European project' and a "tool for modernization or adaptation to changing economic conditions as well as an instrument for cohesiveness with a view to enlargement" (Jepsen, Pascual 2006: 26). The latter, frames the ESM as a dynamic and evolving model which is affected by both national and European forces and processes. The focus in this strand of literature is on the development of a distinctive "transnational model", since for one single country to conduct its own individual social policy can no longer be regarded as viable (Vaughan-Whitehead 2003; Wilding 1997). Alternatively, the ESM may be described as a set of values, principles and methods encapsulated in three essential principles: the recognition of social justice as a policy target; the acknowledgment of the productive role of social policy and its contribution to economic efficiency; and, lastly, the encouragement of bargaining between the social partners (Amitsis et al. 2003). The reduction of the ESM to three universal principles signifies that a normative definition for the ESM has not been attained and that its content is rather contested, dependent on the reactions to the changes affecting the socioeconomic and demographic structures of the EU in general (Amitsis et al. 2003).

Social Europe as an 'Empty Signifier'

A different effort to define 'Social Europe' -prior to and after the crisis- and help dissolve its ambiguity can be obtained by the tools of discourse theory. In its principles, social and political life acquires its meaning via discourse, especially through the articulation of meaning and identities. The process of establishing meaning is thus a political process, entangled by pluralism and struggles for power (Mouffe 1993 / 2005).

Following this line of thought, a fourth distinctive way 'Social Europe' is being discussed in the relevant literature resembles the notion of an 'empty signifier'. Laclau and Mouffe (1985) suggest that 'empty signifiers' are signifiers without a particular signified. For instance, the concepts of 'nationalism' or 'democracy' may serve as examples of 'empty signifiers' (Montessori 2011). Due to their empty character, that is their lack of a direct observable relation to a particular signified, these notions represent an absent and transcendent totality, one that can never be fully captured or obtained. Therefore, because of their necessary emptiness, they can unite a series of different discourses in a chain of equivalence[2]. As a result, different groups can identify in their own particular ways with a universal demand.

In a discourse analysis perspective, 'Social Europe' is the social field that can never be 'congested' or 'closed' wherein several political or non-political practices attempt to fill this 'lack of closure' (Howarth, Stavrakakis 2000). In the logic of 'discursive structuration', diverse political forces may compete in their efforts to present themselves as particularly well-positioned to fill in the 'lack of closure'. For discourse theory, their effort is to *hegemonize* a notion by carrying out this function (Howarth, Stavrakakis 2000; Montessori 2011).

The political discourse of 'Social Europe' seems to take place around the 'empty signifier' it constitutes in the course of time. Indeed, various political and intellectual actors, not least socialist parties and trade unions, venture to indicate the qualities they strive to realize in the EU by identifying with the demand of Social Europe. These actors emphasize social equality, solidarity and the elimination of poverty, along with other traditional social values as part of their vision for Europe, thus opposing the neo-liberalist trajectory that the EU has acquired. Their aim is to offer alternatives to the strict economic and competitive character that Europe encapsulates at present (Rasmussen et al. 2004). Hence, they try to gain acceptance for their particular meaning and succeed in fixing it. In line with discourse theory, charging the empty signifier of 'Social Europe' with their own meaning will gain hegemony for them.

In a similar pattern, the effort to hegemonize the social discourse comes via other actors as well; in the form of various publications, such as the journal with the suggestive title 'Social Europe' published by a group of intellectuals and socialist politicians, and the impressive number of books written as 'a continent's answer to market fundamentalism' (Rasmussen et al. 2004). Additionally, several online blogs, fora

---

[2] According to Laclau and Mouffe, different discourses offer different content to fill an 'empty signifier'. This takes place through "the linking together of signifiers in *chains of equivalence* that establish the identity relationally" (Jørgensen, Phillips 2002: 43).

and academics' voices are trying to charge the empty signifier of 'Social Europe' with their own meaning in cases when new or differing 'socialization' for Europe becomes a question (e.g. OpenDemocracy.net and blogs.lse.ac.uk).

The polysemy that 'Social Europe' puts forward can be thus explained when one tries to classify the meanings it acquires and interpret its 'fluid' and rather 'invisible' nature, especially in the fourth conceptualization of 'Social Europe' as an 'empty signifier'. In that context, both Social Europe and the ESM remain to a great extent political projects that re-emerge and call for adaptation of their content depending on the economic and social circumstances. Consequently, they are able to trigger discourse that often causes ambiguity. However, their assumed 'floating character' is vivid evidence that both concepts have not been depoliticized and as such they are evolving within the political arena.

Before moving on to elaborate on the actual social discourse produced by the EU, the gradual steps taken by the European construction towards its 'socialization' will be considered.

Tracing 'Social Europe' in the European History and the Official EU Documents

There is no doubt that the content of 'Social Europe' and its discourse have been affected by the diverse political agenda, the political vicissitudes and attitudes that have presided over its development as well as the different phases of the European economic integration and its repercussions on the member states. In general, there are experts who, in the early 1990's, regarded the building of social Europe as an "impossible venture on account of the huge diversity in national social systems or else because of the profoundly neoliberal make-up of the EU" while others reflected that "a pattern of industrial relations similar to that in the member states might emerge at the European level" (Goetschy 2006: 49). Undoubtedly, the course of European social history has always been bumpy or has followed a trajectory different from that anticipated by social scientists or experts. In rough lines, "intergovernmentalism hampered by sovereignty and the diversity of national interests, coupled with the weakness of the treaties as a legal basis, is generally invoked to explain the lack of headway made by Social Europe" (Goetschy 2006: 49). In these early decades, the 'social dimension' of Europe is validated mainly thanks to the European Commission's capacity and its cooperation with social players, i.e. trade unions, the European Economic and Social Committee or the European Parliament (Demertzis 2010). Let us briefly review the route of Social Europe during the past decades.

The Treaty of Rome (1957) authorized the Community to act in certain situations, including the movement of labor, the equal salary for both sexes and vocational training. With a view to achieving the common market, a series of legal provisions was adopted in the 1960's and 1970's concerning freedom of movement for workers, equivalence of qualification and coordination of social security systems. In the 1970's the directives on collective redundancies (1975), transfers of undertakings (1977) and employer insolvency were adopted on the basis of Article 100 of the Treaty of Rome. Health and safety at work triggered equally a great number of directives in these years. The Single European Act (1986) instituted European social dialogue, strengthened the power of the Commission and the European Parliament and emphasized the need for economic and social cohesion. However, for many scholars the social counterpart of the economic integration in those past decades was eminently poor as social provisions were actually reflecting the 'market ethos' of the time and did not constitute real social progress (Goetschy 2006).

It was only the establishment of the large internal market planned by the Delors' Commission (1992) that triggered an in-depth reflection about the social dimension needed in order to ensure the acceptance of the enlarged market and counterbalance its harmful consequences (Venturini 1988). Moreover, the adoption of the Community Charter of Fundamental Social Rights of Workers by 11 countries, with the exception of the UK, in 1989 comprised 12 rights and a symbolic declaration that had no immediate legal impact, yet prepared the ground for the social chapter of the Maastricht Treaty (Goetschy 2006; Yfantopoulos 2007).

The Social Policy Agreement in the Maastricht Treaty (1992) was substantial to stretch the reach of Community social competence by means of extending the qualified majority voting (QMV) and initiating collective bargaining along with the possibility of negotiating European collective agreements. Undoubtedly, the Social Policy Agreement upgraded the social targets and put forward a dynamic social trajectory, despite the fact that the adoption of a large number of Community directives was restricted due to the 'subsidiarity' principle that called little or no action in cases where member states had opposing interests. Besides, even though many directives were promoted by the EU Treaty, they were described as "prescriptions" rather than carrying complete content and orientation (Goetschy 2006). On the other hand, the Structural Funds and the Cohesion Fund with their distributive nature tried to maintain the balance between the economic integration and the social policy needs of old and acceding countries.

Finally, the Amsterdam Treaty promoted regulations on the sensitive sector of employment. With 17 million unemployed citizens in 1997, the EU was compelled by public opinion to cater primarily for employment (Articles 125–130) and the elimination of discriminations (Article 13). Article 125 enabled the policy coordination of national employment policies and helped member states to undertake and implement difficult social reforms at the national level in the fields of employment, pensions, health care and social inclusion (Yfantopoulos 2007).

The Social Discourse of Early Europe; from 'Social Practice' to the Emergence of a 'Myth'

Following the first social provisions set by Europe, 'Social Europe' gradually took shape around typically European themes, such as the need for markets to operate properly or transnational social problems caused by the common and the. The majority of social directives relates to health and safety, the labor law on employment conditions and contracts, the gender equality, and finally the directives on freedom of movement. Moreover, the various social OMCs (Open Method of Coordination)[3] that were added in the field of employment, pensions, health care, and long-term care for older people constitute an important step towards policy coordination (Goetschy 2006; Yfantopoulos 2007).

Nonetheless, compared with the elements that map a national social model, the European social agenda is not a coherent entity and appears to be rather fragmented and 'invisible' as an organic set of social policies. It seems that the "European body of legislation can be regarded above all as complementary to national social laws, functioning as a minimum safety net whether it be in a patchy fashion in respect of certain inherently national matters or in relation to typically European matters not dealt with at the national level" (Goetschy 2006: 60). Along with this indiscernible 'patchwork', the different OMCs serve rather as a guide for national policy making and conduct while the non-binding social dialogue is still limited. According to Goetschy, the Community legislative output was of "highly 'cumulative' nature and becomes apparent through multiple changes in the method regulation while earlier outcomes are not called into question" (2006: 60).

Therefore, the fragmented nature of social progress made at this stage is a result of a 'top-down' approach reflected in a series of laws. Change is pursued by the European Community via mainly the treaties and the Commission, but there is neither continuity nor consistency in the nexus of those modifications. The 'market ethos' of Social Europe and a rather 'prescribed social ethos' that followed the Maastricht Treaty result in politics and respectively into social discourse that can be interpreted as a 'social practice'. This is a concept that underlies the post-structuralist discourse analysis.

Following Foucault's theory, a discourse is "the domain of all statements" (1985: 80)[4]. By focusing on the rules that govern the production of such statements, his theory supports that everything that is said and considered within a particular discourse constitutes a 'discursive formation'. However, a 'discursive formation' is not a random

---

[3] `The Open Method of Coordination (OMC) has been defined as an instrument of the Lisbon Strategy (2000). It provides a new framework for cooperation between the member states, whose national policies can thus be directed towards certain common objectives. It takes place in areas which fall within the competence of the member states, such as employment, social protection, social inclusion, education, youth and training. Depending on the areas concerned, the OMC involves so-called "soft law" measures which are binding on the member states in varying degrees but which never take the form of directives, regulations or decisions (EUROPA – Summaries of EU Legislation <http://europa.eu/legislation_summaries/glossary/open_method_coordination_en.htm.>).

[4] In his 'archaeological' phase of works, Foucault discusses discourse as follows: "We shall call discourse a group of statements in so far as they belong to the same discursive formation [...Discourse] is made up of a limited number of statements for which a group of conditions of existence can be defined. Discourse in this sense is not an ideal, timeless form [...] it is, from beginning to end, historical—a fragment of history [...] posing its own limits, its divisions, its transformations, the specific modes of its temporality" (Foucault 1985: 117). For Foucault, there is "an infinite number of ways to formulate statements but the statements that are produced within a specific domain are rather similar and repetitive. There are innumerable statements that are never uttered, and would never be accepted as meaningful. The historical rules of the particular discourse delimit what is possible to say" (Jørgensen, Phillips 2002: 13).

collection of statements but rather the result of a series of rules of formation which provide the conditions of existence, co-existence, regularities and transformations for a particular discourse (Foucault 1985; Torfing 2005). This implies that 'Social Europe' in the first decades of its building had generated rules of formation that regulated "what can be said, how it can be said, who can speak and in which name" (Torfing 2005:7). At this level, discourse is seen as a 'social practice' and the rules of formation are the result of decisions made by authorities, i.e. the Commission or the treaties as an overall outcome of research and evaluation. Considering the discourse as a 'social practice' allows us to obtain the view on the 'social dimension' of Europe as being socially constituted, historical and contingent, rather than essentialist or imperative (Montessori 2011). This implies that discourse can be contested or modified as it does eventually happen within the European social context.

The post-structuralist notions of discourse analysis permit a second characterization of "early social Europe" using the tools of Laclau and Mouffe's theory (1985). At its outset 'Social Europe' can be said to represent a 'myth'[5]. In line with this strand of discourse theory, 'myths' construct new spaces of representation that attempt to suture a 'dislocated space' (Laclau 1990: 61). Yet, dislocated spaces need not be substituted altogether since "they are not solely traumatic experiences" (Howarth, Stavrakakis 2000: 20)[6]. They have a productive side too given that "on one hand they threaten identities, on the other, they are the foundation on which new identities are constituted" thus, creating a lack at the level of meaning that stimulates new discursive constructions (Laclau 1990: 39). 'Myths'' effectiveness is therefore essentially hegemonic, as they involve the formation of "a new objectivity by means of the re-articulation of the dislocated elements" (Laclau 1990: 61). From their emergence until their dissolutions, 'myths' can function as a surface of inscription for a variety of social demands and dislocations (Howarth, Stavrakakis 2000:20). In a parallel line, the dominant economic discourse and the prevailing 'market ethos' in the 1990's, as described above, becomes the 'dislocated space' in question. On the other hand, the first efforts towards Social Europe, despite having emerged at a still fragmented level, compose a 'myth' -a new objectivity by means of the re-articulation of the dislocated elements- wherein all new social demands and imperatives are being inscribed. The end goal is to achieve a higher place in the discourse hegemony.

---

[5] Laclau (1990:61) defines 'myth' as follows: "By 'myth' we mean a space of representation which bears no relation of continuity with the dominant 'structural objectivity'. 'Myth' is thus a principle of reading of a given situation, whose terms are external to what is representable in the objective spatiality constituted by the given structure". Thus, 'myth' refers to a distorted representation of reality which is inevitable and constitutive since it establishes a necessary horizon for our acts (Jørgensen, Phillips 2002: 39-40).

[6] Howarth and Stavrakakis (2000: 20) refer to 'dislocation' as the " 'decentring' of a discursive structure though social processes such as the extension of capitalist relations to new spheres of social life that can shatter already existing identities and which literally induces an identity crisis for the subject". In short, "it is the 'failure' of the structure and the subject positions which are part of such a structure that 'compels' the subject to act, to assert anew its subjectivity in order to suture the dislocated structure"(Howarth, Stavrakakis 2000:20).

Similarly, the early ESM—established by the Commission's White paper on Social Policy (COM (94) 333)- appears as "an alternative to the logical form of the dominant structural discourse", i.e. a 'myth' (Montessori 2011: 172). It emerges as a result of reflection by Delors' cabinet and it is first articulated as a set of European values that were included in the Community Charter of the Fundamental Social Rights of Workers which were for the first time linked to the ESM (Demertzis 2010: 139). Therefore, all social demands, i.e. the commitment to democracy, individual rights, free collective bargaining, equal opportunities for all, social solidarity and welfare were expressed, articulated and inscribed on the almost 'tabula rasa' of social Europe in an effort to build a normative concept, a 'myth', and with a view to 'dislocate' the rigid economic discourse of the time and offer a social counterweight. Thus, emphasis is placed on solidarity that echoes the core-value of the Social Democratic identity along with the voices of socialists, social liberals and Christians (Demertzis 2010: 127). The aim is to put forward a 'myth' at a discourse level along with a political scheme that would discern common values for the new social discourse to be produced conversely or at least alternatively to the dominant market-oriented discourse. At this point there was not much to 'fuse' together and there were wide margins for creating ex novo in terms of social provisions. What is being prioritized is rather the establishment of a European social space to host fundamental social values and rearticulate the social route of Europe.

The Lisbon Strategy: New Logics and Promises

The advent of the new decade was fraught with 'social events', namely concrete events in the European life that dictated a new orientation in the social agenda. The tentative and somewhat experimental social Europe of the 90s was followed by a significant change in EU's discourse trajectory. Indeed, the unfolding history of globalization and rapid technological progress, on one hand, and the assumption that EU economic models needed to change to be more competitive and innovative, on the other, entailed a new political and economic horizon for the Union (Natali 2010: 94). Upon this horizon, as it will be examined in this part, the already inscribed social provisions and transformations read more consistently and coherently in order to address the economic challenges and the diverse ideological referents, thus reshaping the 'social practice' of Europe and turning it eventually into a 'social imaginary'.

Economic and political rationale of the Lisbon Strategy

Despite its eventual strong economic orientation and policies, the Lisbon strategy was primarily devised as a political project with the insight that a more consistent, integrated and balanced approach to sustainable development was needed. It was intended as a ten year coherent medium-term project aspiring to give the Union an edge over the rest of the world by making it, by 2010, "the most competitive and dynamic knowledge-based economy in the world, capable of sustainable economic growth with more and better jobs and greater social cohesion" (Lisbon European Council 2000). This new momentum for EU integration had to be based on both sustaining EU citizens' living conditions and improving EU's institutional legitimacy. Structural reforms had to be followed by a new focus on multilateralism and democratic deepening for new member states (Rodrigues 2010).

Accordingly, one of the key strategies of the Lisbon Strategy was the reform of the ESM so that it would contribute to the enhancement of economic growth and competitiveness. Hence, the European Presidency Conclusions of Lisbon (Council 2000), Feira (Council 2000b) and Nice (Council 2000c) elaborated on the 'modernization' of the ESM and spoke in favor of its mobilizing impetus to cope with new challenges, namely globalization and domestic social and economic difficulties (Demertzis 2010: 133). Such a goal of 'modernization' brought forth the view that the ESM was defined by the common challenges threatening the member states rather than by values intrinsically shared by them (Demertzis 2010: 132). One essential purpose was to drive forward socioeconomic renewal at the national level and thus promote national social reforms. In the discourse that accompanied the ESM, social protection and employment reoccur as essential components of the EU agenda. The Spring 2007 Council (Council 2007) reaffirmed the initial three sides of the Lisbon Triangle, namely growth, employment and social protection and inclusion, "...in order to ensure the continuing support for European integration by the Union's citizens, [....] the common social objectives of member states should be better taken into account within the Lisbon agenda" (§19). The Lisbon Strategy proposed the coordination of social policy as an indispensable constituent of the effort to redefine the European integration process in order to secure "structural coupling" between economic integration and the warranty for social rights, thus generating discourse consistent with high commitment to a 'Social EU' (Pochet 2006; Natali 2010).

Towards these goals, the Lisbon European Council (2000) implemented the 'Open Method of Coordination' (OMC) whose policy-making practices had come into being on the 'employment' procedure in the Amsterdam Treaty (1997). The 'new' method of regulation emphasized the non-mandatory nature of rules and enhanced flexibility and openness to various players and the rules of different social systems. The idea of the OMC was to make "further adjustments and find additional complementary aspects in relation to the normative tools, content and significance of the many and varied themes addressed" (Goetschy 2006: 61). In addition, it sought to push forward the building of social Europe by welding together coordination processes throughout national reforms of social and employment policies. Indeed, the OMC was extensively employed in order to stress the action needed towards very concrete themes: higher rates of employment and measures for job-creation, a skilled labour force, the reform of state pensions, and the reduction of social exclusion and gender discrimination (Trubek, Trubek 2003; Goetschy 2006; Natali 2010).

For many scholars, the hybrid combination of binding law and non-binding OMC regulations was fearful as 'soft law' was the putting forward of a sort of experimental governance, self-regulation, 'depoliticization' or even decentralization of policy making (Scott, Trubek 2002; Héritier 2002; Goetschy 2006). Notwithstanding these views, this move from a predominant legislative perspective—suggested and legitimized mainly by the Commission and the treaties—to a perspective of European governance of national social and employment policies signified a lot about the legitimacy of the social policies. First, the shift appears to be one from 'quantity' that characterized the 1990's to 'quality'. Instead of adopting new measures, the EU is now focusing primarily on the quality of policy implementation, addressing equally policy areas that would potentially be better coordinated with one another. Secondly, regulations were no longer created 'by default' but rather by means of sharing policy experiences and practices through the production of statistics (Eurostat), monitoring and the promotion of benchmarking via the development of a comprehensive number of indicators (Natali 2010). Additionally, the initiation of European social dialogue within the OMC enabled a plurality of actors and stakeholders (civil society, NGOs, business and trade unions) to participate in the stages of the process and take active role in the elaboration of national reports or the guidelines that had to be followed in order to draft them (Natali 2010). This participation guaranteed a 'deliberative polyarchy' that could accommodate a range of interests, the search for common solutions and the avoidance of resistance to change (Sabel, Zeitlin 2007). Therefore, this move from social legislation to public policy governance aspired to enhance the democratic legitimacy of the EU by ensuring the principles of participation, transparency and openness for the stakeholders involved.

The Lisbon Strategy Discourse as a 'Social Imaginary'; from Hegemonic Practice to Hegemonic Formation

The generated discourse on social policies during the Lisbon process demonstrates that the EU has moved beyond the stage of solely technical and market harmonization and purely regulatory policies. Eliminating its rather fragmentary nature, it has, at last, managed to share some common socially foundational features. Even though the OMC does not always guarantee the consultation and participation of stakeholders to the desired extent nor provide leverage to those stakeholders who were already in the "inner circle" of decision making (Natali 2010; Goetschy 2006), the Lisbon Strategy was indeed a revised and more coherent toolkit that constituted a new 'participatory' form of governance. It was substantial in stressing the importance of the participation of citizens in a more 'bottom-up' approach, as opposed to the 'top-down' approach of the past decades. This was a first step towards enhancing its political legitimacy, thus eliminating the 'invisibility' that would prevail in the EU's social landscape so far both as a result of its segmented agenda and the limited civic participation. Undoubtedly, social Europe at this level remains the result of multi-level tensions, i.e. an evolving process or the result of an interrelation of forces between different economic, social, geographical and institutional realities. Nonetheless, the more solid, action-oriented and coherent social policies which put forward 'crystallized' objectives and more concrete priorities, such as the boost of employment and social inclusion, have been able to affirm their hegemonic position in the social discourse.

In line with post-structuralists' conception of discourse as 'social practice', Laclau and Mouffe's theory is grounded on the ultimate impossibility of societal closure, a condition that makes articulatory practices and diverse political action possible (Howarth, Stavrakakis 2000). In order for a 'hegemonic practice' to exist, i.e. an exemplary form of political activity that involves the articulation of different identities and subjectivities into a common project, the two theorists establish two conditions: the existence of antagonistic forces; and the instability of the political frontiers that divide them (Laclau, Mouffe 1985)[7]. Therefore, all hegemonic practices presuppose a social field dominated by antagonisms that are articulated by opposed political projects. This description of 'hegemonic practice' suits the European field and the social discourse that emanated from it in the decades that preceded the Lisbon strategy process as we have showed earlier.

Via the firm re-articulation of Lisbon's social agenda however, this hegemonic practice of "early Europe" can be said to have turned into a 'hegemonic formation' which is the "outcome of a project's endeavors to create new form of social order from a variety of dispersed or dislocated elements" (Howarth, Stavrakakis 2000: 22). Although no discourse is capable of completely hegemonizing a field of discursivity[8], it can be argued that the Lisbon Strategy process has moved from merely attempting to suture the dispersed elements of the earlier discourse to creating a well-established social vision by producing a more effective and inclusive discourse in its attempt to achieve hegemony, turning now the 'myth' into a 'social imaginary'.

In Laclau's words, "when a 'myth' proves to be successful in neutralizing social dislocations and incorporating a great number of social demands, then it can be said to have been transformed into a 'social imaginary'" (1990:64). A collective social imaginary is subsequently defined as "a 'horizon' or absolute limit which structures a field of intelligibility" (Laclau 1990: 64). In other words, a 'myth' can be transformed into a 'social imaginary' if it is hegemonized at a discourse level or when it becomes clearly legitimated at the political one. Indeed, 'Social Europe' in the Lisbon Strategy process puts forward more clarity and depth and has been successful in incorporating a great number of specific social demands in a more coherent fashion as Europe's understanding of the urge for social cohesion and an established social counterweight is now more evident than ever.

---

[7] In the discourse theoretical perspective, conflict and struggle pervade the social, so struggle becomes an important focus in discourse theory. A *social antagonism* occurs when different identities mutually exclude each other. Thus, antagonisms can be found where discourses collide. Antagonisms can be dissolved through *hegemonic interventions*. The hegemonic intervention proves itself successful if one discourse manages to dominate alone, where before there was a conflict, and the antagonism is dissolved (Jørgensen, Phillips 2002: 47–48). I claim here that this is the case with the hegemonic intervention of the Lisbon Strategy process that has rendered the contemporary social discourse into a hegemonic formation.

[8] Jørgensen and Phillips (2002 : 56) note that discourse refers to "the partial fixation of meaning, while 'the field of discursivity' refers to any actual or potential meaning outside the specific discourse […] 'the field of discursivity' is thus understood as the general reservoir of all meaning not included in a specific discourse. The concept is necessary in so far as it emphasises the contingency and the fundamental openness of all social phenomena".

What remains to be seen is whether new social antagonisms will reaffirm its 'social imaginary' identity in the future or will turn the social discourse into a social criss-cross field again.

EU's 'Social Imaginary' within the Crisis Discourse

In terms of Laclau and Mouffe's theory, the recent crisis has neither put forward any 'dislocated elements' nor did it inscribe any brand new social demands. Instead, it demonstrated the need for a more integrated and coordinated approach to economic, social and political governance towards sustainable integrationism. It seems that the 'social imaginary' of Europe has already been established, followed by the liaison between the economic efficiency and social cohesion and justice rationale. At a rhetorical level, the latter has been vividly underlined. Yet, what the early post-crisis period apparently calls for is further enhancement of the postulations of the 'social imaginary' and elaboration on the 'social and political legitimacy rationale' in the context of "a more socially-friendly rearticulated discourse in a novel Europeanized space of interaction" (Ferrera 2010: 46).

It has often been claimed that narratives of the recent crisis have represented, and often misrepresented, the crisis as a predominantly economic one. According to Murray-Leach, "the crisis was portrayed as an abstract given, virtually a 'supernatural phenomenon', and almost exclusively as an economic one. This ruled out discussions of agency, of causes, or how the crisis might be overcome" (2014: 1). Thus, stressing more the economic side of the crisis rather than addressing the political, social and existential concerns underlying its economic nature, Europe's political identity and social partnership turned even more obscure and debatable, emphasizing again the need for democratic legitimacy and a 'new ethos' for EU. Therefore, 'regressing Social Europe' was also a consequence of the crisis discourse that questioned legitimacy. Europe as a political space was never reported to be adequately visible to the European citizens but in the current moment of the crisis, at worst, this political space was considered part of the problem. The framing of the crisis as primarily an economic phenomenon where solutions were left almost exclusively to prominent executive actors and their prescribed solutions, pictured political and social Europe as a distant 'other' to the majority of Europeans. Therefore, the distant 'other' that the EU was often said to be, soon became the 'foreign other' linked to, if not directly blamed for, the suffering of the member states more or less affected by the crisis (Murray-Leach 2014). Within the crisis discourse, not only Europe as a political construction was alienated from its citizens but also member states were 'othered' in relation to the nations that suffered the most, such as Greece, Italy, Ireland and Portugal. Solidarity envisaged by the "early social Europe" proved rare and impenetrable in the politics of vitiating 'unity in diversity'. As emphasized by Ferrera, "there is indeed growing evidence that the EU is now perceived as a potentially dangerous entity by a majority of its citizens, as a threat to national labor markets and social protections systems, as a 'Trojan horse' serving the malevolent interests of globalization" (2010: 47). In line with many scholars then, if EU citizens' anxieties vis-à-vis markets and competition are not alleviated and if voters are not convinced that "the EU cares for its people", the integration process as such may be seriously de-legitimized and jeopardized (Frazer et al. 2010; Ferrera 2010; Natali 2010).

EU's 'Social Imaginary' as a Political Project in the post-Crisis Discourse; New Legitimacy from New Public Discourse

On tackling the onset of crisis in 2008–2009 with measures that would boost economic activity and employment, member-states had to embark upon major programs designed to reduce public expenditure and introduce structural reforms. These reforms related principally to labor law and social protection. At the level of content, suggested changes followed the precepts of many mainstream economists whose tendency has been to regard the ESM as the main cause for the deterioration in the member-states' public finances. Therefore, the content of these reforms was not new but "the political and socioeconomic context opened up an unexpected window of opportunity for the proponents of draconian reforms" (Degryse et al. 2013: 37). While justified by the official 'crisis discourse', these reforms bore virtually no relationship to the economic cycle. They aimed at reconfiguring essential areas of the ESM, namely labor law, collective bargaining, social dialogue, wage formation systems, relations between the two sides of industry and the foundations of social protection, despite the fact that "the best components of this model had proved efficacious in the crisis for avoiding a serious deterioration of the situation within the economy and on the labour market" (Degryse et al. 2013: 38). The countries that experienced the lowest unemployment rates in the wake of crisis were indeed those which had the strongest industrial relations institutions and collective bargaining partnerships (Degryse et al. 2013: 38).

According to specialists, since euro zone countries have failed to commit to a voluntary process of convergence of economic performance and social cohesion, social policies seem to have been designated as the main adjustment variables of monetary union. "What the dominant discourse stated is that forms of internal devaluation—affecting wages, labor law and social protection- must from now on replace the practice of currency devaluation as it was practiced in the past" (Degryse et al. 2013: 38). Apparently enough, the ESM has undergone a serious shrinking during the crisis. In line with many observers, the only means of reversing this dynamic is to put social issues back on the political agenda at both the national and the EU level, reinforcing both the economic and social pillar of the European Union. Towards this goal, completing the economic and monetary union and endowing it with genuine instruments of adjustment and stabilization would bring forward the process of European social and political integration (Degryse et al. 2013: 39).

In the early post crisis era, a considerable number of voices emerged agreeing that 'Social Europe' and the ESM should be discussed anew as a political project. Strengthening or integrating the 'social imaginary' of Europe appears to be twofold. Firstly, there is an urge for a better considered plan towards financing social policies and their sufficient overall coordination. Secondly, there is a need for robust form of allegiance building and democratic legitimacy. Towards the first goal, new opportunities and recommendations have been drafted under the Lisbon Treaty and Europe 2020 Strategy (Frazer et al. 2010). Indeed, the 'Horizontal Social Clause' provides a legal basis for better taking into account the social impact of policies and for mainstreaming social objectives across all policy areas. Moreover, the Europe 2020 Strategy validates headline EU targets and articulates social flagships by stressing more than ever the importance of social issues (Frazer et al. 2010). The new 'angst' for social Europe is to measure real policy outcomes and avoid the risk that in meeting the targets, policy objectives are distorted, forgotten and ignored as it would happen until today (Frazer et al. 2010). Furthermore, there is a requirement often contested to change the direction of economic policies so as to more suitably place them in the service of sustainable and shared prosperity (Degryse et al. 2013: 39). On the other hand, to ensure public and political support, these new social targets should be set following a rigorous and transparent process, clearly taking into account the views of stakeholders. Therefore, the second goal in the political project of Social Europe is to address again the challenge of democratic legitimacy by ensuring that 'socialization' is not moving away from a multilateral and dynamic process to a rather bilateral and technocratic one. Rather it should give emphasis on the engagement of the civil society and partners as well as the stakeholders in their preparation, implementation and assessment of social policies and mutual learning. For instance, various stakeholders' fora linked to the European Platform against Poverty and the Social OMC at both EU and national levels can ensure participation and transparency within the National Reform Programs for Growth and Jobs or the National Strategy Reports on Social Protection and Social Inclusion of Europe 2020 Strategy (Frazer et al. 2010). Thus, democratic legitimacy can be assured if stakeholders are provided with the chance to feel more politically involved and committed in reshaping and hegemonizing the social and political discourse.

In the post-crisis discourse, political commitment is directly related to the emergence of a European public space or a 'transnational' social space. For many scholars, sustainable European integration needs to be based upon "social and cultural constructivism, a permanent feedback loop and political attentiveness to the different and at the same time changing values of stakeholder societies" (Miszlivetz 2012:4). Similarly, a related line of argument that applies to the post-crisis discourse readdresses the need for a 'community of communication' (Habermas 1987) and puts emphasis on the 'horizontal' integration of national public spheres as opposed to a more vertical scheme that has prevailed so far. It is obvious then, that the emergence of a 'communicative infrastructure' between the EU and its people should reoccur as the touchstone for the legitimacy of European governance and enhance the "feeling of belonging" among citizens (Sifft et al. 2007).

Following an even more 'bottom-up' approach, democratic accountability in the post-crisis era, should no longer be linked to a plurality of 'publics' who are defined as the stakeholders in the current European polity (Shore 2011: 298). In this logic, political decision making is to some extent replaced with expertise and science while "what is conspicuously missing in this polycentric regulatory regime of governance is the political concept of a 'demos', understood in the sense of a 'body-politic' and self-recognizing political community that is able to represent itself" (Herrero de Miñón 1996: 25). As politicians and scientists have often pointed out, the problem with the EU's vision, is that democracy without a 'demos' is a contradiction in terms, or worse, a recipe for authoritarianism and elite rule (Herrero de Miñón 1996). In order to contribute to a stronger European identity and the democratization of the European project, the 'inclusive form of community' needs to be transformed into a 'European demos', a clear-cut polity that personifies the European public good by means of a dominant 'bottom–up' approach. Undoubtedly, this is a slow and difficult process and certainly not without conflict. Etienne Balibar (2013:3) endorses this credo in the following words: "…what history shows is not that a 'demos' pre-exists its own political mobilization; on the contrary, it is the ensemble of democratic movements within a social and political content, which really create or generate the 'demos'". Boosting EU's legitimacy calls for an ongoing dialogical and discursive relationship between European citizens and Europe and should not just seek to symbolically transform the disparate peoples of Europe into a unified European people in a rather communicative formula to win over public approval (Shore 2011). Thus, in the post-crisis narratives, 'public discourse' stipulates the democratization of the European political project since it presupposes the politicization of a rather empty European public space (Miszlivetz 2012). Apparently enough, various undercurrent social and cultural processes of Europeanization are taking place via everyday cooperation among civil society activists, professional circles, public intellectuals and journalists. The open question is whether this emerging society will provide enough of a framework for new public discourse in an effort to politicize the European public space in the post-crisis era.

Conclusion

For many scholars, the European Union proved itself in the middle of the crisis as a closed, self-defending universe where the rhetorical 'unity in diversity' failed to adequately address social issues and justify the roots of the crisis. Diversity seemed to be acceptable in so far as it did not jeopardize unity. Nevertheless, it did not deconstruct or blur the 'social imaginary' and the social discourse of Europe at its core, as described in this paper. The EU's assumed 'invisibility' in the early years of its existence emerged from the peculiar position of the European institutions, compelled to seek forms of regulation applicable between diverse economic priorities and undoubtedly, varying ideological registers in the context of the deep ideological, political and social diversity that characterizes the EU. This has contributed at times to a fragmented social agenda and to diverse efforts to define what actually composes 'Social Europe', resulting in ambiguous meanings. Nevertheless, the 'patchwork' of different laws that composed 'Social Europe' turns more coherent and intelligible after the Lisbon Strategy. In some observers' opinion, the advent of the crisis shook EU's 'social imaginary', making it again 'invisible' to its citizens. At a more careful reading though, this 'invisibility' is not so much related to the complex status of the social agenda as to the latter's political validation. In a contrasting viewpoint, this 'invisibility' can prove a new incentive, a rather crucial post-crisis imperative for turning Social Europe into a more coherent whole by readdressing the need for political legitimacy in a 'bottom-up approach' and a rebuilding of the EU's democratic foundations. Using the concepts of ESM and Social Europe as a common denominator, EU's discourse can subsequently move from a political project towards arguing the need for more sustainable social results and shared formulae. Debating, deliberating and identifying the European public good in the framework of Europe's reinforced 'social imaginary' might still conclude in a new politics of a 'social makeover' with more visibility, more solidarity and, in the context of a new Europe, promoting now "Unity in Community".

References

Abélès, M. (2002). 'Political Anthropology of European Institutions: tensions and stereotypes'. In K. Liebhart, E. Menasse and H. Steinert (eds), Fremdbilder-Feindbilder–Zerrbilder: *Zur Wahrnehmung und diskursivern Konstruktion des Fremden*, Klagenfurt: Drava Verlag, 241–254.

Alber, J. (2010). What the European and American Welfare States have in Common and where they Differ: facts and fiction in Comparisons of the European Social Model and the United States, *Journal of European Social Policy, Vol. 20* (2), 102–125.

Amitsis, G., Berghman, J., Hemerijck, A., Sakellaropoulos, T., Stergiou, A. and Stevens, Y. (2003). *Connecting Welfare Diversity within the European Social Model*. Background report for the International Conference of the Hellenic Presidency of the EU on the Modernisation of the ESM, 21–22 May <https://www. eftrofia.gr/Social _Model_report_en.pdf) >

Balibar, E. (2013). *Out of the Interregnum*, <https://www.opendemocracy.net/can-europe-make-it/etienne-balibar/out-of-interregnum > [Accessed 25 November 2014]

Commission (1994). *European Social Policy—A Way Forward for the Union*, A White Paper. COM (94) 333 final, Brussels, 27 July 1994.

Commission. nd. EUROPA—Summaries of EU Legislation. The Open Method of Coordination - Glossary. <http://europa.eu/legislation_summaries/glossary/open_m ethod_coordination_en.htm > [Accessed 18 January 2015]

Council of the European Union (2000). Lisbon Extraordinary European Council. Presidency Conclusions, 23–24 March 2000. <http://europa.eu/european_council/c onclusions/index_en.htm > [Accessed 25 October 2014]

Council of the European Union (2000b). Santa Maria da Feira European Council. Presidency Conclusions, 19–20 June 2000. <http://europa.eu/european_council/co nclusions/index_en.htm > [Accessed 26 October 2014]

Council of the European Union (2000c). Nice European Council. Presidency Conclusions, 7–9 December 2000. <http://europa.eu/european_council/conclusio ns/index_en.htm > [Accessed 26 October 2014]

Council of the European Union (2007). Brussels European Council. Presidency Conclusions, 8–9 March 2007. <http://europa.eu/european_council/conclsuions/index_en.htm > [Accessed 26 October 2014]

Degryse, C., Jepsen, M., Pochet, P. (2013). *The Euro Crisis and its Impact on National and European Social Policies*, Working Paper, May 2013. Brussels: ETUI.

Demertzis, V. (2010). The European Social Model(s) and the Self-image of Europe. In F. Cerutti and S. Lucarelli (eds), *The Search for a European Identity. Values, Policies and Legitimacy of the EU*. Routledge / Garnet Series, 125–141.

Ebbinghaus, B. (1999). Does a European Social Model exist and can it survive?. In Huemer, G., Mesch, M. and Traxler, F. (eds), *The Role of Employer Associations and Labour Union in the EU*. Aldershot: Ashgate, 1–26.

Esping-Andersen, G. (1990). *The Three Worlds of Welfare Capitalism*. Cambridge: Polity Press.

Esposito, R. (2009). *Communitas: The Origin and Destiny of Community*. Translated by Timothy Campbell. Stanford: Stanford University Press.

Ferrera, M., Hemerijck, A., Rhodes, M. (2001). The Future of the Europe 'Social Model' in the Global Economy, *Journal of Comparative Analysis: Research and Practice*, No. 3, 163–190.

Ferrera, M. (2010). Mapping the Components of Social EU: A Critical Analysis of the Current Institutional Patchwork. In Marlier, E., Natali, D. (eds), *Europe 2020: Towards a More Social Europe?* Peter Lang, 45–68.

Foucault, M. (1985). *The Archaeology of Knowledge*. London: Tavistock.

Frazer, H., Marlier, E., Natali, D., Van Dam, R. and Vanhercke, B. (2010). 'Europe 2020: Towards a More Social EU? In E. Marlier, D. Natali (eds), *Europe 2020: Towards a More Social Europe?* Peter Lang, 15–44.

Goetschy, J. (2006). Taking Stock of Social Europe. In M. Jepsen and A. Serrano Pascual (eds), *Unwrapping the European Social Model*. University of Bristol: The Policy Press, 47–72.

Habermas, J. (1987). *The Theory of Communicative Action (Volume 2)*. Translated by Thomas McCarthy. Boston: Beacon Press.

Héritier, A. (2002). New Modes of Governance in Europe: Policy-making without Legislation?. In A. Héritier (ed), *In Common Goods: Reinventing European and International Governance*. Boulder: Rowman and Littlefield, 185–206.

Herrero de Miñón, M. (1996). Europe's Non-Existent Body Politic. In M. Herrero de Miñón and G. Leicester (eds), *Europe: A Time for Pragmatism*, European Policy Forum.

Howarth, D. and Stavrakakis, Y. (2000). Introducing Discourse Theory and Political Analysis. In D. Howarth, A. Norval and Y. Stavrakakis (eds), *Discourse Theory and Political Analysis*. Manchester: Manchester University Press, 1–37.

Jepsen, M. and Serrano Amparo, P. (2006). The Concept of the ESM and Supranational Legitimacy-building. In Jepsen, M. and Serrano, A. P. (eds), *Unwrapping the European Social Model*. University of Bristol: The Policy Press, pp. 25–45.

Jørgensen, M. and Phillips, L. (2002). *Discourse Analysis as Theory and Method*. London / California: Sage Publications.

Laclau, E. (1990). *New Reflections on the Revolution of Our Time*, London: Verso Press.

Laclau, E. and Mouffe, C. (1985). *Hegemony and Socialist Strategy. Towards a Radical Democratic Politics*. London: Verso.

Miszlivetz, F. (2012). The Deep Structure of the European Crisis, <https://www.opendemocracy.net/ferenc-miszlivetz/deep-structure-of-european-crisis > [Accessed 13 September 2014]

Montessori, N. (2011). The Design of a Theoretical, Methodological, Analytical Framework to analyse Hegemony in Discourse, *Critical Discourse Studies, Vol.8* (3), 169–181.

Moreau, M.-A. (ed) (2011). *Before and After the Economic Crisis. What Implications for the 'European Social Model'?*. Cheltenham: Edward Elgar.

Mouffe, C. (1993 / 2005). *The Return of the Political*. London / New York: Verso.

Murray-Leach, T. (2014). *Crisis Discourses in Europe: Media EU-phemisms and Alternative Narratives* <http://blogs.lse.ac.uk/eurocrisispress/2014/11/20/crisis-discourses-in-europe-media-eu-phemisms-and-alternative-narratives/ > [Accessed 26 November 2014]

Natali, D. (2010). The Lisbon Strategy, Europe 2020 and the Crisis in Between. In Marlier, E., Natali, D. (eds), *Europe 2020: Towards a More Social Europe?* Peter Lang, 93–113.

Pochet, P. (2006). Debate around the Social Model: evolving players, strategies and dynamics. In C. Degryse and P. Pochet (eds), *Social Developments in the EU 2005*. Brussels: ETUI, Observatoire social européen and Saltsa, 79–99.

Rasmussen, P., Lynch, K., Brine, J., Boyadjieva, P., Peters, M. and Sünker, H. (2004). *Education, Equality and the European Social Model*. Report for the GENIE Network, Joensuu, Finland, July 2004.

Rodrigues, M.-J. (2010). *The EU Economic Governance at the Crossroads. Policy Paper for Notre Europe* <http://www.notre-europe.eu/media/eu2020-mjr.pdf?pdf=ok > [Accessed 1 December 2014]

Sabel, C. and Zeitlin, J. (2007). Learning from Difference: The New Architecture of Experimentalist Governance in the European Union. *European Governance papers (EUROGOV), No. C-07–02*.

Scott, J. and Trubek, D. (2002). Mind the Gap: Law and New Approaches to Governance in the European Union, *European Law Journal, Vol. 8* (1), 1–18.

Shore, C. (2011). 'European Governance' or Governmentality? The European Commission and the Future of Democratic Government, *European Law Journal, Vol. 17* (3), 287–303.

Sifft, S., Brüggemann, M., Kleinen, K., Peters, B. and Wimmel, A. (2007). Segmented Europeanization: Exploring the Legitimacy of the European Union from a Public Discourse Perspective, *Journal of Common Market Studies, Vol. 45,* (1), pp. 127–155.

Torfing, J. (2005). Discourse Theory: Achievements, Arguments, and Challenges. In Howarth, D., Torfing, J. (eds), *Discourse Theory in European Politics. Identity, Policy and Governance.* Palgrave Macmillan, 1–32.

Trubek, D. and Trubek, L. (2003). *Hard and Soft Law in the Construction of Social Europe: the Role of the OMC.* Paper presented at the workshop 'Opening the OMC'. EUI, Florence, July 2003.

Vaughan-Whitehead, D. (2003). *EU Enlargement versus Social Europe? The Uncertain Future of the European Social Mode.* Cheltenham: Edward Elgar.

Venturini, P. (1988). *Un Espace Social à l' Horizon 1992.* Luxembourg: Commission of the European Communities.

Wilding, P. (1997). Globalisation, Regionalisation and Social Policy, *Social Policy and Administration, Vol. 31* (4), 410–428.

Williams, A. (2010). *The Ethos of Europe. Values, Law and Justice in the EU.* Cambridge: Cambridge University Press.

Yfantopoulos, J. (2007). The Social Policy of EU. In N. Maravegias and M. Tsinisizelis (eds), *New European Union. Organisation and Policies: Fifty Years.* Athens: Themelio Publications, 670–698.

ibidem-Verlag

Melchiorstr. 15

D-70439 Stuttgart

info@ibidem-verlag.de

www.ibidem-verlag.de
www.ibidem.eu
www.edition-noema.de
www.autorenbetreuung.de